# Obedient Journey

## Guided by the Difference-Maker

### by Paul Taylor

*Obedient Journey: Guided by the Difference-Maker*

Trilogy Christian Publishers A Wholly Owned Subsidary of Trinity Broadcasting Network

2442 Michelle Drive Tustin, CA 92780

Rights Department, 2442 Michelle Drive, Tustin, CA 92780.

Trilogy Christian Publishing/TBN and colophon are trademarks of Trinity Broadcasting Network.

Cover design by: Kristy Swank

For information about special discounts for bulk purchases, please contact Trilogy Christian Publishing.

Manufactured in the United States of America

10 9 8 7 6 5 4 3 2 1

Library of Congress Cataloging-in-Publication Data is available.

ISBN: 978-1-68556-498-8

E-ISBN: 978-1-68556-499-5

# Table of Contents

# Foreword

*Obedient Journey: Guided by the Difference-Maker* is far more than a true story of an exemplary human being, which in itself is worth discovering. What I learned reading it literally changed my life. Like many people, I have read hundreds, maybe thousands of books, yet no other book's message ever impacted me in such a positive, profound way as this one did. And if it could do that for me, a seventy-eight-year-old man, far along the path of life, I know it can have an equally beneficial effect on many others. The content, so clearly and beautifully expressed, is that revealing and powerful. What you have before you are the means for releasing the potential in everyone, to excel and be counted, to live up to your full potential, and to find calm and peace and inner strength, and in the process, to share what you have learned and been blessed with to influence and help many more people in positive ways.

Paul's story is a true demonstration of the fulfilled American dream, a Horatio Alger illustration of a boy who grew up in a blue-collar textile-mill family who, despite numerous obstacles, setbacks, and family tragedies, never gave up and became President of Southeastern Freight Lines, one of the most respected trucking companies in America. Blessed with a strong Christian family and encouraged by loving people in his church and community, Paul charged into life, not blessed with wealth, education, or connections, but driven by purpose, confidence, and faith.

Paul was a promising athlete with college football programs knocking on his door, but in an instant, that dream was crushed by a serious knee injury. Gone was the prospect of a "free ride" college education. Present were tough, unanticipated choices. Rebounding, Paul tried the college route, but it didn't work. He knew the cost placed far too much burden on his cash-strapped parents. So ridden with guilt, at nineteen, he dropped out and went job-seeking. His target was Carolina Freight Carriers, one of the best paying firms in town. Twenty-seven times in a row, Paul was rejected as he daily stood in line hoping someone would give him a part-time job on the docks loading trucks.

Then, on the twenty-eighth attempt, he got his opportunity, and he was so grateful. That job may have been the lowest level job in freight operations, but it meant everything to this young man who was so determined to prove his worth. From that humble start, working from the ground level up, Paul earned multiple promotions, step-by-step developing into one of the most trusted, respected, successful leaders in the American trucking industry. That happened in large part because Paul never forgot what it was like to work hard at a job and feel insignificant and taken for granted. He decided to make sure it didn't happen to others. He would honor and take care of people.

I have known Paul for more than thirty years, having met him at Trucking Profitability Strategies, the conference that I led and helped found at the University of Georgia. TPS targeted owners, chairmen, CEOs, presidents, and other senior executives of American trucking companies. Its goal was to help top-level decision-makers not just improve their corporate profitability but also to help them improve every aspect of their businesses, from cost controls to marketing to motivating people to customer service. Its other goal was to help each attendee be all they could be.

Paul may have lacked formal education, but he possessed something far more important—a deep ongoing commitment to learn. When I met him, he was already President of Southeastern Freight Lines, a company I knew little about. I was a professor of Transportation and Logistics, a member of the faculty of UGA's College of Business. Quickly I detected that there was something special about Paul, and he could teach me a great deal about many things from leadership to trucking to faith. And I welcomed his help and counsel, which he always graciously gave me.

Paul exemplified everything good about so many things important to me. He was a true American success story, a man of humble roots, yet so wise. I observed that other attendees looked up to Paul, valued his wisdom, and appreciated, as I did, all of his contributions to TPS, which were many. Over the years, I worked with more than five hundred corporate leaders, from those leading three-truck operations to those running billion-dollar-plus enterprises with thousands of trucks. We were very fortunate to attract the most successful, most accomplished trucking leaders in North America who willingly shared their keys to success with all in attendance. I watched those men and women carefully, listened to them, studied their ways, compared their speech deliveries and messages, and worked with many on our board of advisors. I learned from some of the brightest, most innovative minds in the business. None, though, was better than Paul Taylor. He taught me so much about the right way to lead. And the more I learned about Paul, the more I hungered to know.

Paul was different. He was an unashamed, fully committed, sincere believer in Christ, and as I got to know him better, on many occasions, he explained how his life changed dramatically for the better when at age thirty, he confessed his sins and asked to be saved. This was unusual in an industry known for rough language and tough leadership. Paul, though, consistently maintained a sense of calm confidence, and I noted his praise of others before self and an obvious deep appreciation and love for people, especially for all of his drivers and lower-level associates. Clearly, their welfare and morale meant as much to him as corporate profits and his personal success. And it was clear that this very busy man had his priorities straight. Somehow he always found the time for non-company responsibilities. I just didn't know what had made him that way. So, I pursued the answers I needed. And as I learned more, I urged him to tell his story. The world needed to hear his amazing life story. Apparently, that suggestion sunk in. At eighty-one, Paul began to write. And when he asked me for help with his book, I told him it would be an honor. I respected him so much.

Paul, in his "Preface" and "Introduction: The Purpose of This Book" will tell you the story of why he wrote *Obedient Journey: Guided by the Difference-Maker* and how what started out as an autobiography, a memoir, quickly changed to a story of how his rebirth and faith in God were instrumental in all he accomplished in life, a blessed life guided by prayer and guidance from the Holy Spirit. Until I read Paul's first draft of the manuscript, I had no idea of this change in direction and theme nor that the book primarily was aimed at people like me, intentionally or not, a half-committed, part-time, in all honesty, a pretty ignorant Christian who had missed the boat and needed truth and awakening. But that manuscript and all the subsequent questions that I asked him about his conversion and understanding of faith (for instance, I had no understanding whatsoever about what the Holy Spirit encompassed) produced rich meaning to me.

As I read the chapters, I realized that Paul had become a fine biblical student and, better yet, a skilled teacher. He had a gift for mixing beliefs and wisdom with interesting real-life experiences, some life-threatening, a combination that added clarity and made understanding easy. That manuscript showed me how totally ignorant and oblivious I was to many really important things. And what Paul had, what he had experienced and been blessed by and that he covered so well in his writing, I wanted more of. The book before you was the catalyst that led me, this seventy-eight-year-old man, to seek salvation. And I will always be grateful that God put this disciple, his book, and me together. As I said, Paul and his book profoundly changed my life.

- » May I leave you with a list of questions?
- » Are you satisfied with your life?
- » What's your purpose in life?
- » Do you want to be a better husband or wife, father or mother, grandparent, son or daughter, brother or sister, friend?
- » Do you want to lead and motivate people more effectively?
- » Do you want to achieve at your highest potential?
- » Would you like to know the secrets of running one of the most successful, respected companies in America?
- » Do you want more calm and peacefulness in your life?
- » Are you fearful of the future?

» Do you seek more meaning in your life?

» Do you feel unprepared to deal with life's disappointments, setbacks, and the loss of loved ones?

» Are you sure what being born again and saved really mean?

» Do you want your faith strengthened?

» Do you long for more love, respect, and appreciation?

» Do you want America to fix its problems and secure its future?

» Do you crave more optimism and hope in your life?

» Do you want God one day to say, "Well done, thou good and faithful servant"?

I found truths in Paul's book addressing every question just listed. May you read it and be blessed as I was with its wisdom and guidance.

Fred Stephenson - Ph.D.
Athens, Georgia
June 25, 2021

# PREFACE

I am reluctant to say this is the story of *my* life. After all, I am not a celebrity who has rubbed shoulders with the rich and famous. My face doesn't grace television screens or supermarket tabloids. I am not a world leader, famous athlete, or pop-culture influencer. So why would you want to read this book?

Yes, I was present when the events recounted in this book took place, a witness to them, experienced them. But it's not really my story. It's the story about the One who said, "I am the way, and the truth, and the life. No one comes to the Father except through me" (John 14:6, ESV). This, then, is the story of His powerful and ever-present impact on my life. It's about the difference He has made in transforming my simple life into a marvelous, obedient journey.

Over the years, I have off and on considered writing about the wonderful difference Jesus Christ has made in my life. On the day I decided to move ahead and begin to write this book, I started the day with two different daily devotionals. That day was November 13, 2019. The first devotional gave me the inspiration for one of my own stories, "From a Time of Fear to a Time of Faith." The second devotional solidified God's desire that I was to write my stories to exalt Him for the next generation. In both devotionals, however, God's assurance to me to begin writing was evident.

I began my personal quiet time that day with *Turning Points*, a devotional booklet for the month of November. The message in this first devotional was entitled, "He Leads, We Follow." The scripture was from Psalm 63:7–8 (NKJV): "Because you have been my help, therefore, in the shadow of your wings I will rejoice. My soul follows close behind you; your right hand upholds me." A portion of that devotional went on to say, "Depending on how close we stay to our Guide, a trial can be transformed *from a time of fear to a time of faith*." The focal point for that day was, "Joy is delight at God's grace which enables us to endure our trials." I knew this was God's intended message for me, if not for anyone else. It was this devotional that gave me the assurance I was to write my own story, or rather the story about how Christ has influenced and impacted my life, and also write about an event in our lives concerning our son.

I then picked up a second daily devotional booklet provided by Life Action Ministries, one of America's most effective Christian outreach organizations. The booklet was entitled, *Say Yes to God, a Daily Devotional for November*[1]. The scripture for that day came from Psalm 71:18 (ESV): "So even to old age and gray hairs, O God, do not forsake me until I proclaim your might to another generation, your power to all those to come." The article began, "Saints never age out of relevance. The kingdom needs older voices, people who can relate the word of God through their life experiences, not to elevate themselves because of their experiences but to *exalt God* through those experiences." The article continued, "Many have encountered seasons of loss, grief, setback, and pain. They have also known times of success, celebrations, and change. And as all people have (or will have) remorse and regret, they know what it means to trust God in the fog and to *press into Him in transition*. The aged who have walked with God have much to tell. Honor God by listening to them."

These two wonderful intervening messages left me awestruck. The first devotional helped me to understand that I was to begin to tell the story of God's grace and goodness in my life. Up to this point, Satan had caused me to wonder if this story was exceptional enough to be told. God's Spirit that morning, however, made it clear to me. It should be told because the story was not really a story about my life; it was the story about the wondrous God of the universe, God the Father, God the Son, and God the Holy Spirit. The God of the universe in three persons, with all three honoring each other, meeting all the needs in the lives of Christians. Even still, in my early eighties, where do I start and do justice to such a wonderful God of grace, mercy, and forgiveness?

The second devotional spoke loudly and clearly to my heart. It gave me the assurance of God's desire for me to write the stories of a lifetime. These

---

1       Copyright © crosswalk.com. All rights reserved.

two devotionals read on the same day were both so relevant to what God had already revealed to me. Some may say this is just a coincidence. But I learned many years ago God will take the word "coincidence" out of your vocabulary if you allow Him to. God impressed upon me that day that these two devotionals were no coincidence. I knew I was to write about the experiences in my life, and I was to exalt God by relating those experiences.

God reveals to me every day that if there is to be "a story," it is only to exalt Him. It is not to have any hint of self-promotion. It is to have only highlighted incidents where God has taken care of the gross inadequacies in my life. Even when I did not have a personal relationship with God (though I had a baptismal certificate that indicated I was part of a church), He was orchestrating and protecting me from the self-destruction that Satan planned and desired for me. I had just enough religion to send me to hell. Morality is too often thought of as a substitute for salvation, and it is often confused as salvation. While good moral behavior is an excellent thing, it is not transformational. Only by accepting God's wonderful grace through the shed Blood of Christ can a person be saved. We are then empowered by the Holy Spirit and prepared for eternity in the presence of our Lord.

Can we ever thank God the Father enough for sending us a perfect, sinless Christ to set us free and lead us home?

What a compassionate Savior we have! May He be praised greatly for all the great things recorded in this book!

He alone is worthy!

Paul Taylor
December 1, 2021
Columbia, South Carolina

# Introduction: The Purpose of This Book

Who needs another book? Do we not already live in an era of information overload where we are constantly reading, hearing, and comprehending info? Is there not already more than we can respond to?

In view of the preceding question, why, then, is there such a compulsion on my part to write one more book? After all, what is there that is so important to write about that could possibly be of real significance and value to others?

My response to that question is that it has become hauntingly clear there was such a significant event that occurred to transform my life, even beyond description, that it needs to be shared.

Let me be clear. I am not writing to impress but to express how close I personally came to completely missing out on *real, meaningful purpose in my life.* The real purpose for sharing is to perhaps help many, or at least some, avoid the same deceptions which led up to my significant event. Had that event not occurred, I also would never have come to know one of the most important truths, a truth which is not often spoken of: People can have a most blessed and extraordinary life, and people can do remarkable things! Who said that? God said it, and He still says it. Ephesians 3:20 (KJV) states, "Now unto Him who is able to do exceedingly above all that we ask or think *according to the power that worketh in us* (emphasis mine)." This is conditional, though. This statement of truth is saying God will (and He wants to) make available His power in our lives if we allow Him to.

In my own case, I was seriously charging ahead in life, doing things *my way* as a leader in my workplace. By age thirty, I had decided life for me was about working hard, getting ahead, doing things my way, and enjoying the many things that money could buy. It was also about taking care of my wife and children as a good husband and father. Little did I know then that without proper Godly leadership, influence, and guidance in my own life, I could not lead others effectively, even those I loved the most.

As a child, attending church was something I enjoyed socially. Part of the reason was my schoolmates, friends, and the pretty girls were there. Vacation Bible School was the most enjoyable to me when contrasted with the few other modest social activities that were in my life.

At the age of nine, on the last day of that weeklong VBS, the preacher shared what I now know as the gospel and offered an invitation for us children to become "Christians" and "join the church." Every one of my friends on our pew went forward, and I was left sitting there all alone. I decided it must be a good thing to do, and I went forward also. I became a Christian, joined the church, and was consequently baptized, but I was not really changed and certainly not born again.

From that point on, my church attendance was basically social activity. I had no desire to read the Bible, pray, or listen to sermons, let alone tell someone how Jesus had changed my life. It was not that I was against Jesus; I was just not really for Him, either. I was neither hot nor cold. In the book of Revelation, chapter 3:14–19 (KJV) talks about the Laodicean church as being "lukewarm, neither hot nor cold," a repulsive and precarious state to be in! Do you know anyone like that today? That condition is my reason for this book. I'll explain.

I was a church member but not really a Christian, except in name only. I now realize there are many today in that same condition, and blinding pride keeps them, just as it did for me, from being free and enjoying Christ as Savior and Lord. The most unfortunate thing about being in that condition is that if I had died, at my funeral they probably would have declared me to be in heaven because my name was on the church roll. But without question, that would not have been where I was.

As I grew into my teen years, I attended church only sporadically. Not because I wanted to please the Lord, but again as a social outlet. I had learned nothing about God's unique plan for my life. After all, I already had a plan of my own! Honestly, I did not enjoy much of the truth of the Bible because it made me feel guilty. I wonder why! The truth is that I *was* guilty! I was a fraud. Anyone ever been there and done that? There was no divine power in my life to lead me as a Christian or to keep me focused on the profound truth of the gospel. The gospel describes the horrific price Jesus paid for me to have true "life and to have it more abundantly" (John 10:10, ISV). But I did not have it.

To be completely honest, if I had ever truly desired to be a soldier in the army of God, I was now a deserter. There is no question I was an imposter, although an innocent one. I had followed my friends and "walked the aisle" in Bible School. But I was not ready, nor did I want to be an "Onward Christian Soldier marching as to war." I lacked the knowledge and the desire to represent Jesus in my life, even in a minimal way.

What had happened? Because worldly attractions had become far too seductive for me as a developing young man, I had no desire to follow what I considered being the narrow and restrictive teaching of the Bible. At that time, I had no idea Jesus had spoken these words: "Enter by the narrow gate; for wide is the gate and broad is the way that *leads to destruction*, and there are many who go in by it. Because *narrow* is the gate and difficult is the way which leads to life, (real life), and there are few who find it" (Matthew 7:13–14, NKJV).

In the most truthful terms, I was still a lost church member. I had a piece of paper, an official-looking certificate, showing my membership. But that was all. At the time I joined the church, I did not know the Bible was so clear about what happens when we truly repent, when we are sorry for our sins, and when we humbly ask Jesus to forgive us. Jesus does that instantly, and then the Holy Spirit, the silent enabling power of God, enters the new believers to empower each one to truly live victoriously the liberating born-again life of a Christian.

I also did not know what is clearly explained in Romans 8, verse 8 (NKJV): "Those who are in the flesh" (without God's Spirit) "cannot please God," and verse 9a further explains, "But you are not in the flesh, but in the Spirit, if indeed the Spirit of God dwells in you."

Furthermore, this following powerful truth helped me understand where I really was: "Now if anyone does not have the Spirit of Christ"—the Holy

Spirit—"he is not His" (Romans 8:9b, NKJV). This is an absolute truth, with no wiggle room. The black-and-white gospel truth. No wonder I had no interest in following the Lord. God's Holy Spirit was not within me, and I had absolutely no awareness of Him.

Verse 11 (NKJV) in that chapter further clarifies, "But if the Spirit of Him who raised Jesus from the dead" (again, the Holy Spirit, Whom I will frequently refer to as the Difference-Maker) "dwells in you, *He who raised Christ from the dead* will also give life to your mortal bodies through the *spirit who dwells in you!*"

This truth is now clear to me, and I realize I was pitifully unchanged by my decision at age nine. I did not know then that when God calls us to Himself, He equips us. God provides the Holy Spirit power to equip us to live for Him, represent Him well, and stand firmly and faithfully as His devoted, empowered disciples.

It is unimaginable to me that any person does not desire a life liberated from the bondage of sin. Who does not desire a life that yields the fruit of the indwelling Holy Spirit? That fruit is described in Galatians 5:22 (ESV) as "love, joy, peace, patience, kindness, goodness, faithfulness, gentleness and self-control."

For me, it is a terrifying thought to realize from age nine to age thirty, I had only empty religion, with no power whatsoever to have a truly meaningful life. This is especially upsetting as I realize what an ultimate price Jesus paid in order that I might have so very much more of the "abundant life" as promised in John 10:10 (ISV).

Early on, I had never given thought to this question: If I do not have a real interest in the things of God, why in the world would I ever be allowed into heaven? That empty religion almost caused me to miss out completely on what God so graciously planned for me even before I was born: Psalm 139:13–16 (NKJV) says, "Your eyes saw my substance, being yet unformed. And in your Book, they were all written, the days fashioned for me, as yet there were none of them."

What does this really say? God has a plan, with structure, for each of us, His most beloved creations. From the very beginning, God sees each of us as an only child to be nurtured and developed by His truth and power. No matter how the world treats us, God promises in Hebrews 13:5 (ESV) that He "will never leave nor forsake you."

I had no idea that the Creator of the entire Universe had a plan designed just for me. His promise is, "I know the plans I have for you to prosper you and not to harm you" (Jeremiah 29:11, NIV). How beautiful! How wonderful! The power of God, the Difference-Maker, manifests Himself in our lives and shouts loud and clear, "People can!" People can do amazing things, and people can have an abundant, fulfilling life.

My precious mother had always focused us on the need to live and value the Christian life. She loved the Lord and wanted us to know and love Him also. She knew attending church and hearing the truth of God's Word was good for us. I knew it also. Additionally, I knew being a church goer could create an air of respectability to a person's life from a societal viewpoint. I, therefore, played the role but only partially; I never ever developed as a true disciple of Christ. I did not yet have God's Helper to assist me to do so. God's Word is clear about how dangerous pretending to be a born-again child of God really is. In the book of James, we read this truth: "A doubled-minded man is unstable in all his ways" (James 1:8b, KJV).

Regrettably, my life was about doing my own thing, and I had never given any thought whatsoever to that yet unfound truth as stated above—"double-minded, unstable in all his ways." I was unmindful that God has a precious individually tailored plan to bring purpose and fulfillment to every life. In fact, I had no idea how God could possibly be at work in my life since He, in my mind, was in heaven.

As I look back now, it is easy to see how Satan, the clever deceiver who has had thousands of years of experience, will always work to keep us from knowing God's great love, great promises, great power, and great plan for every single one of us. Unfortunately, at that point in life, I was ignorant of this truth. Besides, in my early manhood, I was determined to enjoy life and make my own way without any religious involvement or encumbrance. There were some major truths of which I was totally unaware.

The purpose of this book is to help anyone who may now be where I was then—a lost, part-time church member with no spiritual power to resist sin. How grateful I am that Christianity was lived out and demonstrated consistently right before my eyes; and not only that, but it was also absolutely so attractive I could not resist accepting Christ's love and forgiveness.

My focus then was clearly on worldly things, and I had preconceived notions that being religious would limit my fun and inhibit me from doing my own thing. Thankfully, the Holy Spirit opened my blind eyes the night I was truly born again as a new creation. All through the gospels, we read of Jesus opening blind eyes, some even blind from birth. When the Pharisees in the temple were trying to discredit Jesus for having restored sight to the eyes of a blind man, the healed blind man made a profound statement: "One thing I know, that whereas I was blind, but now I see" (John 9:25b, ASV). To that, I also say, "Amen"! I have been there and done that—been spiritually blind, but now I see. How precious it is to know and be blessed by these major truths, revealed by God's Holy Spirit. They cannot be denied in me.

All too often, Christianity is talked about as "religion." However, I learned that Christianity really is a "love relationship" with an indescribable living, loving Savior who paid my sin debt and thereby restored me to my divinely planned position! He then gave me a Helper, the Holy Spirit, to equip me to represent Him well in a lost world.

On the other hand, "religion" is much, much, more so about works, what man can do to earn another deity's favor. Christianity is so vastly different because it is about the wonderful *worthiness* of Jesus and what He has *already done*. Jesus has provided the way to forgive, restore, and empower anyone to live in victory with divine, precious peace, both here and in eternity.

Be very certain about which one you rely on—an enslaving religion or a liberating love relationship with Jesus Christ. One of these "leads to destruction and torment" while "Christianity leads to liberty and delight."

Another often misunderstood yet vitally important truth is when we repent and accept Jesus' gift of forgiveness, He not only pays our sin debt, but He also provides the indescribable power of the Holy Spirit to indwell within us and fill our being. The Holy Spirit empowers us to represent Christ and live in victory over sin full time. My, how I needed to know these powerful truths!

What a joy to experience that great comforting, enabling power in my own life when I quit pretending about who I really was. I then asked Him to forgive my sins and false pretense as a Christian and to be truly and fully my Lord and Master. I finally decided to become an authentic disciple of Jesus. And that is when He set me free! I rejoice every time I read, "Where the Spirit of the Lord is, there is liberty" (2 Corinthians 3:17, KJV).

Because God made man in His own image for Himself, and to walk in fellowship with Him, He provides a way for us to do so. God sent Jesus to restore us from our sinful state, and the Holy Spirit is that power that then dwells within us and empowers each of us to live faithfully and victoriously until He calls us home. He provides that Power within each of us that we might fulfill His wonderful plan and be a faithful witness to others in our earthly life.

Satan, the arch-enemy of God and cunning deceiver of man, does not want us to know of God's precious gift of divine power, and Satan certainly will do all he can to keep us from relying on that power. Satan loves it when we labor in the impotent and feeble flesh!

It was a great revelation when I fully realized that, because of God's great plan and provision, *people can!* Can do what? *Excel and Walk Obediently!* Because we are empowered to excel as we walk the obedient journey with Him in fellowship, we can shine in unimaginable ways. He opened my eyes to that exciting truth and gave me the great joy of being a part of seeing so many people come to that profound awareness of their God-granted capability to excel! What a precious gift from our Creator! He is truly the Difference-Maker.

*Empowered to excel and to walk obediently, because of the Difference-Maker*—this is one of the greatest untold stories in the world today. Our Creator offers us three great gifts to ensure that people can—the forgiveness through the sacrifice of Jesus; the wisdom and guidance from the Owner's Manual, the Holy Bible; and the indwelling Holy Spirit. God gives us all we need to excel, and He loves it when we do so. Our gracious God did not create us and then not provide the means to excel. He provided His Spirit to make a difference along our journey.

In summary, the purpose of this book is twofold:

To make clear, every one of us has been created to excel *in life*. We can never truly excel by being mere "part-timers" with the Lord. It is clear people can excel and live empowered in God's peace when we allow Jesus to be Lord! He saves us to represent Him full-time and enjoy eternity in His precious presence (no pretense).

To share this enlightening truth: He provides the Power of the Holy Spirit—the Difference-Maker—to enable us to "have life... and have it more abundantly" (John 10:10b, NKJV).

It is a simple choice. Will I accept His precious blessing through faith in Jesus as my Savior and receive His precious power, blessing, and peace *which surpasses all understanding?* I would never write or speak these truths if I, by His grace, had not experienced this transformation.

*Obedient Journey* describes my genuine willingness to be obedient to Jesus Christ at the center of my life and unveils my efforts to be faithful. Once I committed my life to Jesus, I no longer walked alone because His Spirit guided me and walked within me. I found that His Spirit was more powerful than the enemy of God and man who had previously blinded me and held me captive to sin. We are promised in 1 John 4:4 (NKJV), "He who is in you is greater than he (Satan) who is in the world." God opened my eyes to what a powerful *Difference-Maker* He provides when we surrender our lives to Him. I speak from experience that God revolutionized my life and His plan, when followed, will produce a life at your highest potential, as well as a life of unspeakable peace, fulfillment, excellence, and liberty. Trusting Jesus and putting His instructions into practice brings rewarding blessings and outcomes.

My guiding belief, because it both happened to me and I saw how it transformed many others, is that *people can* achieve beyond what they imagine possible if they give their lives to Jesus Christ, allow Holy Spirit to guide their steps, and follow the best owner's manual ever written, the Bible. Far too many people underestimate their capabilities and how to develop to their fullest satisfying potential. Ephesians 3:20 (NKJV) promises, "Now to Him who is able to do exceedingly abundantly above all that we ask or think, according to the power at work within us." Whatever our Creator calls us to do, He supplies and provides the needed resources.

This book is uplifting and positively encouraging, and it's absolutely true. And *Obedient Journey* is for anyone who desires a truly more purposeful, fulfilling, and abundantly victorious life, as well as for anyone who desires insight into spiritual matters with real life examples and application. My question to you is, why should I not share this enlightening book of truth with anyone else to help them gain insight and to help them be certain of their salvation in the wonderful eternal Kingdom of God...forever?

God made us to live victoriously, and He provides us with the great power to do so with the Holy Spirit power. People can excel in life along the path of our *obedient journey* because God our Creator enables and equips us to do so. He makes a difference in our lives. He is our *Difference-Maker*!

# CHAPTER 1

# My Hometown

I would like to share some information about early days in my hometown and what made it so special. Although I grew up lacking an abundance of material possessions, no one ever told me I was disadvantaged. So I was never scarred. There were a number of families just like mine in Cherryville, so I was not alone and did not dwell on what I did not have. Besides, when you don't have much as a child, you develop a wonderful imagination.

We lived in a home provided by the textile mill, which employed my mother and father. It did not have central heating or air or hardwood floors. Our floors were covered with linoleum, which looked nice but was not very durable. You might describe our house as being painfully plain, but it was home.

With no extra money for toys for us children, Christmas was the only time we expected to receive a gift. I never had a bicycle until I was twelve years old. A friend, Franklin Wright, got a new bike, and his dad sold our family his old one for, I believe, ten dollars. It wasn't pretty and shiny, but it was mine, and I was so happy to have it.

I had three sets of clothes, shirts and pants. Although they were not fancy, my mom always kept them clean and ironed. One set had to be kept ready for Sunday to wear to church. My shoes were high-top brogans, not stylish but durable, and new ones seemed to be a long time coming.

While we were not, by any means, possessors of many material things, I was rich in the way it matters most. First, I grew up in a home filled with love, faith, and generosity. I also grew up with one of the greatest blessings parents can give their children; I knew they loved me! The effort they put forth to provide all they possibly could lingers to this day in my remembrance of them. Above everything, they taught me to be a grateful and honorable person.

I was further blessed by being surrounded by a wonderful, supportive, encouraging community of good, caring people. Additionally, my parents taught us to work hard, and when problems arose, to use our intelligence and capabilities to deal with them. We learned to focus on finding solutions and moving ahead, not whining about injustices or anything else. God doesn't want that, and neither did my parents. Collectively, these blessings laid the foundation for a life not built on sand but on granite. All these factors shape a young person's character, attitude, priorities, and thinking.

There are many elements, in addition to family, that joined forces to shape my journey in my small North Carolina hometown of Cherryville. And while I didn't understand or grasp the role of the Holy Spirit that was to later come into my life, I did understand the blessings of Christianity as demonstrated by my family and those in my hometown. Many lessons were learned that I'll share here. But let me begin by discussing what I call "environmental factors" before addressing my family's impact.

Cherryville had no unique identity, nor outstanding tourist attraction, nor any other greatly acknowledged significance. But it was my hometown. Nestled in the Piedmont section of North Carolina, on land between the ocean and mountains, it was a community almost completely dependent on the textile manufacturing industry. But as far as I was concerned, it was the perfect place to grow up. It was never too hot in the summer to play outside, and it was never too cold in the winter to be outside, except perhaps to make the trek from my bed to the unheated bathroom on the back porch. Even in my long underwear, it was a dreaded journey in mid-winter. For forty-six years, Cherryville was my home until a very significant event caused my relocation.

Just what made my hometown so special? Actually, it was many things.

## Church

Cherryville had many churches, both large and small, including four large, beautiful churches representing different denominations. While there were only about 2,500 people living in Cherryville in my early years, the churches had loyal, active members, dedicated and faithful, who served as positive role models for me. Regular emphasis was placed on revival, spiritual renewal, and faithfulness to our Savior and Lord. Collectively, the churches in town put emphasis on evangelism and even held effective crusades at the high school stadium with the objectives of strengthening the faith of believers and adding new followers of Jesus Christ to the church rolls. Churches also provided Vacation Bible School, an event in midsummer attended by many children in the community.

Yes, church members were committed. Even for funerals, on weekdays, there would be nearly as many choir members participating as there were for Sunday morning worship services. Funerals were no small affair in my hometown, for in Cherryville the dead were dutifully honored. Sunday was a day set aside to worship God and to spend with family. As a child, we even had "Sunday clothes" that we wore only on Sunday in honor of our Savior and as a show of respect for God's church. There was a significant effort to "remember the Sabbath and to keep it holy." I thank God for those who were grateful enough for their salvation (liberation) to love and preserve God's churches. In my hometown, people did not work on Sunday. Here's something to chew on: "It is more than interesting that scientists say our bodies are genetically wired to require one day out of every seven for physical, emotional, and spiritual restoration in order to perform at our highest potential."[1] Yes, that is an interesting fact, but then it should not surprise us because we also have divine DNA and are made in His image. Our brilliant God told us to rest on the Sabbath.

Our area of Cherryville was what we called a "mill village." These communities, predominately in the South, were built around a textile mill that employed almost everyone in the town. The town supported the mill, and the mill gave life to the town. Mill villages were often characterized by rows of modest, identical houses built by the mill to house its employees. Working in a textile mill was hard work, and the wages were meager.

People who grew up in a mill village would be quick to tell you there were very limited social opportunities available. Since children didn't work in the mill, there just wasn't much to keep children occupied; toys and games

---

1     From *The Word for You Today* © Celebration Inc.

were at a minimum in most families, simply because of finances. The ruts were deep, and the routine of boredom was well-entrenched.

Each summer, First Baptist Church, like most churches in Cherryville, held a weeklong Vacation Bible School that I looked forward to. For those of us who had limited social and extracurricular opportunities elsewhere, VBS was an eagerly anticipated event. During Vacation Bible School in the summer of 1948, the pastor shared the gospel and gave an invitation to become a Christian. As previously discussed, everyone on my pew responded, and consequently, so did I. *This must be the right thing to do*, I figured.

A few days later, at the age of nine, I was baptized and started attending church regularly, but church was more of a social activity for me than anything else. Gradually I drifted away, rarely ever picked up my Bible, and prayed only in extreme emergencies. I displayed no evidence of being "born again" because I simply had not been. I had not been changed. In essence, I was a "lost" church member. At that time, I was probably too young and had too little training to comprehend the truth about such an important step in one's life. I have since learned the complete process in "regeneration."

Being created anew consists of the following:

» Conviction—the understanding that I have broken God's law with sin.

» Repentance—responding to conviction of my guilt.

» Deliverance—being set free of the penalty of sin by my Savior, Jesus Christ.

» Obedience—obeying, with God's power, out of gratitude for God's grace and undeserved favor.

» Peace—living as God gave us life to live, free of guilt and fear.

During those early days, Reverend and Mrs. E.S. Elliot of First Baptist Church regularly visited families who lived in our mill village, and they talked to our parents about bringing us to church. They reminded us that Jesus loved us and wanted us to be part of this church. They were dear, kind people who loved God and consequently loved us children, even though we could make no monetary contribution to God's church. One might describe us kids in those days as scruffy and unrefined, common mill village ruffians. Nevertheless, the Elliots knew we needed to be loved and nurtured as a part of same.

Since then, I have learned that in the eyes of a just and righteous God, there is no such thing as common people. We are all limited editions of one, each special with unique fingerprints, voice prints, DNA, and unique irises of our eyes. Each of us is always on His mind!

Mrs. Elliot, known as Pearl to most everyone, was a tender and kind-hearted disciple of the Lord. Her affection for children could easily be described by the verses in the book of Matthew when Jesus told His disciples, "Let the little children come unto me, and do not forbid them, for such is the kingdom of heaven." Pearl and Reverend Elliot visited our home often and never seemed discouraged that we rarely attended church as an entire family. Even though my parents couldn't always attend, they made sure we kids were provided transportation so we could attend. The Elliotts came to visit because they really cared, and they knew their compassion honored the Lord. To this day, I am convinced that their unconditional love for children, like me, awakened an awareness in me that I could never get over and only my Creator could complete.

## Community

Cherryville schools were staffed by very competent teachers who loved their profession (their lifetime calling) and loved their students. All were so gifted. And oh, how the teachers loved to see their students excel. Every Monday morning, a gold star was placed on the chart beside the name of each person who attended Sunday school the day before. To me, this conveyed that they were as concerned with our spiritual development and moral conduct as they were with our intellectual development. There was no political correctness at the time, and that alone is reason enough to call them "the good old days."

Cherryville also had a school board comprised only of local people who loved the school and loved the students. They also respected the teachers. Because the board members were involved locally, they made informed and wise decisions. The result was that students were ultimately very well-equipped for our next steps in life.

I cannot say enough, or ever be grateful enough, for the sound, fundamental education I received there, especially in English. Having been grounded in reading and writing later became invaluable to me as a business leader in an industry where effective communication was so vitally important.

The Cherryville police knew everyone in town, and they were respected as essential protectors of us all. They often took young first-time lawbreakers home to their parents for appropriate punishment and correction rather than to the police station. They simply wanted the best for the youth. And we respected them for this and trusted them.

The doctors in my hometown were so absolutely committed to helping the sick they made themselves available 'round the clock. I remember Dr. F. M. Houser, a wonderful, friendly doctor who had been crippled in an auto accident by a careless driver. His being crippled did not change his wonderful outlook on life. Because of that accident, he had to wear braces on both legs for the rest of his life. On many occasions, when one of us children would become worse during the night, even two or three in the morning, he came willingly—and cheerfully—to our home to help a sick child for very little pay. His reward has now come in his promised eternal home!

Most people slept never locking the doors and let their children play outside without fear for their safety. I have learned over many years that one of the best ways to know more about our Creator is to spend more time outside enjoying His magnificent creation. "The heavens declare the glory of God," the Psalmist wrote. With great fondness, I recall those wonderful days playing outside all day, making up games, climbing trees to see if baby birds were still in the nest, and catching lightning bugs at dusk. We all found ways to entertain ourselves and enjoyed every minute of it.

Since illegal drugs were unheard of, drug-related crimes were nonexistent. More people were content with life, and there was no need for the mind-altering and life-destroying drugs which are wreaking havoc in our society today. Dogs and cats ran loose and got along better than most of our politicians get along these days. It was an age of patience, even when the neighbor next door was not exactly like you. People knew things went better when we were neighborly with one another.

By now, you are likely concluding Cherryville was a very wholesome place to grow up. Between the many good churches, the fine schools and teachers, the honorable police, the wonderful doctors, the absence of harmful drugs, and the safe environment my hometown provided, we felt very secure.

## Blessings

Family and friends visited and did not have to "text" to see if it was acceptable. They visited without appointments, even at mealtime, and all shared in whatever food had been prepared. Relatives were not an intrusion, and we all knew our relatives more completely because we all had time for each other.

Our classmates were almost like family. We spent year after year together, all the while establishing lifelong friendships. Many of us started the first grade together and graduated twelve years later together. My friends were always welcome in my home, and I was always welcome in theirs. Their parents had many of the same beliefs and moral values that my parents had, so there was consistency all around. Many of our houses were modest, but they were blessed with the love and respect of family. The old adage "the house doesn't make the home" is so true. We were grateful for what we had, and no one ever told us how "disadvantaged" we were. If they had, we would've had to have had an explanation as well, since it was a word most of us had never heard. It is so overused today!

We also learned many lessons the hard way. We learned from "stone bruises" that, while going barefoot, you'd better "look before you leap." That is still a valuable lesson for life even to this day, whether you are buying, flying, or marrying.

We did lack the wonderful devices and advancements of today, but we had something better—a genuine peace and contentment about our lives in my hometown. When I think about progress, I'm always reminded of what humorist Ogden Nash once said, "progress might have been good once, but it has gone on far too long." What some today consider "progressive" is clearly regressive. It is not progress when we abandon values, especially Christian values, that have served us so well in the past.

We have all heard the expression, "you should never look back because all of that is behind you." Experience has shown me sometimes we should look back, and when we do, we find a place called *my hometown* that so well prepared us for a life of peace, fulfillment, and satisfaction. My hometown was wholesome. It was a place that never gave up on people and a place where the church reached out, and in the process, introduced me and multitudes to my Master, the Lord Jesus Christ. Because a Christian reached out to me, and because I attended a revival service, and because other Christians were praying for me, my life was revolutionized and redirected by that wondrous event. That event alone, the night I truly gave my life to Jesus at age thirty, is enough to appreciate what a great place my hometown was for me. Yes, we can, and should, look back and see just how blessed we were to live in a small town called Cherryville. My hometown shaped us over those early years to be grateful, thankful, and richly blessed people with special friends forever.

Was my hometown perfect? No, because no perfect people resided there, but still, it was special. Yes, yes, yes it was. And I owe so many people there in that sweet town who believed in me, invested time in me, and modeled Christ before me. I can only say it was where God, in His infinite wisdom, put me and where I needed to grow up and come to know my real purpose in life. I consider it and know it to be nothing less than the beautiful grace of God, His unmerited favor that He allowed me to grow up in my hometown. Furthermore, it was also by grace He allowed me to be born into the family that He placed me in. Yes, blessed I was. In my early years, little did I know that God had any plans for me. But as I matured and after I started studying God's Word, it was enlightening and exciting when I read for the first time that precious promise "The steps of a good man are ordered by the Lord" (Psalm 37:23, KJV). Every true child of God knows for anyone to become righteous; it is only by the sinless blood of Christ. Our righteousness was paid for at a high price! However, once we are His and seek His ways, He orders our steps. That is so wonderful!

I realize my small town and our modest means limited many aspects of our lives. For example, we had "school clothes," usually two or three sets of shirts and pants which our parents bought at Galloways or Goldiners, the two department stores close to us. As you can imagine, selections were very limited, and so were our finances. I remember very specifically when Mom bought me three seersucker short-sleeved shirts with large flowers and green leaves. One of them was lime green with very large orange flowers and green leaves, and another was brilliant blue with huge orange flowers. The third was green with red flowers. I did not love them, but they were new, and they clearly gave me a unique identity. In fact, it's probably a good thing the Department of Social Services had not been instituted yet, else they may have removed me from my home for "abuse" when wearing those loud, ostentatious shirts.

I have never forgotten how much I coveted just one pair of knickers which were knee-length and worn with knee-high socks. I also desired a pair of penny loafers. They were both stylish in those days, but our meager budget called for overalls and brogans, which were high-top work shoes. The worst thing about brogans was you could never wear them out, especially if they had the name "Wolverines" on them. I learned later in life they were made of horsehide. No wonder I thought they were eternal! The durability of the brogans also reduced the frequency of replacement shoes and the slim hope that those shoes might be the coveted penny loafers. Children of wealthy parents wore those fancy slippers. They placed a coin in the tongue of the shoe, and I wanted to project the same style as those who wore them.

Through all of this, though, I did learn a life lesson: it is better to learn how to share and "do without" at home than to have the world teach you the hard lessons later, after being coddled too much. Our modest means made us children grateful for what we did have—parents who loved us, friends who enjoyed our company, and neighbors who cared about us and wanted the best for us, just like they wanted for their own children. I had not yet learned at that early age that there was a book of truth, thousands of years old, which declares this paraphrased truth: "It is better to have little in a place of love than wealth in a place of strife." What a great blessing for me to have been born to parents who lacked a whole lot of worldly goods but loved their family and consistently taught us right from wrong and to take the Golden Rule to heart by always trying to do the right thing.

## Family

Our family consisted of my parents and five children. Edwin was my older brother, and Martha and Ruth were my older sisters. Ann was my younger sister, and—you guessed it—she came along at a very inopportune time. She spoiled my very coveted position in our family as the baby. Life never was quite the same for me after her arrival.

*Paul's Parents, Lester and Velma Taylor*

*Paul and his Siblings: front row;*
*Ruth and Paul, back row; Martha, Edwin and Ann*

Our father, Charles Lester Taylor, was born in 1905 in the small mountain community of Todd, North Carolina. When we would ask him about his education, he would always laughingly say, "I went in through the front door and out the back door, and that was it. I knew all I needed to know." We never knew the real truth, whether he had any formal education or not, but we were well aware that he had a profound mechanical mind, and he could accomplish anything he set his mind to. He clearly verified that God truly is the Difference-Maker.

My father never had the life of ease anytime or anywhere along the way. He was one of nine children born to his parents between 1902 and 1919. Times were exceptionally hard, especially in the mountains of North Carolina. But my dad's lifetime of serving, giving, and growing has helped me to clearly define an answer to the question I have been asked on numerous occasions. That question is, "Paul, what is the most important thing you have learned over the course of your business life?" My answer is very simple: "people can!" And my good father's life absolutely reinforces that truth. He took what life gave him, decided not to be a victim, and with very little education, worked hard and invented two different textile machinery attachments for patents. They were registered in the U.S. Patent Office. They were never worth much money, but they spoke volumes to me about his keen mind and technical ability.

You see, my dad was special because he was "fearfully and wonderfully made" (Psalm 139:4, KJV) and "made in the image of God" (Genesis 1:26, KJV). Even though, as a child, I had never read that truth, I realize it now. No one else ever had, or will have, his DNA, his fingerprints, voiceprints, or unique iris of his eyes. He was a limited edition of one, and he is still my precious dad!

My dad was a gentle, kind man who was physically powerfully strong. He was known for his ability to lift and carry what it took two people on the opposite end to carry. He believed in hard work, loyalty to his employer, and, even more so, loyalty to his family. He did whatever it took to feed his family of five children, and if he ever complained, we never knew it. He spent almost all his adult working life in the textile mills in and around Cherryville, North Carolina, primarily for the Rhyne-Houser Manufacturing Company, where he became the head mechanic.

Because of their lower economic status, mill people were somewhat stigmatized. But we were too uninformed to be victims. And we did not have the politicians always capitalizing on it and pretending to care about victimization. We never knew if, in fact, we were underprivileged. Perhaps the old adage "ignorance is bliss" was our way of avoidance.

I grew up in a modestly-furnished shotgun-style narrow-width mill house with a hallway down the center. Our kitchen was the largest and warmest room in the house. I remember when sleeping in my small bed, perhaps as a four-year-old child, that I had nightmares because the Second World War was under way, and the era of the atomic bomb was just beginning. I would awaken from my nightmare and being too afraid to move and almost to breathe; I would call out to my daddy. He would respond with, "What's the matter, son?" To which I would whimper, "I'm afraid." He always came and sat on the side of my bed. He would lay that large, muscular arm over my small frame and tell me, "Son, it's alright, and I am right here with you. Go back to sleep." I knew I could trust my daddy, and I would go right back to sleep.

I will never forget my dad's faithfulness. It was almost as if he slept lightly so as to be there for me. In Psalm 121 (ESV), we read our Heavenly Father's promise: "He who keeps Israel [you] will neither slumber nor sleep." The psalmist also assures us that our Heavenly Father is our keeper and clings fast to our souls. "The Lord will keep your going out and your coming in from this time forth and forevermore."

Psalm 27:1 (NKJV) is also a question with a promise. It says, "The Lord is my light and my salvation, whom shall I fear? The Lord is the strength of my life, of whom shall I be afraid?"

My earthly father always came and always comforted me in my time of need. My heavenly Father has now taken his place, and I cling to the promise of the psalmist: He who keeps me will not slumber.

Daddy never learned to write before he left school in his early teens to start working. He went to Bluefield, Virginia, to work in the coal mines at about age fifteen. In those pre-Depression days, there were no electrical or gas-operated machines. They literally collected the coal by hand; their only tool was a pickax. Can you think of a better example of manual labor? "When a seam of coal narrowed and would be maybe three or four feet high," he told us, "I would lie on my side to pick at it until it opened again." He had the arms and pectoral muscles to prove it. There were few other jobs available, especially in the blue-collar mountainous area where he grew up. But Daddy worked, and he worked hard, and he was grateful for the work.

Daddy never told me why he left the coal mines, but he came with several of his friends to Cherryville in search of work. He found a job at the textile mill, and he spent the rest of his working life there. Although Daddy started at an entry-level position, he advanced to head mechanic at this same mill, Rhyne-Houser Manufacturing Company.

Then life changed. The mill that Daddy had worked in for so many years was purchased by a corporate conglomerate, and even though my dad was the head mechanic and knew all there was to know about the various types of machinery, he was discharged after a lifetime of loyalty because he could not write and could not fill out the reports that the new owner required. After that, Daddy always seemed to feel a little inadequate. He did not go to work for another mill. Instead, he bought and operated some knitting machines over his garage, making socks for a living until he experienced heart failure a few years later. Eventually, he had a coronary and passed away in 1965, at the age of fifty-nine. Upon my dad's passing, the abundant flowers, the plentiful sympathy cards, the crocks of food, and all the many visits attested to the respect in which he was held by so many. When we, his children, look back on him now, we see what a wonderful father he was and how much he loved his children. Daddy never complained, whined, nor lamented about the hard life he had. He was never a victim of a stolen childhood. He dealt with whatever came his way and was a rock for his grateful children. At the time, we failed to recognize the adversity he had to overcome; all we saw was his thankful, positive outlook on life. The only thing I can remember that he ever really complained about was a tight collar and a necktie. That's a pretty good legacy to leave.

When my father came to my hometown looking for work, he not only found a job at the mill, but also he found the love of his life—my special mom!

My mother, Velma Pernice Hicks, was one of six girls born to Albert and Ada Hicks in Cherryville. She was born in 1909. Mom's father was a carpenter of German descent. He had helped build many of the mill houses for the Rhyne-Houser Manufacturing Company. And while he contracted typhoid fever and passed away before I ever personally knew him, I still learned much about him as I grew older. One thing I learned was that when my father wanted to date his pretty blonde daughter, Velma, he had to ask permission from her father. My grandfather consented with one stipulation—my dad must "court her at home".

Our mother's mother lived next door to us, which was a wonderful blessing for me. In those days, the food from a previous meal would be left on the table and covered with a white tablecloth to keep flies away. After I had eaten breakfast at home, it became a ritual for me to slip away to Grandma's, hoping she would have some of her wonderful biscuits and bacon under the white tablecloth. She always knew why I had come so early, but for the longest time pretended she didn't know I had already eaten at home. She coyly provided me a second breakfast, and it was our little secret. Eventually, second breakfast was so common for me that grandma would take me straight to the table and make certain I cleaned out the leftovers. It was a blissful time, a time before anyone had ever heard of cholesterol, which may be another one of the reasons we call those "the good old days."

Grandmother was a wonderful gardener, and she also loved flowers. Her vegetable garden was between our house and hers, a well-worn walking path snaked from one house to the other. Her flower garden was one of my favorite places as a young boy. She loved gladiolas and dahlias, and so did I, but for different reasons. These flowers grew to a height of two-and-a-half to three feet with beautiful large blooms. The butterflies could not resist these pollen-rich beauties.

To this day, there are two things that, for as long as I can remember, I have loved and enjoyed. Those things are birds and—you guessed it—butterflies. In my mind, they are some of God's finest creations. My attraction and love for them have never wavered. Perhaps I innately knew God created something very fascinating when He made the caterpillar that could spin a cocoon around itself and emerge transformed as a beautiful butterfly. It's an astounding demonstration of God's wise and complex creation.

Anyway, the "glads" in particular were about as tall as I was, and they attracted multitudes of beautiful butterflies. I stood between the rows with butterflies fluttering around me, catching one after another. I tried not to harm their delicate wings, but I am reasonably sure I didn't help them. After I gazed at their beauty then released them, they didn't manage to fly quite as well. But I marvel when I think that God created them to carry pollen from one flower to another, sharing their astounding beauty with us. To this day, I love flowers, much like my mother did, and am continually fascinated by their gorgeous God-designed beauty.

*Paul taking care of his flowers*

My mother and father were married at ages nineteen and twenty-four, respectively, during the early years of the Great Depression. It was an indescribable time, a time of depression of the economy and even more so, depression of the spirit. Suicide was widespread, and people did not know how to cope in an era when there was little work, little food, little help, and even less hope. There was great human suffering. Unemployment rose above twenty percent. Most stocks became worthless. And to make matters worse, the Dustbowl followed immediately thereafter. It is difficult for us to comprehend the pervasive pessimism that hung like a fog over the country. Yet I never heard either of my parents ever complain. They remained steadfastly grateful for what we had, sparse as it was.

My mother had only a seventh-grade education. Her family needed what money they could get, so she started working in the mill at the age of twelve. Her earnings went to support her family. She never got to keep any of the money she earned until after she was married. And it was while working at the mill that she met my father. In addition to working in the mill after she married, she picked cotton on her uncle's farm. It was hard, back-breaking work, requiring much stooping, and the pay was meager. Every little bit helped support our family, which now consisted of five children.

Mom planted a garden which she worked after her shifts at the mill, and whatever she was able to grow in the garden that we did not eat immediately, she would work late into the night canning vegetables to eat at a later time. These days—and nights—were long and demanding. And like my father, Mom worked tirelessly to provide for her precious family.

*Paul's mother gardening*

She loved to be outdoors, working the soil, always growing a vegetable garden or two, and flowers as well. My, how she loved her flowers! She was also continually fascinated by their Godly-designed beauty. Perhaps her great love for nature and passion for flowers was what ignited the very same passions within me. I have developed the same appreciation for flowers. Every time I work with flowers now, I always remember Mom and how she loved them.

There is an event pertaining to Mom and flowers that is burned in my heart and mind. On an early March day in the mid-1980s, a year or two after I had left Cherryville, we were visiting Mom when she said, "Paul, I want to show you something outside." We walked out to what appeared to be an empty flower bed. Mom stooped and delicately removed a tiny bit of earth, then pointed to a very small plant, a crocus, just emerging. As she pointed to it, she excitingly said, "Now, that's God." My mom reverenced God, and she realized He was in everything beautiful that was created. She believed we could discover the wisdom and brilliance, and power of God in all created things, especially beautiful flowers, which she loved. I treasure the memory of knowing that my special mom saw God in everything, even the smallest of things, like the slight green bud reaching through the moist earth toward heaven.

My mother's faith was beyond description. She endured the sudden and painful loss of her firstborn son, my brother Edwin, who died when he was twenty-nine, and then the loss of a kind and loving daughter, my sister Ruth, who passed at age forty-two. My mom was anguished as my sister suffered terribly from cancer, but she never blamed God or lost her faith. She also lost my father, who died of a coronary before his sixtieth birthday. All of her six sisters preceded my mom in death, yet she never lost her wonderful appreciation of life and expressed it with joy and laughter every day.

After my father's passing, Mother would, on nice days, work for hours in the garden tending to the vegetables or the flowers. She was tough. She worked a heavy tiller, and she had endurance, passion, and God's peace, which made what she did a labor of love. After she had worked all day, she would come in and prepare the evening meal. Afterward, she would listen to Bible preachers on the radio, and even with failing eyesight, she would crochet as "sincere but unrefined" voices from the radio proclaimed the Gospel. She created crocheted masterpieces, almost by feel. Now, as I think back, I realize the Master helped her create masterpieces because she was—and is—a Masterpiece, now in her eternal home.

Mom not only had the patience of Job but the faith as well. She lived with Job's words in her heart and mind every day: "Though He slay me, yet will I hope in Him" (trust Him) (Job 13:15, NIV).

For the last twelve or thirteen years of her life, Mom suffered from Alzheimer's, yet she never became angry or uncooperative. Her last few years were spent in an assisted living facility. Finally, at 96, she worsened, and it was evident the Lord would soon call her home.

My son and I went to the hospital that day, knowing she would probably not live another day. As I started out of the house, I was prompted to get my

45

Bible. When we arrived at her bedside, her eyes were closed. I touched her hand and whispered in her ear, "Mom, have you had any good news today?" "Mom" was a cue word for her, and she whispered, "Paul, is that you?"

"Yes, It's me."

Then in response to my question about good news, she whispered, "Not really."

"Mom, I have some," I said, and I began to read the 23rd Psalm. "The Lord is—"

"My shepherd," she whispered.

"I shall not want," I continued.

Together, we cited the remainder of that beautiful psalm. Not one voice then the other, but together, our voices as one, in unison, this exquisite, sacred poetry flowing from our lips:

*He maketh me to lie down in green pastures:*

*He leadeth me beside the still waters.*

*He restoreth my soul:*

*He leadeth me in the paths of righteousness for His name's sake.*

*Yea, though I walk through the valley of the shadow of death,*

*I will fear no evil: For thou art with me;*

*Thy rod and thy staff, they comfort me.*

*Thou preparest a table before me in the presence of mine enemies;*

*Thou annointest my head with oil; My cup runneth over.*

*Surely goodness and mercy shall follow me all the days of my life...*

Together, we proclaimed the psalm's final verse:

*"And I shall dwell in the house of the Lord forever."*

She closed her eyes and never opened them. Those were the last words she ever spoke.

Here was a beautiful person whose memory at ninety-six was practically nonexistent, and yet, she could remember the powerful promises and truths of God's Holy Bible. She had stored them in her heart! If there never had been another blessing in my life, my precious mom would have been enough. She loved life, and more importantly, she loved dearly the One who said, "I am the Way, the Truth, and the Life" (John 14:6, KJV). What a blessed heritage she left for us.

My mom had an exceedingly difficult life, probably harder than we can all realize. Though she suffered a great loss with the passing of her husband and two of her children, as well as her parents and all of her sisters before her, and though she worked extremely hard physically, she was not a victim. She was a victor, positive and pleasant. And if you knew her, you knew how victoriously she lived!

Even though times were very hard during my early years, my positive mother never told me I was "disadvantaged" or "discriminated against." She knew one of the worst things any parent can ever say to a child is, "You can't do that. People will not let you." I, therefore, felt completely secure and at ease in my circumstances as a contented child who knew he was loved and who believed he could succeed. Perhaps I was naïve, but I am crediting my Maker for protecting me from those most restrictive and demoralizing words—disadvantaged, discriminated against. God knew what my mother knew then and what I've learned later: people are empowered to excel by God's Holy Spirit, the Difference-Maker, but they need to be encouraged, not discouraged, to believe it and strive for it. God has enabled me as His child to have such an eventful life, despite never having taken a single business or Bible course. There is a powerful truth that God promises, "Greater is He that is in you, than he who is in the world" (1 John 4:4, KJV).

I have one sister, Ann, still living. She reminds me a great deal of my tenacious mother. Nothing is too difficult or challenging for her. For years, she operated her own catering company and then managed the food services for a large social club. Obviously, she is an incredibly great cook! Ann has the same "overcomer" spirit as our good mom. If something is challenging or a new undertaking, and if she doesn't already know how to do it, she will simply work at it until she does. Like Mother, Ann has always known that *people can*, and she is therefore never unwilling to undertake whatever the challenge is. She has the rare common sense of our father. She is an extremely talented lady.

When our daughters were small girls, Ann would make intricate detailed Barbie doll clothes for their dolls, sewing on beautiful tiny beads and other decorative items. From her early adult life, she became proficient in making masterfully gorgeous birthday cakes and wedding cakes. For our mother's seventy-fifth birthday celebration, Ann made nearly a hundred cake squares, each decorated with a different colored pansy. She made a large cake, too, adorned with varying beautifully colored pansies. As you might suspect, pansies were one of Mom's favorite flowers. The cakes were a work of art! She made an equally gorgeous Bible cake for my seventy-fifth birthday with my favorite Bible verse on it. Without a doubt, Ann is gifted artistically and is a tenacious hard worker, but most of all, she has a very kind heart and loves people. She was beyond devoted and unfailing to tirelessly help care for each of our family members before they passed. Ann was especially attentive to one sister, Ruth, who suffered from cancer for eighteen long months. When I see Ann, or Annie, as our children still call her, I often think of our very special mother, and it's a precious reminder, as they remind me of one another.

Ruth, one of my older sisters, was a humble woman, kind and generous of spirit. She never married, and I'm persuaded it was because both she and God knew my mother would need her. When my dad passed and my older brother Edwin passed, Ruthie was there with her during those very difficult times. Our children thought Aunt Ruthie could walk on water, and for them, I think she would have tried if asked. She would do anything to entertain them and play with them. She loved them as if they were her own and played whatever make-believe games they wanted to play. She lavished gifts on our children at Christmas. She whistled regularly to "The Sound of Music," and her whistle was like a beautiful flute. Sadly, Ruth developed cancer, and God welcomed her home at the age of forty-two. She faced her illness with much grace, never questioning God. She loved Jesus and continually assured us during her illness that it was alright, not to be sad, and that she was going to be well again in heaven. In all of those forty-two years, I never heard her say one unkind thing about anyone! That's quite a legacy for anyone to leave. Never could anyone be blessed more than to have someone so kind, gentle, and humble as family.

My brother Edwin was ten years older than me and just the kind of brother anyone would want to have. I looked up to him because he was just a wonderful brother—loving, unpretentious, and a happy guy. Edwin joined the Navy with three of his best friends, and they served together. He played the accordion and was a kind and gentle man. At twenty-nine, he found the love of his life and was soon engaged. Although Edwin had never been ill before, Edwin suffered a massive coronary and died the same day. My mom and dad were devastated. Yet they never blamed God. They knew life had its ups and downs, its disappointments and blessings. Their experiences and their faith had taught them how to deal with tragedy, and they did not let it destroy their love of life.

Finally, I had another older sister, Martha, who married young. She and her husband worked hard. They never had children, and they did well financially. Probably because they didn't have children of their own, they enjoyed inviting our children to do some things with them. Our children felt it was a treat to get to spend the night at their house because it was so much "fancier" than ours. They often took a couple of them at a time to Lineberger's Fish Camp. In addition to serving the best seafood in Western North Carolina, it housed a large candy shop. Going there was truly a special treat.

I continually feel especially blessed to have grown up in my small, wholesome hometown of Cherryville, North Carolina. Most importantly,

I realize how blessed I am to have been born into such a wonderful family of good, kind-hearted, positive, grateful, hardworking, joyful people. They showed me that God does indeed make a difference in one's life, and their perseverance led me to know *people can*, and with certainty, how powerfully true that statement is.

# CHAPTER 2

# Best Laid Plans

You already know of my great love of being outdoors and enjoying God's majestic creation. "The heavens declare the glory of God!" wrote the Psalmist. It's something you just cannot fully experience and appreciate from the rocking chair. So quite naturally, I was an active child, frequently outside, always running, playing, and growing healthier and stronger as a result. I remember even as early as the seventh grade, I regularly ran home from school and back at lunchtime for several reasons, not the least of which was because it was refreshing for me, and it energized me to run. No one in those days had yet heard of Forrest Gump, the subject of the 1986 Winston Groom novel and subsequent 1994 film that made famous the phrase "Run, Forrest, run!" Yet, that was me. At least as far as the running was concerned. It only took me about seven minutes to run home, fifteen minutes to eat, then turn around and run back to school. Plus, I even got to see my dog, Rocky, every day at lunch. Best of all, my mom always, even when she was working, had good, healthy food for my lunch.

Sports and athletics were important activities in my hometown. Most of the textile mills fielded a semi-pro baseball team from among their employees. Cherryville, to this very day, is widely recognized as a baseball town, home to high school state champions and American Legion World Series playoff teams. Undoubtedly, there are few other small towns with the same fan interest and consistently positive winning results.

Equally as interesting was the commitment made to the Cherryville high school football program. In the early years of the program, 1934, they had only fifteen players on the team, and most of those fifteen players took to the field for the full sixty minutes, playing both offense and defense. Remarkably, they won the State Championship that year. Thus, the name appropriately given to the Cherryville High School athletes with such endurance was and still is "Ironmen." Becoming an Ironman was a superlative accomplishment and is worthily coveted to this day. For those who grew up hearing about the wonderful tradition those athletes began, it was rather easy to idolize the Ironmen and then begin to look forward to a time when we might be proudly called Ironmen as well. I must admit that, in my own case, I imagined one day that I might even qualify and become an authentic Ironman. So as I ran back and forth home for lunch, I often thought this was just part of my preparation to be a part of this great tradition. I suppose all of us have boyhood ambitions that sometimes seem almost unreachable, but as we grow and mature, we come to realize a critical and vitally important truth—*People can!*

*The Original Ironmen*

In my preteen and early teen years, my body began to develop, and by the time I was sixteen years old, I was nearly six feet tall and weighed 185 pounds. All of my running over the early years lengthened my stride to the point that I was the second-fastest runner in competitive races in my school. Indeed, my Maker had given me a healthy athletic body, and even though I did not realize it at the time, it was by His divine grace and favor that I did become a strong and competitive Ironman.

During my junior and senior years, I was encouraged to join the track and field team since that sport would help me stay in great shape for the football season in the fall. I competed in two track events—the 100-yard dash and the mile relay (team) events. I also competed in two field events, the shotput and the discus throw. It was all very enjoyable, with one exception—the mile relay race. For some unknown reason, I was normally the anchor leg, the last runner to run. The reason this was less enjoyable was because the anchor runner was expected to maintain or regain the lead and win the race. If the third runner had passed the baton as the leader to me, I was expected to protect that lead. On the other hand, and in a worst-case scenario, if I received the baton from our third-place runner, who was behind, I was expected to make up the difference and win the race!

Let me tell you, even if you are in great shape, the quarter-mile (440-yard run) is a runner's nightmare. It is almost a full sprint all the way. It was also usually our last event, and my dread of having to run it sometimes took away the enjoyment of competing in the other events, namely the discus throw, my specialty. As expected, however, track and field did help keep the football players who participated in shape for the coming season.

## The Summer Before

In a textile village like ours, there would be summer work available at the mills for some of us older teenagers. This was the case in the summer of 1955. The work we were hired to do was hard, heavy work, which is exactly what I needed for this summer before my final senior football season.

Cotton mills in those days had raw cotton, baled in large, heavy bales, delivered constantly. My particular job this summer was to unload the cotton truck when the bales arrived and then to transfer the cotton from the "cotton house" to the processing part of the mill as needed. The bales consistently weighed between four and five hundred pounds.

One thing that made this extra challenging was that there were no elevators, only long inclined ramps to both the "cotton house" and the mill itself. They were not necessarily steep inclines, but they were lengthy, which required a good "running" start and steady push with hand trucks, with no let-up, in order to get the bales all the way up the ramps. This, as stated before, was exactly what I needed in preparation for football, but oh! What a price to pay! How my legs burned at the top of that ramp, bale after bale.

But did it ever pay off! When football practice started my senior year, I was in the best shape of my life. I was fearless, maybe foolishly, but I knew it was all about readiness, and I was ready. After all, this was going to be my ticket to college. No one in my family had ever attended college, so it wasn't necessarily a high priority for my family, but for me, it was important. I have always enjoyed reading and learning. Further, most of my friends had already selected their colleges, and I was now ready for one to select me, so I could go there with a football scholarship!

The local and county papers had already begun to speculate that this was going to be a banner season for the Ironmen. After all, it was very unusual for a high school team in 1955 to average almost 200 pounds per player like our team did. We also had a new coach who had played professionally for the Washington Redskins, and he was very knowledgeable about the game of football.

Our first game was against Mount Holly. Even though we were expected to do well, we were not favored to win this first game. The final score was 33–19, in our favor. We gained 362 yards rushing, and when it was all over, we felt like true Ironmen. In those days, most of the stronger players played both offense and defense. In my case, I was an offensive fullback and a defensive linebacker. How delighted I was to intercept in that first game, our team's single intercepted pass as a linebacker.

In the county paper the next morning, the sports headline read, "Taylor Scores Three, Ironmen win 33–19." I remember that game well. At halftime, our coach put in two new plays around the ends. One was for me, and the other was for Ronald Turner, a halfback. At the risk of being misunderstood or sounding arrogant, I will tell you—we were unstoppable.

My most immediate thought after the game was, *I just hope some of the colleges become aware of this.* Sure enough, during the next week, three pieces of mail came to my mailbox. They were letters of interest from UNC-Chapel Hill, The University of Tennessee, and Davidson College, who fielded a football team at that time.

How exciting! My grandiose plans to play college football were underway. But sadly, it was only a week later that they were shattered. I certainly did not know it then, but after almost a lifetime, I know it as one of the most certain truths: Our Creator and Life-giver will always have a better and more perfect plan than we can ever have alone.

*What in the world happened?* you ask. In a game against Belmont High, I carried the ball and wound up in a pileup on the ground. Before I could get up, someone deliberately grabbed my foot, twisted hard, and tore the ACL of my left knee. In those days, you were not assisted off the field, without weight bearing on the knee, as is now the safe practice. I limped off, which did not help my serious injury. In fact, when I got back to the sideline, the question then was, "Paul, are you about ready to go back in?" I could barely stand on it, let alone play. However, I continued to take the field for the rest of the season but never managed more than a few plays each game before the pain became unbearable. I was devastated, without any perspective of what my life could now become. My dreams were crushed. But unknown to me then, my Heavenly Father had a better plan. He always has!

"For I know the plans I have for you," declares The Lord. "Plans to prosper you and not to harm you, plans to give you hope and a future" (Jeremiah 29:11, NIV). Who can claim this promise from God Himself? Every person who has been made righteous by the sinless blood of Jesus Christ! Sometimes we may feel like we are struggling along on our own, but that's just a feeling. God answers that feeling with this unbreakable promise: "I will never leave nor forsake you" (Hebrews 13:5, ESV).

## The Real Plan

Since the opportunity to attend college on an athletic scholarship had vanished in a single football play, the immediate question for me was, "What now?" Our family had no extra money set aside for college, so what was I to do? Knowing how badly I wanted to attend college, my parents borrowed (and in the process did without some of their own needs) enough money for me to attend Western Carolina University for one year. It was enjoyable, but honestly, I felt too badly about their sacrifice on my behalf. In those days, there were not a lot of resources for student loans, and financial assistance as there are today. At the end of that year, I decided to stay at home and not return.

In our small town where the textile industry was dominant, there was only one place where the wages were considerably better than textiles, and that was Carolina Freight Carriers Corporation. This company had been founded in Cherryville by the Beam brothers and, because of reliable service from a lot of dedicated employees, it had developed into a large East Coast motor carrier. This hometown trucking company business was consistently using part-time day laborers to load and unload trailers at the large service center located there. This seemed to be the best place to make a satisfactory wage. Yet, there was only one problem, and it was big—everyone saw the opportunity, so there were many more applicants than there were jobs. My parents, having worked in textiles all their lives, knew none of the decision-makers at Carolina Freight. They, therefore, had no influence on Carolina Freight, and they could not help me get noticed for an opportunity.

The process to get hired to work was for the day laborers to show up at 7 a.m., 3 p.m., and 11 p.m., in case they needed more workers, "extras," to process the cargo on that day or at that time. We would all go—and wait—and hope that we might finally be given an opportunity to work on that shift that day. It was frustrating for me because I had shown up on twenty-seven consecutive occasions with no success in getting to work. It was like college athletics; I was a walk-on athlete, and I would have to earn whatever I got if I could only get a chance. Finally, on the twenty-eighth attempt, the job foreman looked at me and said, "You, boy, work with J. D. today." I did not know J. D. was the most difficult one of all to please. J. D. seemed to trust no one, maybe even including his mother, and he despised having to teach new and inexperienced workers like me. But I was so glad to finally get work that I think I would've worked for the devil himself. I had already made up my mind beforehand without reservation; I had *truly decided* that if I ever get to work one day, I would prove myself, and they would ask me to come back for work the next day. Sure enough, I worked forty hours per week for the next six weeks. It was heavy, sweaty, manual labor, and extremely hot in the summer. As I later learned, it was also a bitter cold job in the winter, which was equally as tough to endure. But it was a beginning for me, a chance to prove my worth, and I was grateful to have the job. It also taught me something about perseverance. Over a lifetime, I have encountered many people who wanted to accomplish something. I'm sure you have, too. But I find it interesting that those who actually *did* accomplish something are the ones who *decided to.* There is a huge difference between wanting to accomplish something and deciding to accomplish something.

My friends would come home from college and ask me, "What are you doing now, Paul?" I would answer, "I'm loading trucks." All too often, I saw in their faces a cast-down look, almost as if I had declared I had leprosy. I'm sure they did not mean harm, but it helped me to know even then that an important part of my calling in life was to empathize with and consider the hard workers. I knew, in every way that I could, I needed to see that honest, hard-working, down-to-earth people were appreciated and given the dignity they deserve. They all too often do the tough things others feel they are above doing themselves and receive too little appreciation for their effort.

That first job as a day laborer was where I clearly saw the extreme importance of right leadership (encouragement, respect, and motivation) versus management (control and lack of respect and trust).

## Family

My precious wife Lynette and I had eloped and married in 1957 and in another year started our family. We began our marriage with twenty dollars in my pocket, but I knew without question she was the one God had created for me. I knew this for a number of reasons, not the least of these being the way she made me feel in her presence. Her genuineness and affection were different from any other girl's I had ever known. She loved life, loved her family, loved her friends, and then, when we were blessed with them, loved our children. Lynette proved her love, over and over, by how much she sacrificed as she nurtured our six children. We were so blessed that all six children were born healthy, and each one was so special and unique to us. While I was working many hours to provide economically, Lynette handled the bulk of the responsibilities at home. As you can imagine, the tasks were many for a family of eight. Laundry was plenty, and in our early years, we could not afford a clothes dryer; washed clothes were hung out to dry on a clothesline, which required lots of ironing on Lynette's part for a family of eight. Lynette didn't have the luxury of a dishwasher, either, but they weren't readily available then.

Lynette was a natural mother, contented to play the role God created her to play. She taught our children how to love each other and to get along. She taught them the importance of obedience and good manners. Our children were close in age, and they grew up entertaining and caring for each other. They were not lavished with tons of toys, but they were creative and played joyously with one another, and shared the things they had. We had a very happy home. When our last two children (twin girls) arrived, our older four children thought our Lord had sent them as their "special" baby doll sisters. Rarely were there times when the children did not play and entertain themselves without being kind to one another. They really loved each other, and God had given each of them kind but unique dispositions that made each child sweet special blessings to their mother and me.

*Paul and Lynette's young children:*
*Eugenia, Edwina, Sandra, Bo, Paula and Melinda*

Life was busy as the children grew. Lynette juggled her responsibilities at home with her part-time position as "head chauffeur," coordinating the complex logistics of getting each of the six children to all of his or her own activities. Our children were very involved in our church, in school activities, and in the community, participating in everything from sports and cheerleading to choir and piano. As it was with any family, everything was not always rosy. Our six were not perfect. When discipline was in order, Lynette was never so politically correct as to send one of the children to "time out." When necessary, she was a practitioner of old-fashioned discipline, often with the time-tested smack on the bottom or the occasional hickory switch, the way God's instruction book (the Holy Bible) instructs.

It was a tremendous blessing to have been given a helpmate who loves children. She told me early on in our marriage the only two things she would ever want were a happy home and a dining room suite. Eventually, I could provide the dining room suite, but our Lord God had to provide the happy home.

I lack the words to properly write the feelings in my heart for how much I love her and for all that she sacrificed so that I might have a career. Many times she gave me counsel when I was discouraged, and her advice kept me from quitting my job more than once. In essence, she forewent her own potential that I might give the extra hours and extra effort to continue to progress in my career in order to take care of our family. Never once did I hear an ultimatum to help her more with six young children. God gave her to me because she is one of probably very few who could do what she did and still have a glad heart and a happy disposition. She went for lengthy periods without any new clothes because the kids needed new shoes; she ate smaller portions to make the food go farther, or so that our children might have extra helpings, all the while keeping a positive, upbeat outlook on life. Lynette loved being a mother, and I believe that is God's call on her life. No one except Jesus can say "I love you" with more truth than a Godly mother. She is my heroine. She is a natural mother, and just like everything else that is good, she was sent from heaven.

*Lynette and Paul, 2013*

## A Good-Paying Job

All of these challenging years were teaching me many things, but there is one that has served me better than any of the others. That truth has shaped my whole life—people can!

I had never read that mankind is "fearfully and wonderfully made" and "made in the image of God." I had, however, in my early twenties, learned that determination was an important part of accomplishment. While I lacked higher education, my Creator had given me an extra measure of determination. Over the years, I have also learned that determination with divine direction is an unbeatable formula! God made us in His image in order that people can be successful in a profound way.

Thankful to finally have a good-paying job with a good company, I began to really try to learn all that I could in hopes that perhaps I could even advance at some point within the company. My plan was to work as hard as I could every day and read all that I could because I lacked higher education, which is normally so helpful in corporate advancement. It was also my intent to treat everyone I encountered with real respect. Clearly, I realized only a superlative effort would allow me to grow into a better job or next step, but somehow, innately, I knew this—people can! And I could, too.

After about three years as a freight handler, the service center manager approached me and asked me if I would like to learn to fill in as a shift foreman. This excited me for several reasons—there was acknowledgment of the extra effort I had put into a hard and tiring job, and, of even greater significance, it would lead to a pay increase. Only God in heaven knew how important at least a little extra money would be for my growing family.

Before I go any farther, an explanation might be in order as to how my long-time friend, Bob Austell, and I earned our first promotions. We did our part, and God did His part.

When we both began as freight handlers, there was a crew system in place. It consisted of four people: a checker to process the paperwork (individual freight bills); a sender who unloads the inbound trailer and sorts the freight into individual and complete shipments; and two crew wheelers who would take the complete shipments to a designated outbound trailer and load it. There was a considerable amount of wasted time with the four-man crew system since the checker did not physically handle any freight at all. In view of this, the company negotiated with the Teamsters local union to implement a two-man system. With the two-man system, each person would perform the entire process: checking, sending, wheeling, and reloading each shipment.

My friend and I were selected to carry out the experiment. It was right up our alleys. Bob was physically strong and smart. I, too, was strong and had reasonably good common sense. The experiment made a hard, difficult job into a contest, a race, to see just how much freight we could move in an eight-hour shift. The results exceeded everyone's expectations. As you can imagine, the change to a two-man system created some unrest among less physically able workers and those who could not read or write to the extent they could handle the paperwork.

And while it created some fracture in relationships, it did benefit us to show our employer we could do even more challenging jobs in the future. As we worked, we asked ourselves, "How are we ever going to get out from behind these hand trucks?" On that day, we agreed, "We will work our way out," and once we decided to, our gracious God helped us do so.

There was a very memorable event during that period of time. It involved the local Teamsters union. I belonged to the union, even though my father had told me, "Son, don't ever join a union unless you absolutely have to." But Carolina Freight was a "closed shop" with union dues collected by the company and remitted to the union. For this reason, I had to become a union member to be a full-time employee. I never attended a union meeting, though, primarily because I never needed intervention with my company. As I have thought about it over the years, I believe my father's advice had come as a result of an effort he witnessed to organize a large textile mill in Gastonia, North Carolina, many years earlier. That effort had escalated into violence with injuries and deaths. Another factor was that my father, though often overworked and underpaid, believed strongly in unwavering loyalty to your employer.

Jesus, the source of all wisdom, declared a profound truth in Matthew 12:25 (NKJV). He said, "A kingdom divided against itself is brought to desolation, and every city or house divided against itself will not stand." The apostle Luke also tells us this truth: "No servant can serve two masters; for either he will hate the one and love the other, or else he will be loyal to the one and despise the other" (Luke 16:13a, NKJV).

The point is clearly made that division is a destroyer and/or restrictor of anything. All parties must be working *together* to make things better for all participants.

The experiment of using a two-man crew rather than a four-man crew became a contest. This change had sped up the work substantially. Bob and I wanted to see how much we could get done in an eight-hour shift. That increased productivity then caused an unanticipated situation. Apparently, someone had complained to the local union that we were working too fast and carelessly, running up and down the warehouse floor. We were working hard, but we were not running, and whoever it was who complained about us never complained directly to Bob or to me. But the head of the local union sent a messenger to speak with us. He said to me, "You need to slow down before you hurt someone." We had never come close to hurting anyone, so I sent word back to the official in language I am now ashamed of: "When I get a paycheck with your name on it, I will start listening to your directions." My statement probably also contained a few choice profanities because, at that time, I had developed the vocabulary of the proverbial sailor. It was somewhat common on the service center floor.

I write all of this to say that it is indicative of where I was in life, doing things my way, young and strong, with a healthy family, and now beginning to make ends meet. I did not need religion, either. Actually, I have learned no one needs "religion," a conduct consisting of rules, regulations, and rituals. I did, however, need Christianity, which is not about rules, regulations, and rituals. It is about a love relationship with the Living Savior, Jesus, who has paid my sin debt and the sin debt of anyone else who will accept His precious gift of forgiveness. Oh, how I needed that! At that time in my life, I desperately needed that relationship with the Risen Christ.

I think now of a Bible verse which I did not know then: "Whatsoever thy hand findeth to do, do it with all thy might [heartily] for there is no work, or device or knowledge or wisdom in the grave where you are going" (Ecclesiastes 9:10, NKJV). That tremendous truth was written by the second wisest man who ever lived, King Solomon. Solomon was teaching this truth: that now is the time to work with energy and purpose to get the most and best from life and to prepare for eternity, for time is fleeting. In case you are wondering, the wisest man who ever lived was Jesus, who came to earth as a man.

Let me tell you, I was not only into doing my work heartily but also was *heartily* into worldliness, and *heartily* is the best description of my lost behavior. And by the way, *worldliness* is just another name for sin.

Regardless, I was convinced I had arrived. Now I was my own man. I thought I didn't particularly need anybody or anything except my own family. Things were finally going my way. The saddest part was that I thought I was living it up. But I did not know I was a dead man. Ephesians 2:1a (NKJV) tells me I was "dead in trespasses and sins." My language had become coarse and profane. This is no excuse, but that was the norm in that era when work was hard and heavy. It was a place and time where the culture was gradually etched into me until I had become absorbed in it. The language was not always intended to be as bad as it was, but it had become habitual.

Really, it is a profound wonder that I ever advanced at all at Carolina Freight. In my effort to earn badly needed extra money, I did sign-writing and painting in the little spare time I had. The Vice President of Operations, Mr. Russ Cook, called me one day and indicated there was a large sign for Carolina Freight that needed to be repainted. I inquired as to what he wanted me to paint on the sign, and his answer was, "Paint it back just as it is." It was approximately twenty-five feet long and four feet high, and I was excited for the extra money a sign this size would bring for us. Diligently I worked three or four hours daily for six or seven days. On the eighth day, I got up early, went to the trailer maintenance shop where the sign was and began to finish the black striping on the large red letters. As I had almost completed it, out of the corner of my eye, I saw a short, older man wearing a hat approaching. It was Mr. C. G. Beam, the primary founder and Chairman of the Board of the company. Mr. Beam loved the maintenance end of the trucking business and always, first thing in the morning, visited the maintenance shop. I had never met him, but I thought to myself, "that must be Mr. Beam, and he is going to really like this sign." The sign was striking, with a gleaming white background and large red letters now being outlined in black. He walked up and looked it over. He did not say "good morning." He then bluntly asked me a question that startled me, "Who told you to paint that?" I replied it was Mr. Cook. He then asked, "Who told you what to put on it?" To which I replied, "Mr. Cook." He then turned to me and unsmilingly said, "That d–n thing ain't going up nowhere!" I thought to myself, *This is an angry human being*. I knew he had an uncanny way of challenging people, but this, to me, was way overboard. Then I had another thought—*My family needs the extra money, but not this badly*. So I responded, "Well, if the d–n thing ain't going up, I ain't gonna finish the d–n thing!" I began to clean my brushes and left the premises. Mr. Beam knew how to bring out the best in folks and, in my case, the worst, but it certainly was unorthodox. I now realize in that early entrepreneurial age, many founders of businesses felt they had to be overly demanding since funding was very limited, and any kind of waste or loafing had to be prevented. Their bark was far worse than their bite. I had to mature a great deal before I realized that method was the way many founders approached their businesses. The depression years had made a profound impression on them that reinforced that approach.

I was still a freight handler at this time and didn't know if I would even have a job when I reported for my regular shift that afternoon. My language, profanity, and quick temper were consistent demonstrations of my lostness. Thank God, He didn't give up on me.

As God later elevated me in the company, Mr. Beam and I, as we got to know each other, became very respectful of one other. The day came when he even referred to me as *son*. He had a brilliant mind and could ask the most penetrating questions. He had his way of challenging people to excellence, and I had mine. He was a great mentor, and I am indebted to him for his patience with me.

Thank God, and I mean, literally, *thank God* that there were a few exceptional people in my workplace who had something different about them. Their actions resonated with character and integrity. They never seemed to be pulled into degrading dialogue, loud talk, or quick-tempered conflicts. It was clearly noticeable to all the rest of us who were of different habits. No matter what the consequences, they exhibited a professional calmness about them. That consistency was so unusual and rare; it made it even more obvious and attractive. They were bright lights in a dark environment. I did not know then that they had a unique identity the God of all creation had bestowed upon them. "You are the light of the world" (Matthew 5:14, NKJV). They lived with *resolute purpose* and consistency to reflect the light of the Risen Savior. Their quiet peace, I realized later, came from obedience to their Master.

Anyway, I had been making small plans for my future on my own, without wisdom. I did not then know the source of wisdom. When you lack wisdom for decision-making, then you have to live with whatever comes your way. Nonetheless, I saw and worked with a man who had peace that I did not have. His profoundly consistent behavior caused me to realize he had something I desperately needed. He was a man I so admired. His peace I respected, coveted, and wanted. At the time, I did not realize it was a peace God, our Life-Giver, our Difference-Maker, intended for all created in His image to have. I also did not know at that time that God's great plan for mankind is for mankind to excel and live with God's plan, provision, and resultant peace that "passeth all understanding" (Philippians 4:7, ASV).

# CHAPTER 3

# Free, Indeed!

In my early working days as a supervisor at Carolina Freight, my Heavenly Father put a very special man in my life as a coworker. I am convinced God sent me to Carolina Freight to be in this man's presence. His name is Joe Alexander, and his job was as a hostler. A hostler is someone who moves the trailers from place to place as they are loaded and unloaded. There were constant departure-time deadlines and constant calls, in not so nice a language, to get a certain unit moved "on the double." It was the challenging nature of that job. Courtesy was not the order of the day—urgency was. What was fascinating to me was that Joe never, ever allowed others to change his demeanor, nor cause him to lose his temper, nor respond to anyone in a disrespectful way. I admired the calmness and consistency of his life, while others, including myself, let circumstances alter the way we interacted with each other. Joe possessed self-control that was so different. If I had to use a single descriptive phrase, it is *he possessed then and still does such a peaceful presence.* Joe was not the only "light" in that place, but he was the most consistent one. He is also the one who persevered and never let me back away from my appointment with my Savior. Joe was obedient to what Jesus has instructed all of us Christians to do. That is to tell others how wonderful God's grace through Jesus is! It is difficult for me to describe the respect I had then for him and even more so now. I was amazed at the consistency in his life. It did not matter what the surrounding circumstances were. He is, to this day, telling others about the wonderful blessings of being saved.

I knew Joe was a member of First Baptist Church, where I had been baptized and attended sporadically through the early teen years. I also knew he was highly respected for the way he lived out his faith. He was consistently talking to others about their faith, church attendance, and living the Christian life. Although he worked in a challenging environment, he was un-influenced by it. I realized later; once I was saved, it was the Holy Spirit of God (the *Difference-Maker*) who was so very evident in my admired friend. Joe was never the typical "natural" man. He knew, however, that I was.

It is even more astounding that a person, who had such a difficult childhood as Joe had, would have such a positive and kind demeanor. Joe's mother had died when he was a very young child, and he had been passed from one relative's home to another during that childhood. His siblings had been separated also, and yet he was neither bitter nor angry with God. Joe was grateful that God sent Jesus as his Savior, and I never knew him to miss an opportunity to share his faith with anyone.

In early 1969, Joe invited me to revival services which were going to be held some six weeks or so later. I am sure he knew how much I needed to be "under new leadership." So, out of respect for his distinctively attractive life, even when he was in the heat of battle, I agreed to attend. After all, it was weeks and weeks in the future, and I could worry about that when the time came.

As you might have guessed, the first thing I knew, Joe was reminding me that revival services were going to begin in a week. I tried to avoid him as much as I could over the next few days. The services were set to last an entire week. Early in the revival week, perhaps on Tuesday, Joe pinned me down. "Now, Paul," he said, "you promised you would come to revival services. Why can't you come tonight?" I tried to make excuses, but he reminded me again: "You promised." Reluctantly I agreed, primarily out of respect for the way this man lived out his faith—so faithfully and admirably—and I had promised him I would go. After all, I reasoned, I could endure anything for one night. That was my plan—to go only as a spectator, not as a participant.

The time came, and I went to the church, barely arriving on time, and seated myself in the back with no intent to do anything but endure. Lynette and the children were already there and seated nearer the front of the church. I felt my going would satisfy my promise to my respected friend. But I learned something that night—a lost person should never take a seat in the back of a

Baptist church. When you are under conviction because of sin in your life, it is a long walk to the altar.

The visiting preacher preached. I cannot tell you anything he said, but the choir sang, and I do remember the title of the invitation hymn. It was "Lord, I'm Coming Home."

Suddenly, I began to uncontrollably weep as I thought about how lost and sinful I was. I was powerless to resist (nor, strangely, did I want to resist) going to the altar and submitting my life in forgiveness and repentance to my Lord and Savior Jesus Christ. God's Holy Spirit convicted me of my need to be forgiven. Then the words of this powerful hymn spoke to my sinful heart.

*I've wandered far away from God, Now I'm coming home.*

*The paths of sin too long I've trod, Lord I'm coming home;*

*I've wasted many precious years, Now, I'm coming home;*

*I now repent with bitter tears, Lord, I'm coming home;*

*I've tired of sin and straying, Lord, Now I'm coming home;*

*I'll trust Thy love, believe Thy love, Lord, I'm coming home;*

*My soul is sick, my heart is sore, Now, I'm coming home;*

*My strength renew, my hope restore, Lord, I'm coming home.*

This refrain, or chorus, was sung after each of the above verses: *"Coming home, coming home, Never more to roam, Open wide thine arms of love, Lord, I'm coming home."* The hymn was written by William J. Kirkpatrick, who lived between 1838 and 1921. It is a very old hymn, but it further verifies truth lives and prevails for eternity.

Jesus said, "I am The Way, The Truth, and The Life, and no one comes to the Father, but through Me" (John 14:6, NASB).

I also remember as the invitational hymn started, looking at my watch and saying, "two more minutes, and I'm out of here." But God had a better plan for me. I have, over a lifetime, discovered this simple truth—*He always does!*

The burden of my sin had overwhelmed me with guilt, and I knew I must yield to the loving Savior. I was compelled to accept His precious gift of forgiveness for my many sins.

Beforehand, I had no awareness of this important truth about the Holy Spirit I had just experienced. When Jesus was dead in a sealed and guarded tomb, God the Father sent His Holy Spirit to raise Jesus back to life. When Jesus ascended back to the Father, He sent the Holy Spirit to focus lost people on Himself, Jesus. The Holy Spirit also reveals to people the great sacrifice Jesus has made that we might be born again, forgiven, saved, and made whole. The Holy Spirit is also the One who empowers true believers to live victoriously over habitual sin and be obedient to His word.

God's Holy Spirit had overwhelmed me as I sat in God's church. He, the Holy Spirit, caused me to realize it was "my sins" that caused Jesus to willingly go to the cross for me personally. He, the Holy Spirit, caused me to see myself as I really was. The Holy Spirit reminded me how desperately I needed to repent and become a true child of God, not just an uninvolved church member listed on the membership roll. In fact, if no one had done anymore to obey the Lord and to support the church than myself, the church would have no longer existed. As I read my Bible later on, I discovered this truth in John 16:14 (NKJV): "He [the Holy Spirit] will glorify me." This is what Jesus told His disciples then and what He says to you and me today. Thus, our primary role is to live in such a way, by Holy Spirit power, that others can see Christ in each one of us, just as I had seen Christ in Joe Alexander's exemplary life.

I knew my children deserved a father who would be led by the Holy Spirit of God instead of a father who saw the world's way so very attractively. Every child, since they did not decide to be born, deserves parents who will teach and lead them by God's Spirit. Then, what a wonderful life awaits anyone if they will follow Christ and let Him be Lord. When Christ is our Lord, as promised, we can hear "what God the Lord will speak, for He will speak peace to His people" (Psalm 85:8, ESV).

# CHAPTER 4

# The Best Advice Ever

On that wonderful night when the Holy Spirit of God showed me who I was and how much I needed to repent and be forgiven, I made my way tearfully to the front of the church, where the pastor awaited those who had made a decision.

When the pastor learned of my decision to follow Christ Jesus, he said, "Paul, I want you to stay with me as the people leave so that I can talk with you after they are gone." That meant he expected me to stand with him at the front door as all the people left and said goodbye. I wasn't excited about doing that because my tear filled eyes were red, my nose was running, and I was thoroughly ashamed of whom I had become since becoming a church member twenty-one years earlier. Becoming so aware of my sin and the need for my Lord's forgiveness had humbled me. I had become helpless by some indescribable Power that I could not resist. I *could* not resist that Power, nor did I *want* to resist that Power.

In a small town like Cherryville, as you know, secrets are scarce. As various little old ladies left the church and passed by preacher Carter and me, they would give me a hug or take my hand and hold it tightly. "Paul," one lady said, "I'm so happy for you. I've been praying for you for fifteen years." Another told me, "I've been praying for ten years." I received several similar comments as the congregation filed out into the night, and I was stunned that anyone cared enough about me to pray for years and years that I would be born again, set free, and finally become a real Christian. I wept more as I realized how the true people of God care more indeed about others than we realize. I did not know then that this is exactly what God expects and empowers you and me to do as His followers. Little did I know this church, in preparation for revival and renewal services, had prepared a list of people who were either "fallen away" or needed to be saved. Dozens of people had prayed earnestly over those names for weeks and months, and God heard and honored the prayers of His people.

Dr. Carter then said, "I asked you to stay so we could talk about how to grow spiritually. I want to tell you what God expects of you and what I expect also, in order for you to grow in your love for Christ and in spiritual maturity." It would not have mattered what he might have said, for I was prepared to do it, to follow his instruction, *whatever it might be*! I was so glad to be free of Me and my selfish worldly wants and the guilt associated with those sinful wants.

He said, "You be in Sunday school every Sunday morning, and you be in worship service every Sunday morning also. You should be in BTU (Baptist Training Union, a weekly Bible study held at the church) on Sunday evening. Be in worship service on Sunday night. When you are not traveling, you be in midweek prayer service on Wednesday night and learn how to pray. Start reading your Bible every day to know God's will for your life. Start telling people right away what a difference Jesus has made in your life."

I thought he had finished and started to walk away, and the last thing he said to me was, "Oh, by the way, bring a tithe next Sunday."

My first thought after all these instructions was, *Wow, it's too bad that Bible has already been written because if I can do all he has just explained, it would qualify as another Biblical miracle.* At the time, I knew nothing about the power of God's Holy Spirit, Who had now become resident in me at the moment I finally repented and accepted Jesus as my Savior. Yes, I had been a church member for a long time but now I was truly a member in the kingdom of God. Jesus had promised to send His Holy Spirit to all His disciples. He said to them, "He will glorify Me" (meaning the Holy Spirit would always point people to Jesus and what Jesus had done for mankind). Only now was I beginning to understand that Jesus had forgiven me, cleansed me of sin, and had sent His Holy Spirit to empower me to live victoriously and represent Jesus effectively.

Giving me that instruction was clearly the most wonderful thing anyone could have ever done for me. My pastor made it plain, and I was ready to hear it. He said, "It will cost you something to be a *practicing* Christian, but you will never regret it." I am so indebted to him for having the courage to tell me *straightforwardly* how I could and should honor God and have God's peace in my heart through obedience.

I am completely convinced what he said to me that night should be said to every person, even today, who accepts Jesus Christ, in repentance, as their Savior.

Dr. Carter explained to me that evening how to make Jesus not only Savior but Lord as well. He didn't call it making Jesus Lord, but that is what he was describing. Dr. Carter was making it clear to me what God expected of me and how important it was that I do so. The best news of all was that God had so touched and cleansed me; I wanted to do anything I could out of respect and gratitude for being set free of Satan's power in my life. Dr. Carter was kind but candid, and I will forever be indebted to him for his obedience in his calling as God's bold and faithful messenger.

I cannot explain "the peace of God which surpasses all understanding" (Philippians 4:7, NKJV) as I drove home to be with my family. But it was tangible. It was real. And it was true. When I got home, we sat around the kitchen table and celebrated what had just happened to me and, thus, our family.

This night had become a time not when I *wanted* to do something, but a time when I *decided* to, and I *gave myself wholly to the Lord*, habits and all. I was happy and thrilled to do so. A prodigal had come home to a loving Father. And they had literally prayed me out of an awaiting hell as a lost church member into the loving care of my Savior, with God's Holy Spirit as my Helper and my Difference-Maker. My precious wife and I, on the next Saturday night, also wrote out our first tithe check. It was a great blessing to do so.

Over the many years since the Holy Spirit awakened me, I have tried to learn all I could about this powerful One, and this I know beyond any doubt whatsoever that the Holy Spirit will help any person hear God's truth about

Jesus and be convicted by it. The Holy Spirit will then empower the hearer to respond and obey the truth. The Holy Spirit also helps us fully realize what a horrific price Jesus paid that we might be forgiven. Conviction of our personal sin that put Jesus on the cross in our place and His overwhelming enabling power are two things the Holy Spirit provides abundantly, as we determine to make Jesus Lord.

# CHAPTER 5

# Deliverance in the Chapel

It was at the First Baptist Church in Cherryville, North Carolina, that I made the decision to make Jesus Christ not just my Savior but the Lord of my life as well. After going home, my family sat around the kitchen table, and we talked about my experience and what the Lord expected of me. Then the Holy Spirit led me to go back to the chapel—which remained open for prayer twenty-four hours a day during revival week—to pray about getting everything in my life in sync with Him. I felt I needed to go back and pray and ask God to help me stay faithful now that I was truly His child.

Jesus had, on this special night, become real in my life, and I was now being led to humble myself before my Savior. It was amazing how at this point, I felt such an intense sense of peace. His refreshing presence was like nothing I had ever experienced. God's Holy Spirit was seriously at work in this forgiven sinner's life. I cannot begin to describe how His presence impacted me in such a positive manner. I had not yet read this promise from God's Word, "Where the Spirit of the Lord is there is liberty" (2 Corinthians 3:17, KJV), but I knew I was now free of Satan's hold on my life forever.

As I opened the double doors to the chapel and started to walk down the aisle, I saw something that almost overwhelmed me. When I was a young teenager, I had sketched a black and white drawing of "The Praying Hands" at the request of Mrs. Wilma Hickson, the Women's Missionary Union Director who must have been aware of my love of art, drawing, and doing creative things. I had never given that drawing another thought until that moment in the chapel. My drawing was done so many years earlier, and now that framed picture sat squarely in the center of the Chapel's altar table. My seeing that drawing verified in my heart and soul that this was my time to allow the Lord to get my life right. If there ever was a confirmation of God's being at work in a life, this was it for me. I could almost hear—and I certainly did sense—

God saying, "I will strengthen you, my born-again child, to take a stand and live faithfully for me." I was so overwhelmed that I knelt, wept with joy, and prayed earnestly for His liberating presence to always be evident in my life.

*Paul's Praying Hands drawing in the chapel*

As I knelt, I noticed my nicotine-stained fingers. Working long hours in a very active capacity in a time-sensitive environment drove me to become a heavy smoker. In my capacity now, with dozens of deadlines to meet, I had become heavily addicted, smoking almost three packs a day. I knew Christ would not be honored, nor would He be fully my Lord, if I continued to cling to such an addiction (a truth not just applicable to my nicotine addiction, but with any other addiction, unhealthy habit, or idol). So as I prayed, I acknowledged my enslaving addiction to cigarettes. And God's Spirit gave me this prayer: "Lord, I know you do not want me enslaved, but I know I am too weak to stop this habit. If I can serve you like this, so be it, but if I cannot, I hereby put this in your strong hands. I give it to you." The prayer was sincere and heartfelt, and as I rose from the altar, I felt as free as a person can be. I felt confident and encouraged that my addiction was done with. It was a magnificent deliverance beyond description.

That was over fifty years ago, and I have never even thought about smoking again. Cigarettes had bound me, enslaved me, and much like Christ breaks the chains of sin for those who make him Lord of their lives, so too had Christ freed me from this addiction. Since that day, cigarettes have had no hold over me. The temptation to smoke is gone. Jesus delivered me, cold turkey. There is such truth and power in the promise that I referred to earlier in 2 Corinthians 3:17 (KJV), "Where the Spirit of the Lord is there is liberty."

As I began to read God's Word, pray, and study, I learned of His promise to send the Holy Spirit into the lives of His children. Jesus had forgiven and cleansed me. Now God's Holy Spirit was resident within me to help me *stay free* from any enslaving sin. That night the Lord set me free from a habit that had become greater than my own physical willpower. I had been set free of *me*. The Holy Spirit had enlightened, satisfied, and given me a "peace that passeth all understanding" (Philippians 4:7b, ASV). That night God demonstrated His deliverance to me in the Chapel. I did not have to earn it; I did not have to work at it. No, He did it instantly and perfectly. Deliverance was available to me, and I asked for it and accepted it. I was now eternally free and under my Lord's watch care.

Yes, deliverance is available to whoever will believe and receive, regardless of one's past—but it comes only through complete submission to our Savior, the Lord Jesus Christ.

When the Holy Spirit of God comes into the life of a believer as promised, you can know for certain that people can resist any evil with the heavenly power that has already defeated Satan by way of the resurrection of our Savior. God's Holy Spirit spoke peace to me that night, and He has continued to do so ever since, reinforcing that peace through His Holy Word.

I learned a great truth that night—Jesus cannot truly be Lord of our lives until we crown Him with our will—literally giving it over to Him, as He is trustworthy.

What is this peace that passes all understanding? It is freedom from any disquieting thought or worrisome emotion. It is also knowing that the Holy Spirit within me is greater than any temptation that Satan will put in my path. Now that is true *deliverance*. The indwelling Holy Spirit of God, the Difference-Maker, guarantees people can "have life and have it more abundantly," just as Jesus promises in John 10:10b (NKJV).

Praise God for His indescribable power!

# CHAPTER 6

# Beyond My Imagination

Those early days as a truly born-again, forgiven child of God were among the most memorable and fulfilling in my entire life. The guilt of past sins had been removed, as Jesus had cleansed me from a worldly past. He had also taken away my "want to" as far as being worldly.

I remember rejoicing in my heart when I, for the first time, read 2 Corinthians 5:17–18 (NKJV): "Therefore if anyone is in Christ, he is a new creation; old things have passed away; behold, all things have become new. Now, all things are of God, who has reconciled us to Himself through Jesus Christ, and has given us the ministry of reconciliation." Only a forgiven sinner who has been loosened from the bonds of Satan can know the joy that this scriptural truth and promise brings. All of a sudden, I was at a brand new and wonderful place. I had been delivered from Satan's captivity and evil influence after several decades as a lost church member.

There is another passage that equally brought a profound peace and joy to my soul in those early days as a true child of the Living God. It is 1 Peter 2:9–10b (NKJV). "But you are a chosen generation, a royal priesthood, a holy nation, His own special people, that you may proclaim the praises of Him who called you *out of darkness into His marvelous light* (emphasis mine)." What profound truth this explained and described for me.

Overnight, the promises of God had become unbelievably exciting and encouraging. Also, the people of God, our local church people, had become so warm and helpful as I began my new journey from a once flagrant sinner to a now forgiven saint. I never really felt worthy of being called a saint, but if that is what God declares His repentant Children to be, that's certainly all right with me.

Those early days of liberty for me were wonderful. I felt so liberated even though I had not yet, at least as I remember it, read this promise: "Where the

Spirit of the Lord is there is liberty" (2 Corinthians 3:17, KJV). I just knew I was free (from me), and it was then - and still is - wonderful to have a new life of peace and fulfillment. I was beginning to understand what a precious gift my Savior had bought for me at His own expense (becoming sin for me) and had so graciously then given to me. I also knew there was a wonderful new empowering influence in my life that I could not comprehend or begin to explain. For the sake of better words, that powerful influence gave me "God-confidence," which replaced my foolish "self-confidence."

The Lord began to bless our family as we worshipped regularly together. All of our children grew up in a church where the Bible was taught and preached without reservation or compromise, and we all began to grow as a Christian family.

God also began to bless my work and consistently gave me whatever I needed whenever I needed it to be able to help and lead the people I had responsibility for. Most of all, He gave me great respect for these people who came to work day after day and did their jobs so well, even though they had no clear or certain career path to a more desirable future. I am so thankful for that day when I practically begged for a chance to work and was then subsequently given the opportunity to do so. I firmly believe that was God's great plan for me - to start at the bottom - and experience what it is like to labor at the same hard job year after year. After all, how could I ever appreciate hardworking, loyal associates if I had not experienced the same environment and perspective as they do daily?

I still remember the times when my friends who had not seen me in a while would ask, "Paul, what are you doing now?" My answer would be, "I am loading freight at Carolina Freight." They did not conceal how surprised they appeared to be. I am sure they had no wrong intent, but their reaction was a dead giveaway of their bewilderment at my answer. I learned one of my most important lessons as a manual laborer—God gave me life to always do my very best to give hard-working people absolute dignity and respect in the workplace. Neither they nor I knew that God had a wonderful plan for me.

And that plan included giving me a great admiration for the people who work at hard jobs for long periods of time. Those hard-working people, most often, do so with loyalty and a grateful attitude. Those arc the very people who have played the greatest role in developing our great country.

Perhaps my respect was because I had observed both of my parents work so hard, yet they seemed to be unappreciated for their loyalty, tenure, and effort. Or, maybe, it was because Jesus Himself demonstrated great love and respect for the "common" people (although I dislike this term), and He expects His followers to do likewise. The book of Genesis tells us that we, mankind, are "fearfully and wonderfully made." There is nothing common about any man! Now I am convinced He was preparing me, by working as a day laborer, for a later assignment with another great company. There, valuing people completely (VPC) was (and is even more so today) the foundation of that company's great success.

In all the early formative years at Carolina Freight, the great majority of the freight that moved between the Northeast and the South moved through the Cherryville, North Carolina complex where our corporate headquarters was also located. There was a very large sorting operation that took place there also. Shipments for a particular destination would be taken from an inbound unit and reloaded together on a unit designated for that particular destination. This involved millions and millions of pounds of freight per day, and it required a twenty-four/seven operation. There was also much career opportunity associated with this extensive activity.

My first promotional opportunity came as a warehouse foreman and then quickly led to a shift supervisor position, then load control manager, then assistant service center manager. Unbelievably within a very few years, God gave me opportunity to become the service center manager of that entire facility. I had been given the opportunity to lead an entire operation in less than ten years after I never thought I'd ever even get an opportunity to work there as a day laborer.

As a service center manager, I was responsible for the leadership of more than two hundred people. This facility served as the site where all the cargo from the Northeast and all the cargo from the Southeast flowed into, in order to be sorted to the various destinations within the entire Carolina service area that included the New England, Middle-Atlantic, Carolinas, Georgia, and Florida regions.

There was a constant flow of LTL shipments. LTL identifies smaller, less than full truckload shipments. These were sorted and assembled at this facility. LTL trucking is not an easy business, but it is much easier if you have personnel who are treated with respect and dignity.

In addition, there was an extensive pickup and delivery operation because the shipments originating within the Cherryville service center's radius would be quickly offloaded to their destinations, usually before midnight. Locally picked up shipments were quickly "in the flow." Also, besides the sorting operation, which was extensive, there was a substantial pickup and delivery operation, which I also had responsibility for.

Transposing the information from shipping orders to standard freight bills was also the service center manager's responsibility.

It was a very challenging, never easy, but always gratifying job. Truly there never was a dull moment. And one of the things that made it challenging was being able to safely load fragile items like light fixtures with much heavier cargo such as pipe fittings without damage. It required a considerable amount of skill to load hundreds of full loads every day that could arrive at the destination without damage.

My responsibility was for the entire pickup and delivery operation, including the salespeople serving same. Additionally, a primary responsibility was to keep the incoming LTL loads sorted and reloaded as outbound loads without delay.

I never dreamed this would ever be my opportunity as the one responsible for all this activity. There again, I dare not take credit for what my Savior has done. There was one thing for sure I certainly knew, my Lord and Savior expected me to treat these diligent workers and friends courteously and respectfully. And I did. We had a great team who loved their company and the great opportunity Carolina Freight Carriers provided with good-paying jobs. The absolutely most enjoyable part of this period was being able to encourage and appreciate those people I had worked "elbow to elbow" with over the years. They respected me, and I respected them. That is God's plan for all businesses. It is not always carried out, but where that mutual respect is an established consistent practice, it always produces a win/win.

Please do not misunderstand me because it is important to know it was the grace of God that made all these wonderful opportunities realities. I was simply a young man seeking to live for the Lord, who had little training in leading others, especially in a collective business effort. I had worked diligently and faithfully with long hours because my earthly father had taught me to always give everything my best effort. Now my Heavenly Father had made my best effort acceptable because of His gracious guidance, influence, and power.

As I reflect on those days, it becomes clear God had a plan for my life. I would never have known that plan if an obedient Christian, Joe Alexander, had not cared enough about me to invite me to a church where the Holy Spirit of God showed me how much I needed to be transformed. On that night, I asked Jesus to forgive me and become my Lord and Savior and how graciously He did so. And I followed Him in grateful obedience, loving His guidance, as I began a miraculous journey of peace and fulfillment.

There is a great truism that is now clear. God has made us all for Himself, and He has a wonderful plan for "success" for each of us. However, it is conditional. I cannot know His plan and enjoy His divine guidance and influence unless I know Him! Jesus makes that possible for anyone who is genuinely repentant of sin and needs forgiveness, and then He offers His "peace of God which surpasses all understanding" (Philippians 4:7b, ESV).

God's Holy Spirit is the One who causes us to see the great price Jesus paid that we might "have life and... may have it more abundantly" (John 10:10, NKJV). The Holy Spirit is the One who becomes resident after we have been saved. His purpose is as a Counselor, Helper, Advocate, Comforter, and a source of strength. He is the One, the Difference-Maker, who had steadily guided me along my road of progress and helped me stay faithful to my Savior when Satan's temptations were so prevalent.

It is fascinating now when I think about it (but at that time, I did not realize) that on that night when I was overcome with guilt and sorrow, it was God's Holy Spirit who brought that conviction. The Holy Spirit always points to Jesus and reminds us of the great price Jesus paid with His own sinless life, that we might be free and forgiven. It is also so important to understand that the Holy Spirit is the incredible power that God provides to every true believer in order that we might represent Jesus willfully, faithfully, consistently, and powerfully.

It took me a while to fully understand why I had no power in my life to live for Christ when I became a church member at age nine. It was simply because I was not truly born again. The Word of God is very clear on this matter. Every true Christian is indwelt by the Holy Spirit. Romans 8:14 (ESV) says, "Those who are led by the Spirit of God are sons of God." Verse 8:9b (NKJV) also declares an absolute truth: "Now if anyone does not have the Spirit of Christ [in other words, the Holy Spirit], he is not His." It also took a while for me to realize the same power (again, the Holy Spirit) that raised a dead Christ from the tomb is resident in every repentant sinner. That is a huge source of power. I had the Spirit of God guiding me through all those years of advancement at Carolina Freight. It was no longer unexplainable as to how my progress had been so continuing. It was simple. I had done my part in seeking to be obedient to Him, and I had worked hard with my best effort, and the Holy Spirit had done all that I could not do.

What a precious Gift and Helper had come into my life.

As our company continued to grow, it was divided into geographical regions with designated regional managers for each of these regions. Each of these regional managers would have complete responsibility for the performance in each of the service centers in the various regions.

After several years as service center manager of the large sorting operation, I was given the opportunity to become regional manager of the North and South Carolina service centers. It was an exciting step forward and an exciting event for me. Now I had the opportunity to get to know many more people and hopefully help all the managers in that region become better at motivating, leading, and encouraging people.

Several years later, in the mid-to-late-seventies, the opportunity arose for me as the Middle Atlantic Regional Manager. This included service centers in Pennsylvania, New Jersey, and New York, and this advancement was a much more challenging task for several reasons. The region had been overseen for many years by a single individual who had now decided to retire. The man was well-known and familiar with all the local unions who represented our people in these terminals. He had a working relationship with all the officials, and we enjoyed what we called *labor peace*. It was, however, at a price. This *price* was essentially a compromise that was not advantageous to our company, with concessions that ultimately turned into past practices.

Perhaps you would not have thought so, but another reason for the challenge I faced was the cultural differences that were present in those days. I had no idea the Civil War was still in play; I was identified as a "rebel" from the South, a label that did not convey respect. The fact that our company had strong Southern roots was not a plus for certain numbers of people, both in our workforce and with the union officials. The company also was identified by some labor union officials as a "rebel company."

This only fed suspicion and mistrust.

At any rate, as we began to look more deeply into abnormally high labor costs, it became evident something was very much out of the ordinary. It appeared this had been out of control for a good while, and the cost of "labor peace" had become considerably too high. To be fair, the manager who preceded me was able to get favors from some of the union officials if they were not requested too often, but as a result, our cost of doing business in this Mid-Atlantic region was beginning to make us less competitive than we needed to be. It fell on me to try to do something reasonable about improving same.

Labor practices in those Mid-Atlantic states were far different than in the South. At our Brooklyn terminal, we had somehow created a "non-working" union steward position—with twenty hours overtime built into it! The steward, Thomas Hogan, and I had serious small differences, but this practice continued. Every time I tried to push harder to make improvements, the result would be a slower pace in getting the work accomplished. I was literally out of my element and not making enough headway. It was increasingly difficult to believe we should be paying such an outrageous sum and receive no work in return.

Meantime, our internal audit department had begun an intensive payroll audit of each of these terminals. As they searched personnel, payroll, and social security records, they uncovered findings that I found astonishing. As a result of that audit, one of our sharpest auditors, Joe, and I decided we would show up at one of our Pennsylvania service centers at midnight in order to do a surprise actual headcount of workers who were present. Our purpose was to determine if the numbers of actual people who showed up for work matched the payroll.

We told no one except those who scheduled our reservations. Joe and I flew into Pennsylvania and traveled to that location at midnight. I entered from the back while he entered from the front. We corralled everyone into a group and asked for drivers' licenses and social security identifications from each of the sixteen people present. Astonishingly, everyone had both of these documents on their person. Obviously, a bit perplexed, we scratched our heads in disbelief as we left the facility.

Since we had told no one we were coming, we were mystified. But one thing we had noticed within the office was the file cabinets and service center manager's desk drawer had all been damaged as they were pried open. None of this had ever been reported, so we knew something was amiss.

The next morning we returned to the Pennsylvania service center, but as we were about to leave to go to another facility, one of the office workers handed me a phone and said, "This call is for you, Mr. Taylor." The person on the other line identified himself as Jack McGrath and said, "I am a private investigator, and I am asking you to trust me. I hear you are an honest man, and I can help you." He then said, "I understand you did a headcount last night and found everyone there. Is that right?" I responded, "Yes." He then said, "Don't you think it is a little strange that Raymond Bertucchi was on your dock at the same time he is incarcerated in Holmesburg Prison?"

You can imagine how my jaw dropped when this was said. I chose to trust Jack, canceled my flight home, and we had dinner. As it turned out, he was a very skilled and reliable private investigator, and because one of his best friends was one of the first handwriting experts with the FBI, Jack McGrath had access to resources that would help us clean up this serious cesspool of deceit. We could now begin to match signatures on canceled checks and other identifying documents.

Jack explained to me that there was an honest employee, whom I'll call Tim, working at that terminal who was aware that a fraudulent scheme had been taking place. Tim was dismayed by the questionable practices occurring at his workplace. When Tim saw us the night we made our surprise inspection, he made a difficult choice. He believed us to be truthful people who were making an effort to clean up the graft, and he decided to help.

Through Tim's courage and with Jack's help, we learned that a relatively simple scheme was taking place with the awareness of the facility manager. We discovered that the manager had been strong-armed to participate because he supposedly had become indebted to the resident loan shark after playing the horses at the nearby track. Ultimately, we learned that when one of the workers would go to prison, they would send their driver's license and social security identification to "stand-ins" who were on our company payroll, but these stand-ins only showed up to work when they were tipped off. I never learned how the paychecks for the stand-ins were split among the prisoners, union steward, and the stand-ins. All I know is that it was a challenging time for this "rebel" from Cherryville, North Carolina. Life for me at that time certainly was not a bowl of cherries.

Once we cleaned up the mess, the facility operated well for a long time thereafter. Make no mistake about it—Carolina Freight Carriers was a great company that provided so well for so many for so long. This was simply a transitory situation at a location while the company became more and more effective in improving efficiency in the entire operation. I will always be grateful for that loyal associate taking such a risk to do the right thing. That honest person proved again: "Honesty is always the best policy."

Also, let it be clear, for every one of those who would steal or deceive, there were hundreds and thousands of fine employees who worked diligently and loyally to grow a great company.

The Carolina Freight Brooklyn, New York, operation had always been a challenge for some of the same cultural reasons, particularly because the labor loyalties to the unions were always much greater in this location than in other locations. The strength of the unions was a substantial factor as well. It seemed the appreciation for a good-paying job with a reputable company was not nearly as prevalent in this location as it was in many of our other locations. Theft and security were always concerns because we handled large amounts of clothing to and from the garment district in downtown Manhattan. Collusion with corrupt law enforcement and mob enforcers added to the difficulty. In essence, the culture there was substantially different than in most of the southern states, and yet, it was a market that carriers needed to serve along with the other states that were less challenging. Customers expected a carrier to have complete geographical coverage, including into the most difficult areas.

In addition to all the above, it was alleged that a promised payoff of some kind had not been honored in the past. Whether it was true or not, the union used this serious claim and held it over our heads and was extremely difficult to deal with.

We had some very loyal associates at the Brooklyn facility but substantially more associates who appeared to have no appreciation for the company at all. It seemed to me, whether this is accurate or not, that, as a whole, they couldn't have cared less about the rest of the company. Their focus seemed to be only about what they wanted and decided. Here is the result. The theft of designer clothing was atrocious. Now it had fallen on me to begin to try to regain control and stop such robbery. Truthfully, every time I was there, I was uncertain about my personal safety. Nonetheless, I knew if worse came to worse, I would end up in a place where the word "problem" does not exist. I was certain the God who had sent His Son to save me—and after I was forgiven, sent His Holy Spirit to guide and empower me as I represented Him full time—would watch over me. And He did!

Security of the property in order to keep outsiders from stealing was one issue. The greater concern was theft by our own people. Even security services, which provided gate security, were often bribed by organized crime, and the organized crime forces in those days had enforcers whose cruelty had set them apart as the ones to pay attention to. They were good at fooling people, presenting themselves to businesses as legitimate security services. Essentially, though, you never knew whom you were really employing. Also, they made it plain, "We can and will stop your theft because people have respect for us." Indeed, they substantially reduced the theft at the terminal. However, when it became absolutely certain they were a part of organized crime, we had to deal with the reality of knowing these are the same people who murder, extort, prostitute young people, sell drugs to teenagers, and so on. It was a haunting awareness.

While I traveled often to New York, Pennsylvania, and New Jersey, I had six children at home in Cherryville whom I desired to see grow as strong Christians. I was leading a Bible study every Sunday and even offering my testimony on occasion on how God had transformed my life. Yet, at this point, I discovered, though inadvertently, this situation existed. There was only one remedy: trust God, who said, "I will never leave nor forsake you" (Hebrews13:5, NKJV) and go terminate their services. It was a sobering time as I thought about it then—and still is today—as I recall how cruel the enforcers in this organization were those many years ago. On occasion, I would receive in the mail from an anonymous source a New York newspaper clipping about some person being killed in the mob wars. It was a message to me and more than a bit eerie.

Somehow, the security service always knew when I was coming to the Brooklyn service center. Sure enough, I remember a particular day I drove up and went inside where they were waiting for me. They greeted me warmly and then said, "Mr. Paul, did you bring us a G-note today?" I replied, "No, I did not. In fact, I have some less than good news. We are terminating your services." It was a tense moment, not knowing what would happen next. The younger of the two said, "You should reconsider. Have we not done the job?" My response was, "Yes, you have, but this decision is final."

Then came this assertion, "You will be sorry. We are going down to the union hall and tell them how stupid you are." I could sense what was going to happen next—labor unrest when the union officials learned we had terminated their friends' services. Perhaps, their security "friends" shared the proceeds.

I waited three hours before going to the union office, which was a bastion, to tell union officials about the changes. There was a large steel door, no windows, and a buzzer and camera. Once someone upstairs opened the door, an elevator was available, but it had to be released also.

This incident occurred during a period when rival mafia families were feuding and were killing rival members with some degree of regularity. Therefore, this place was heavily secured, and no one entered without observation first and then authorization to get into the elevator. It was intimidating, but thank God, I was on a mission to do what was right. Upon arrival, I was surprised to see how cordial, as like never before, the three of them were. They offered me a seat and then said, "We have some mutual friends in the next room." My heart sank a bit as they opened the door, and the other two I had just terminated joined the group. Now I was surrounded by five very angry people in a secured building. Alone... or so it appeared.

The union president had been designated to be the spokesperson. He said, in essence, "They have told me about your decision, and because it is a bad decision, we *expect* you to change it. Let me explain why. Your people who steal have no fear of the police, or of the safe and loft squad [garment center police], or of the FBI. But for P. and D.," he continued, referring to the two men who had been at our facility as security agents, "they have respect." You will regret this decision, and we expect you to change it now." I replied that the decision was made, and the RICO Act, which is anti-organized crime legislation was real. "Therefore," I stated finally, "the decision is done." Yes, they had stopped the theft and had been compensated for it, but it was over. With that, the union president became enraged, and they each began to taunt me, curse, and call me every ugly thing you could think of. It was brutal. But the peace of God was in my heart, and I did not respond, as I am sure they had wished I might. If I had, likely they would have beaten me to a bloody pulp. I had not walked into that place alone. After thinking about it for many years, I know the Lord put a protective hedge around me. He was there with me. He had quieted my heart when He said, "Be still and know that I am God" (Psalm 46:10, KJV).

That incident was, I believe, on a Thursday. I left Brooklyn the next morning after sleeping with a chair wedged under the door latch of my hotel room. This additional safeguard was a standard procedure for me for many months, even before this event. My thoughts were that if I am going to die, at least I will be awakened when the chair is dislodged before I am killed.

The week after my Brooklyn encounter, I had planned to spend a week camping and fishing on a beautiful mountain lake with my son. We'd done this for many years, and it was a highlight of the summer. I traveled so much with my job that this respite offered us a chance to spend a whole week catching up on our relationship, and we both looked forward to it expectantly. The location where we camped was remote, and there were no cell phones in those days. As you can imagine, I was glad to be away from job concerns for a break; however, I did decide to call in to the office on Tuesday and see how things were going. My son and I took the boat to the landing, where I used a payphone. My secretary told me, "We had a load of cigars hijacked in Brooklyn yesterday." The load was a regular weekly movement of Cuban cigars for distribution in the New York area with a value of around $175,000. Immediately I knew this was retaliatory and probably just the first of more than one payment for the stand I had taken to fire the corrupt service. It was a lot of money at that time for my company to pay as a result of us doing the right thing.

Obviously, the thieves involved had inside information. The way it usually went was when our driver stopped at a traffic light; the hijacker would jump on the running board with gun in hand and have the driver drive to a more secluded place. The hijacker would then take the driver's identification, threaten the driver that if he ever cooperated with the police, and tell him, "We know where you and your children live." The driver would then be released, and then the truck would be driven to an enclosed warehouse, unloaded, driven miles away, and abandoned. A driver, understandably, for fear of his family being harmed, could not afford to ignore the hijacker's warning.

The second load that was hijacked was a partial load of calculators valued at about $70,000. It was taken a week later. In those days, it was alleged that the mob had bought and paid for favoritism from law enforcement for a lot of territory in and around New York City, and many of these practices were not uncommon.

My company and I had been required to make a decision, which was whether or not we would cooperate with the criminal element and buy protection for temporary financial well-being. It was a soul-searching, perilous period, but I am so glad today we had the conviction to do the right thing. In essence, and paraphrased, would we take the narrow gate (the narrow way) or the broad way that leads to destruction (Matthew7:13, NKJV)? Ultimately, we overcame the problem of lenient management in those terminals by hiring capable, experienced leadership to overcome the omissions of the past.

I was growing professionally and spiritually. My work was challenging but rewarding. I had worked diligently and persistently to create greater respect for all the many hard-working people who did the tough work of manual labor, interfacing with the customers, and providing consistently good service. I knew this truth in my heart—you will never get people to willingly give their best discretionary effort unless they feel they are respected and valued.

It was a real joy to see how people reacted as they were respected more and more and as we applied Christian principles in the workplace. After all, I had discovered the Holy Bible is the best Leadership and Human Relations Book ever written. It had become of optimal value to me. I had come to realize just how awesome the Author is!

*Paul at CFCC, in 1968*

# CHAPTER 7

# Let Him Lead... He Knows the Way

Sometimes it is difficult for us to imagine how intimately God is involved in the details of our lives. When we are reborn into the kingdom of God, the Holy Spirit becomes resident within every child of God. The Holy Spirit then guides, empowers, protects, and helps us demonstrate in our daily lives those things the Word of God has told us to do and to be... in order to be obedient.

Our humanity still causes us to not always obey what the Holy Spirit is teaching and leading us to be and do. Because that is a reality, we do not always make correct decisions, especially when we are overtired, in need of rest, and perhaps even trying to do more than we can do well. It is on these occasions that we are prone to make the poorest of decisions. I was at such a place in my life, to the point that I had begun to think Carolina Freight, perhaps, was not the place where I was supposed to be vocationally, even though I definitely did realize this company had given me so many wonderful opportunities and I was grateful for them. For some reason, I was somewhat uncertain about several work-related issues and struggled with a few matters of ethics with just a person or two. When you are overtired, in need of rest, it is easy to make hasty and most often unwise decisions. At these times of exhaustion, decisions may not always be thought out fully, and unfortunately, are often made without the guidance of the Holy Spirit's wise counsel. In this case, I had not sought to honor God's will for me nearly as fervently in prayer as I should have.

On a given Friday afternoon, I was driving home to Cherryville from Fayetteville, North Carolina, where I had met with one of our better customers to be certain everything was in order and so that we clearly understood their expectations. This was in our company's best interest since this customer was interested in giving Carolina Freight a larger share of their products to transport. That day we had clearly defined the details which needed to be taken care of as the market share for us was substantially increased.

But as I drove along, my restlessness about the future, which had been prevalent for several weeks, began to really become burdensome. Somehow, I had come to the conclusion that this was not the place I was supposed to be. It was a very challenging period for me with the questionable issues that were prevalent as well as the very, very long hours. I admit now that my reasoning was reckless, to say the least. Nonetheless, I reached a decision as I drove: "I am going to resign on Monday morning. I will trust God to help me find my place so I can take care of my family." This decision was now a settled matter, at least in my mind.

When I arrived back home, it was after the dinner hour, and the family had already eaten, so I sat down to eat alone. While I was eating, the phone rang, and it was a coworker calling for me. He began the conversation with, "Paul, you will never guess what happened today." "What?" I replied. His answer shocked me: "Your boss got fired!" He had no other details, and I returned to my meal. The phone rang again, and it was Mr. C. G. Beam. Mr. Beam was our founder and Chairman of the Board who chastised me for painting the sign. He was a very wise, plain-spoken person, but not one easy to get to know because he was a man of few words. He proceeded to tell me what I had just learned from my coworker, and he then asked me a question: "Can you meet with me in my office at one-thirty tomorrow?" Obviously, not knowing what was going on, I acknowledged that I would be there. The lawn that needed to be mowed would have to wait.

I had a worrisome Friday evening, simply not knowing what events had triggered all that had transpired. It was also a bit unnerving to think about a possible demotion for me, or even a dismissal could be forthcoming. It certainly helped me put into perspective my foolish idea to resign on Monday. All of a sudden, I realized—there might be nothing for me to resign from.

As planned, we met in his office, and he told me what had happened with my boss. They had either terminated him or allowed him to resign his position. I am not sure which. His position was the Director of Operations for the entire company. As a Northern Division Manager, I had reported directly to him. Mr. Beam did not elaborate on any details but said to me, "We think you might be able to do this job. Would you like to try it?" To say I was floored would be an understatement. To be at any higher level in the organizational structure had never even crossed my mind except to work my way up from loading the trucks. In fact, I had never asked for nor ever expected any promotion. The only job I ever coveted was that first one as a day laborer. Amazing! Climbing the corporate ladder was never an objective of mine. All I ever did was to do the job I currently had as well and as conscientiously as I possibly could. I owed my Savior that stewardship since I now represented Him full time. He would provide for me whatever was best for me and my family.

Mr. Beam went on to say, "If you want to try it, your title will be Acting Director of Operations, then if you perform it like I think you can, we will officially make you Director of Operations." In all honesty, I was almost in a state of shock, but I answered with, "Yes, sir. I would like to try it." Not only did I want to try it to be able to provide more monetarily for my large family, but also because it was an opportunity that would allow me to give recognition to and appreciate more of the hard-working people who had faithfully built that great company. I knew it was the hard-working people who had made Carolina Freight one of the more respected motor carriers in the United States. This promotion would also be an opportunity for me to represent my Savior to many more of the associates, just like Joe Alexander previously had done so well for me.

When I arrived home, my precious wife was waiting anxiously to know if "we" still had a job. Needless to say, she was overjoyed as we thought about how gracious God had been to us. His provision through all the years had been almost miraculous, and this last event was even more so. I must admit, however, I was somewhat ashamed of my entertaining the idea of resigning on Monday and embarrassed it had even been a reality.

Remarkably, on Monday morning, we began a new chapter in our lives. We asked for God's blessings in this new and more challenging endeavor, and as usual, He provided everything we needed to meet the requirements of the new job. In a little more than six months, at the annual meeting, they announced a title change for yours truly, to Director of Operations. My Savior and Redeemer deserves all the credit.

Successively, at the next annual meeting, they announced my next promotion to Vice President of Operations. And at the next annual meeting, they announced another promotion for me to Senior Vice President of Operations. This was no less happening in 1978, a little over twenty years later, in the company where I had shown up twenty-eight times just wanting to load freight before ever getting to work a single day.

I realize I really owe so much to all the people who supported me, believed in me, and helped me over the years. But most of all, I owe praise to my Blessed Savior, who guided me and grew me over the years. He also kept me from a foolish decision and probable disaster of "resigning" with no job. In addition, He gave me a wonderful way to represent Him as a satisfied and fulfilled Christian to a great many more people. I am truly beyond grateful.

When I think about this eventful time in my life, there are two promises in God's Word that come to mind. Ephesians 3:20 (NKJV) is one promise: "Now unto Him, who is able to do exceedingly abundantly above all we ask or think, according to the Power that works in us," and Psalm 139:13–16 (NKJV) is another: "For you formed my inward parts; you covered me in my mother's womb. I will praise *You*, for I am fearfully and wonderfully made; marvelous are *Your* works, and that, my soul knows very well. My frame was not hidden from *You*, when I was made in secret, and skillfully wrought in the lowest parts of the earth. *Your* eyes saw my substance, being yet unformed, and in *Your* book, they were written." In essence, these words express the truth that the life of a person, and the structure and meaning of that person's life, are all established from the beginning by God.

Yes, *People can!* But, in order to do our very best, we must know it can only be done by following the Owner's Manual, in obedience. That manual states, "All scripture is given by inspiration of God, and is profitable for doctrine [teaching], for reproof [conviction], for correction [getting something straight], for instruction [training] in righteousness [right living] that the man of God may be complete [capable], thoroughly equipped [fully prepared] for every good work" (2 Timothy 3:16–17, NKJV). These are our God-breathed instructions and comforting, calming words. It is a comforting thing to think about how none of us who have accepted Jesus' wonderful gift of forgiveness are ever out of God's thoughts. At different times we may feel desperation, but we can be comforted with His promise: "I will never leave nor forsake you" (Hebrews 13:5–6, NKJV). How reassuring it is to know that promise when we are facing uncertainty. This was a time when I learned an important truth which is the title of this chapter: "Let Him lead... He knows the Way."

# CHAPTER 8

# The Challenging Choice

There are times in everyone's life when taking a strong stand on principle is in order. God desires for people to live by the highest moral and ethical standards, and He provides the strength to do so. Not only that, all associates deserve to work at the direction of someone who has the character that real leadership demonstrates. As I indicated previously and additionally in my career, character and integrity were issues to be dealt with, albeit undesired. At this time, I was the Senior Vice-President of Operations at Carolina Freight Carriers, and I had to take a strong stand relative to integrity. This incident was one of those times I remember rather vividly because it involved my *unemployment* for seventeen hours.

Before trucking was deregulated in 1980, a carrier could not operate just anywhere, only where their original certificate of authority was granted by the Interstate Commerce Commission, or ICC. Purchasing another carrier's certificate or another freight company altogether was the only way to enter a new geographic area. So, for expansion purposes, we bought a small carrier to fill a geographic gap in our operating authority. In order to integrate that carrier as efficiently and promptly into the Carolina Freight system, we sent an experienced person, whom I will call "George," who reported to me, to oversee the integration of this new area.

While my family and I were on vacation, George persuaded several corporate officers that he should not report directly to me. Furthermore, he persuaded them that he should be allowed complete freedom to do whatever he deemed appropriate relative to the transition. Unfortunately, George had conveniently forgotten to discuss any of this with me. Not only had George violated the chain of command, but discarded any semblance of respect and courtesy in the process. When I returned to work on Monday morning, a loyal friend informed me of the "changes" George suggested to be made to the business plan. This friend also told me there would be a meeting with the Executive Committee that afternoon at 3 p.m. to discuss the matter. Needless to say, I was shocked, disappointed, and frustrated by the deception. It had always been my practice to discuss anything concerning any other leader directly with him or her and then rely on logic to be the persuader in that specific matter. This had not been the reciprocal case here.

During that 3 o'clock meeting at which I was present, one of the other officers (a friend of George's) in the organization made the case in support of the proposed change of responsibility. It was, to say the least, illogical. I say that because everyone knew the sooner we could integrate and fill the new lanes with freight, the better off the company would be. But this was not what the proposal being discussed would support. I have never quite understood what caused anyone to be persuaded that the proposed course of action would be advantageous for our company. Granting George a lesser degree of accountability would certainly not support definitively and efficiently integrating the new lanes of business as expeditiously as possible. I also recognized this ploy as an effort for George (the person requesting the change) to have less accountability and more unchecked freedom. That lack of culpability would certainly hinder and/or delay proficient integration into our existing system.

After the presentation was made, the officer who had made same, turned to me and said, "Paul, don't you think this would work better?"

I was ready with the correct answer: "It is illogical, unnecessary, and it is not only a poor idea—it is a lousy idea." You must remember, I had been simmering since about 10 a.m. that morning, and I had been patient throughout the presentation (summoning more patience than I ever knew I had). In fact, I honestly felt I would have been personally better off no longer having responsibility for my subordinate, but that decision was not necessarily better for the company. Anyway, you can imagine my response had prompted some startled looks on the faces of some in the room.

They discussed the pros and cons with several other executives in the meeting, with some of them continually trying to convince me to concede to this change in structure. I suspect some of that support for George was because of friendship, but I also believed they were unaware of some of his compromising behavior. We discussed it at length, and as we did, the clearer my decision became. The straw that broke the camel's back for me—and what I could not get past—was that I knew about the improprieties of the person, George, who devised this plan. This subordinate of mine had come behind my back to propose this strategy in an effort to escape the essential accountability established to produce the integration of this new purchase as quickly and efficiently as possible. There was no benefit whatsoever for the company to make such a change.

I had finally had enough, and I politely said, "Some of you want me to make a decision, so I have made one. Either George is leaving the company today, or I am leaving this company—today." As you can imagine, that remark created a rather tense setting. Especially when I said, "You decide which one it will be."

I was not trying to do anything heroic, nor did I feel good about having to take such a strong stand against the desires of some of my respected superiors. Always, I have been a team player because it takes unity to excel. And my stern position was not easy to maintain. I would never be insubordinate, but when you know morality and smart business principles are being compromised with a decision, a real leader will be resolute.

Apparently, they were shocked at my expectation. Yes, it was awkward, but I had finally had enough. After another thirty minutes or so of back and forth between them with no resolution, I felt I had my answer.

I then said, "I do not belong here. I hereby resign." I turned and asked a friend if he would drive me home so that I could leave my company car there. Then I courteously told everyone goodbye and left the premises. Lynette and I went out to dinner in Charlotte that evening with our pastor and his wife. We ate at a wonderful Chinese restaurant. Understandably, Lynette did not enjoy her meal as much as I did because I had told her, "We're now unemployed." I suppose that did cause some indigestion. Later, I thanked the Lord for His many blessings and watchcare over the years, and I slept soundly that night.

At 7:15 the next morning, our phone rang, and my boss was on the line. He requested that I come to the company for a brief meeting, to which I replied without sarcasm, "I don't work there anymore." He said, "Come for just fifteen minutes." I asked how many people would be there. He named the three who would be there, and I agreed to go for the short, fifteen-minute meeting.

When I got there, there were actually five people in the office of Mr. Beam, the Chairman of the Board, and Mr. Beam had been selected to do the talking. He said, "Paul, we have this thing worked out," to which I responded, "Why are you telling me? I don't work here anymore." I wasn't intending to be rude, just honest.

He then said, "We need both you and George, and we will keep George for ninety days and then let him go." My response was, "That's too bad because you aren't going to have both of us." He responded with, "Paul, do you know what your d—n trouble is?" Hoping I would not be considered a wise guy, I replied, "Mr. Beam, I am aware of some of my deficiencies, but I will be glad to listen to your evaluation." He said, "You are just plain d—n hard-headed." My very confident, but not arrogant, reply was, "Yes, Mr. Beam, you are exactly right. But when I have been hard-headed, ninety-nine times out of one hundred, it has put money into your pocket, not mine."

With that said, Mr. Beam looked at one of the other executives and stated, "Tell George he's done. And give him that d—n old car." He then looked at me and said, "Now get your butt to your office and get back to work."

You never feel good about anyone being dismissed, but when unity, success for your company, or character are the issues, it is sometimes necessary. I did not feel like a hero. I felt like I addressed a serious issue within our company with my own job security. It clearly required having the moral confidence, even though difficult, that it was the right thing to do. Not only that, we know we can always better live with ourselves when we have done the right thing, whether challenging or not. People were created to excel. But an important part of living up to our potential is taking an unwavering stand for what is morally, ethically, and spiritually right.

It was a less-than-pleasant experience for all the parties. However, there will be times when leaders must take a strong stand to defend a principle and what is right.

While this was a terribly unpleasant experience for all involved, I was more than pleased to learn George became a practicing Christian later in his life. Perhaps this was God's divine plan all along to help bring George to Himself. We are never, regardless of our actions, out of His thoughts or His desire for us to turn to Him.

# CHAPTER 9

# From a Time of Fear to a Time of Faith

My employer, Carolina Freight Carriers, had just purchased GI Trucking in 1983, and as a result, I was in California visiting some of the new facilities. I called home to check in with my family, especially about my only son, Paul Jr., whom we call "Bo." He was twenty-three at the time and had been having some problems swallowing. We had been to several different doctors before going to one of the very best ear, nose and throat specialists in Charlotte, N.C. I was anxious to hear the diagnosis, but I was not prepared to hear what I was told. Lynette struggled to keep from weeping when she told me what the specialist had determined. She said, "It is a large, fast-growing malignancy." At her words, I felt the blood drain from my face as it registered. Now my only son was in the battle for his very life.

I finished touring the facility in California almost as a zombie as I began to process what all this might mean in the days ahead. The cross-country flight home was consumed with worry and prayer. Even though I knew the God who had transformed my life could also heal my son, it was a new place for my family and me. And I was deeply terrified. After all, my son had been healthy, athletic, and strong all of his life.

Once back home, the details made me even more uneasy. Four different doctors had made scans, and all had come to the same diagnosis: *a large, fast-growing, malignant mass.*

At the time, my immediate leader, Ken Younger, was on the Board of Directors at Duke Medical Center. I asked for his help, and he was most gracious to step in and make a request on my behalf. Duke Medical Center was at the forefront in treating cancer at that time, and getting an appointment there was not easy to obtain. However, Ken called on Friday, and we had an appointment the following Monday. It was a long weekend, but the wonderful church we were a part of encouraged us with the commitment of continual prayer.

My son and I left on Monday morning for Duke. It was about a four-hour trip. While we were driving, we reminisced about the wonderful times camping together on the beautiful, clear, cold Lake James in the foothills of Western North Carolina. Since there was so much travel in my work, I would always plan our trip soon after his school season ended. We would go catch up while we roughed it, camping and fishing for an entire week. They were wonderful times. I clung to those wonderful times that day, knowing what may be coming.

We arrived in Durham, North Carolina, and, after we ate a small breakfast, went straight to the hospital. The head of thoracic surgery, Dr. Farmer, received us promptly. He had already reviewed the findings of the other doctors, and he ordered additional X-rays and scans. The doctor examined our son over a period of several hours. Once all was completed, he gave us the long-awaited news. "I must confirm the diagnosis of the other doctors," he said, matter-of-factly. "It is a large, fast-growing malignant mass. We will schedule surgery in a couple of days, but we want to go ahead and admit Bo. Please have your family come up, and you all have dinner the night before." His words projected an ominous probability.

Others had joined me and my family in praying the diagnosis would be different from what we had already been told. But Dr. Farmer clearly indicated that the previous medical conclusions had been correct, and he restated these conclusions with a great sense of urgency. He said, "This is a serious surgery. The growth is wrapped around vital arteries and nerves, and a number of things can happen. We will have to go slowly. There could be various results. For example, he may lose the use of one or both arms. He may have to be assisted with breathing for the rest of his life. Or he could have a stroke." The doctor did not have to tell us it could even be fatal. When he instructed us to have our family come for dinner the night before surgery, we all knew how serious this was. He also told us this surgery, because of the location of the mass, could take more than several hours. How I dreaded to call his sweet mother with such bad news! I was absolutely devastated and crushed beyond description. I had always been able to deal with the difficulties in life with hard work, perseverance, and strong effort. This time, however, my faith was challenged. I realized this was beyond me.

I called my wife with the dreadful news. She was also crushed and then later relayed the information to our extended family and church. Our church was an exceptional body of believers. They believed in prayer and were diligent about praying. So, our church established a 24-hour continual prayer chain, beseeching God's mercy upon our son. We were bathed in prayer day after day throughout this journey.

By the end of that first day in Durham, I began to prepare to leave my son's room for the evening. We embraced, and I told him not to worry. I told him, "Good night, Bo. I love you," and I left the hospital. I was a nervous wreck and felt as if I were dying on the inside. There was a Sheraton Hotel onsite, and, fortunately, they had a room. As physically weary and discouraged as I was, I skipped dinner and went straight to my room. I felt so alone. Ironically, I had been so shaken that morning that I did not anticipate the doctor admitting Bo, and I had made no provision for myself to spend the night. Honestly, I did not know what to do.

As I sat in this hotel room, I began to think back to the time of my father's death. When he passed, I was my father's only living son. I felt I had to be strong for everyone else and not weep, and determined to stay strong through the whole burial process for my mom and my sisters. However, about a week later, when I walked into my grandmother's home, the dam burst. I finally wept and wept hard, and the grieving process began. At that point, after grieving, God gave me indescribable peace. As I thought about my father's death in the quiet of my hotel room, it occurred to me that I should go ahead and just weep now for my only son. So, I got down on my knees to weep and grieve, but I somehow could not shed a single tear. In an instant, I was involuntarily standing with my hands raised *in praise*. I praised my Lord and Savior as never before in my life. I was led and empowered by the Holy Spirit of God to do so. I cannot explain it; I can only describe it. Next to the night when God set me free and gave me real life in Christ, it was the most glorious thing that ever happened to me. I experienced Psalm 85:8 (NKJV), "I will hear what God the Lord will speak, for He will speak peace to His people." He spoke indescribable peace to me that night.

As I have thought about that time in my life and really wondered how it all happened and exactly what did happen, it has finally become clear. When nothing else would suffice, God gave me, his sinful child, *a God hug*. During the time of my uncertainty, worry, and sorrow, my blessed Lord did a most remarkable thing—He hugged me. "Hug" is defined in the Webster's dictionary as follows: "to hold fast, to stay close, and to press tightly in the arms." (And by the way, Daniel Webster, the publisher of the Webster's dictionary, also said, "The greatest thought that can occupy a man's mind is His accountability to God"). I experienced that night, in the midst of grief, the "peace of God which surpasses all understanding," just as it is described in Philippians 4:7 (NKJV).

When all of our family gathered at the hospital for Bo's surgery the morning of, our pastor, Dr. Mike Minnix, led us in prayer. Following that prayer and based on what God had done for me the night before, I could honestly say to all my family who were gathered there that morning, "I am confident Bo is going to be okay." I am not certain how many others really felt that way since I could still see grave concern on their faces. I'm not certain they could understand why I was genuinely positive that God would be glorified and Bo would be okay. But because of the divine peace He had given the evening before, I believed this would turn out better than we could imagine. God had replaced my worry with peaceful faith.

Based on what Dr. Farmer had told us, we were all prepared for a long surgery. Therefore, we were very surprised when after only a little more than an hour, the doctor emerged with a smile on his face and said, "I have never witnessed this before! It miraculously was not a malignancy. It was a very rare abscess, and I've never seen this type of abscess in this part of the body before in all my years of practice. So, while I was in there, I took out his tonsils. He will be fine."

Needless to say, we could not praise and thank our gracious God enough. The God hug I had received the night before made me certain He would see us through. God had miraculously assured us that our son would be spared.

Because of this experience, I realized the least I could do is share what I have experienced with our gracious God. We will never know if because of prayers God changed the certain malignant mass to an abscess. But what I do know is when we have become desperate because of situations beyond our control, the God we know and love stands ready to do exactly what He promised. Again, Psalm 85:8 (NKJV) states these precious words, "I will hear what God the Lord will speak for He will speak peace to His people." In our calamitous world, how we need to hear that divine presence speaking peace.

God took me from a time of fear to a time of faith and did so with an unforgettable God hug. Since He loves each one of us, knows everything about every one of us, every minute of every day, we should not be surprised when He comforts our deepest need, at our most desperate time, with a God hug.

# CHAPTER 10

# Fully Yielded in 1984

In 1984, I was well-settled in to my position as Senior Vice President of Operations at Carolina Freight Carriers Corporation. Since my work week was full of travel and appointments, Saturday mornings were usually used to catch up on paperwork.

Over the years, I worked hard creating mutually beneficial relationships with people from all ranks of employment with whom I interacted. I began my career as a day laborer and had no real sponsor. Therefore, I wanted to make it somewhat easier to interface with those who were not in a leadership position. I believe most of the workers who knew me also knew within my heart there was great respect for the hard, and somewhat seemingly thankless, work they did so willingly day after day. They seemed to realize I truly appreciated them since I had once been there myself. Basically, there was a great deal of mutual respect. I knew something about the consistently hard effort it took on their part to keep our company strong.

Therefore, I tried to keep my door open as much as possible. On this particular day, I looked up, and there stood two over-the-road drivers in the hallway outside of my office. One stepped inside and asked if I had a few minutes to hear them. I assured them I would be glad to listen.

These drivers were two of the hundreds who moved the fully loaded trailers from one service center to another. Some of these round trips were made while most of us slept. As team drivers, one would drive for four hours while the other slept on the built-in-bunk in the upper back of the tractor cab. During the journey, they would exchange places. This kept the cargo moving without delay, but it was not an easy life. Unfortunately, there were many things that interfered with sleeping in the cab. A few examples were rough roads, horns, and noises from other trucks. In reality, it was a hard way to earn a living, especially since the mattress on which they slept was on top of a solid metal base. This meant road impact was substantial without any extra suspension.

The first thing the gentleman said was, "I know you probably can't or won't do anything about our problem, but we want you to hear it, anyway." At that moment, I decided if there was anything under the sun that could be done for these worn-out travelers, it would be done. So I listened attentively to them about the tractor bunks they rested in. I am convinced they were surprised when I said, "Have you guys got time to go down to the maintenance shop with me?" They answered, "Right now?" to which I affirmed, "Right now." They seemed shocked by my response.

The Senior Vice President of Maintenance was in his office, and he was our first point of contact. Not only was he a very knowledgeable maintenance person, but also he was a very cooperative senior leadership team player. So, I explained to him these two hard-working drivers had developed an idea to install a suspended bunk. This suspended bunk would help absorb the road shock. They explained their idea in more detail. He said, "I will be glad to equip a prototype. We will get right on it."

You would have thought I had just given them the keys to the U.S. Mint. These drivers left there feeling like they had really been valued as people. However, if you want to know the truth, I felt even better because I was able to help these hard-working, loyal associates. I realized it was these people who could be counted on to get the job done day after day, month after month, and year after year, even though they had no career path to a greater future. These people, in fact, build companies. They are the catalysts necessary in a company for companies to keep promises and grow. They play a very important role in making prosperity available to all who are a part of the same.

What I did that day was not particularly outstanding on my part. It was just the right thing to do for them. If one of them had been my son, I would have wanted his leader to do the same thing for him. Doing the right thing should always be the criteria for leadership decisions.

God taught me over a period of time that Christianity (which I define as following the teachings of Jesus, to "do to others as you would have them to do to you," Luke 6:31, NIV) is not just to be taught as a way to live part of the time. It is to be applied in the workplace, just as it is in the Sunday school room. Faith is applicable everywhere, *especially* in the workplace, where unity is so critical. God's ways will always be appropriate and produce the best results.

After I became a born-again Christian in 1969, I began to look forward to reading God's Word every day. The more I read, the more I realized my need to make application of the teaching of Christ, the Apostles, and the Prophets. It became a fascination, almost an obsession, to read and study this book of truth. It became so very clear to me that this book, when read and applied, was the very best way to create a healthy business environment. To me, it was and continues to be the best leadership and human relations book ever written. I was never disappointed in the outcome when I applied and trusted a principle from this book of wisdom and truth. And I knew it pleased my Savior.

After my salvation, God expected me to grow up in Christ and to live for Him faithfully. And I was truly so glad to be free of the old self that I wanted to be faithful. Those were wonderful, spiritual developmental years for me. The more I read and studied the Word, listened to and learned from anointed preachers, spent time in earnest prayer, and shared my faith with others who needed to also be set free in Christ, the more I completely opened my life to the perfect will of my Savior. Why could I or should I not trust a Savior who died in my place?

In the spring of 1984, I went to my office on another Saturday morning with the intention of catching up with paperwork and planning my calendar. However, this particular Saturday, something more important happened as I began to think how wonderfully God had graced my life over the last fourteen years. Those thoughts caused me to close my eyes and pray. I sat at my desk, with my door partly open, and prayed this simple prayer, "Lord, I praise you for your wonderful liberation, guidance, and influence in my life.

I now submit myself completely to your perfect will. If this is not the place I can serve you best, show me where it is, and I will go there, no matter where or what." I really meant it! The strange thing was that I was not unhappy or mistreated, or disillusioned about the great company I was a part of. Those were not the reasons I prayed that heartfelt prayer. The Holy Spirit guided me, and I just wanted to be where God wanted me to be. Anyway, God knew I was sincere, and I knew it, too.

Then a strange thing happened, which I attribute to God's Holy Spirit within me. He did not speak audibly but simply made me aware of his message: "Paul, you need to humble yourself." It was a clear directive. My door was open, and I remember thinking, *If I get on my knees to humble myself, some passerby may think I am ill or that something is wrong.* However, I did not hesitate. I got on my knees, willingly and obediently, and prayed the very same prayer again, "Lord, I praise you for your wonderful liberation, guidance, and influence in my life. I now submit myself completely to your perfect will. If this is not the place I can serve you best, show me where it is, and I will go there, no matter where or what." I then got up with a "peace of God which surpasses all understanding" (Philippians 4:7, NKJV).

My company had been so very good to give someone like me one opportunity after another to grow and develop. My Lord, on the other hand, had helped me realize what 2 Corinthians 5:17–18 (KJV) promises,

> *Therefore, if any man be in Christ, he is a new creation; old things are passed away; behold, all things are become new. And all things are of God, who hath reconciled us to Himself by Jesus Christ, and hath given to us the ministry of reconciliation.*

I was in a strange place, yet I knew there was nothing to fear. I knew, and God knew that I was willing to do whatever He deemed best for me. I wanted to be obedient. It was indescribable. I can tell you I experienced Psalm 85:8 (KJV), "I will hear what God the Lord will speak, for He will speak peace unto His people." It indeed was "a peace of God which surpasses all understanding" (Philippians 4:7, NKJV).

It is impossible for me to explain this paradox. When I was the most yielded to His will, I was also the most liberated. I did not realize this truth at the time. Once I realized my need to become a faithful disciple of Jesus, what was the first thing I needed to do? I had to decide that I would follow Him, be obedient to Him. I had to follow Him not just as my Savior, but I had to crown Him Lord with a totally submitted life. It is a term we do not hear often enough today—lordship. If I truly trust Him and want all God has prepared for me and desires for me, I can only have it by way of complete submission. I reiterate purposely; it is called lordship!

I better understand now what was happening in my life. I had never really thought about and absorbed God's promise in Psalm 139:15–16 (NASV):

*My frame was not hidden from You, When I was made in secret, And skillfully wrought in the depths of the earth; Your eyes have seen my unformed substance; And in Your book were all written the days that were ordained for me, When as yet there was not one of them.*

This is a promise for you also if you are a disciple of Jesus Christ. God was orchestrating things and keeping His promises. I was the blessed recipient of His grace and goodness. God has a unique plan for each of us. It's called a partnership. This partnership involves us doing our part—submitting, yielding, with nothing held back, and Him doing His part—blessing, protecting, and guiding.

I have come to know this truth from His words that our God is the *only* true God whom we can always trust. We are to let God guide our lives and show us the path, even if that path is filled with uncertainty and risks. Unconditionally! Christianity is a full-time privilege, and God expects us to work at it, grow into it, and excel at it. We can always trust God to lead us.

You may be wondering, "Can I really trust Him with my blanket promise to obey wherever He directs?" The answer is profoundly simple: "How can

I *not* trust the One who has already paid a sin debt I could not pay and has taken my sin away and died in my place?"

I did not particularly want to leave a company that had been so very good to me, but I had learned over the years that my Savior would not allow me to make a mistake if I was continuously seeking Him and His direction. It was a very special time I will never forget.

God is an awesome, trusted Provider and Difference-Maker.

# Chapter 11

# A Divine Release

Approximately three weeks after the Saturday morning experience of yielding my future to my Lord and Savior, no strings attached, I was visiting with Lynette in the hospital where she was recovering from surgery. There I told her what I had done that Saturday morning a few weeks before when I prayed. Then I commented to her that it would not surprise me if I got a call from W. T. Cassels, Jr., President of Southeastern Freight Lines. I had learned about an existing open position there, but no one had mentioned I might be considered for it. It was the Difference-Maker in my spirit giving me this awareness. Lynette inquired why.

I told her I was somewhat familiar with Southeastern, and they were a very strong competitor in the portion of the Southeastern U.S. which they served. The Cassels family who owned Southeastern was held in extremely high regard by their customers and especially by the associates who made up the fine company. I had never heard anything but especially favorable comments concerning Southeastern. One of those who had told me about the company was a former associate of mine at Carolina, who now worked at Southeastern. I trusted his judgment because he knew how to lead people. His name is Romie Cox, and he never got over the esprit de corps that existed within the people of Southeastern. Obviously, that great environment existed because of the genuine respect for and care of the associates by the Cassels family.

Some of my knowledge about Southeastern had also come from Bud Dressel, the Vice President of Operations for Southeastern. He and I had served together on the Board of Directors of the Operations Council of the American Trucking Association (ATA). We saw each other from time to time at our board meetings. Bud seemed especially interested in the Quality Improvement Process I had learned about at 3M headquarters that I'll elaborate on later. I had shared with him my own more than passing interest in same. I had no idea if Bud had shared any of that information with his President and owner, Mr. W. T. Cassels, Jr. However, years later, as I thought about it, I felt like he surely had done so.

Anyway, Lynette and I continued our conversation about Southeastern Freight and what all would be involved if Mr. Cassels called or if any of that happened, namely relocation. Since we were lifelong residents of Cherryville, to say the least, she was shocked to hear what I was saying. The great majority of our families, our parents, and most all of our friends resided there. All of our childhood memories would not be left behind, but they would be a challenge to remember as fondly if we moved away. All of the people, who had been so kind to us over the years, as well as our closest neighbors, would no longer be present in the same way in our lives. Our spiritual mentors would no longer have a weekly and almost daily presence in our lives. The people who had given me opportunity at Carolina Freight Carriers would no longer be a regular part of my life.

This was a lot to leave behind. It was indeed difficult to consider all of these many factors as we talked about a re-location to a place where we knew practically no one. For sure, it was more difficult for my good wife to consider than for me. She was a bit taken back since she had not yet received the same peaceful reassurance which I had received on my knees in my office that Saturday morning three weeks before when I gave my Savior His rightful privilege of guiding all my decisions, including vocational decision, in the future.

That Saturday surrender was another of the most liberating things I had ever experienced. The first was in the church during a revival service when God's Spirit brought awareness of how much I needed to be genuinely born again as God's saved child. There, I had personally experienced in a powerful way, the truth of that wonderful Bible verse found in 2 Corinthians 3:17 (KJV), "Where the spirit of the Lord is, there is liberty." But on this Saturday morning years later, when I genuinely surrendered, I had finally come to know that "liberty" was—not just a biblical phrase, but a revolutionary life-changing truth. It can happen only when we yield our will completely to Jesus in Lordship.

After Lynette had been at home from the hospital for a few days, shortly after dinner one evening, the phone rang. I answered, and a voice on the other phone said, "Paul, this is Bill Cassels. My father founded Southeastern Freight Lines. I have been given your name as someone I should get to know. Would you consider having dinner with me, no strings attached?" My heart began to beat a little faster as I said, "Mr. Cassels, I had begun to think you might never call." I now realize if I had been Mr. Cassels and heard that presumptive statement, I might be thinking, *what kind of idiot or egotist is this that I am speaking with?*

We made arrangements to meet a few evenings later in Rock Hill, South Carolina, which is about the mid-point between Cherryville and Columbia. Throughout our meeting, I was not surprised to see what I had expected—a humble, quiet, but articulate gentleman. He possessed an air of genuineness. He explained that he was interested in hiring a Senior Vice President of Operations since Mr. Bud Dressel had just suddenly passed away. Bud, as mentioned earlier, was a good personal friend of mine and had told me much about Southeastern Freight and its unique characteristics.

Mr. Cassels went on to say he realized Southeastern must begin to expand rather quickly in order to meet customer expectations. Next, he stated another priority: Southeastern Freight needed to build many more service center facilities. Mr. Cassels also indicated the company owned a Bell Jet Ranger helicopter because frequent travel to facilities was so important to preserve and enhance the Southeastern culture. He knew well how important the regular presence of leadership was. People needed and welcomed that attention and encouragement regularly. Every word he spoke was meaningful, and there were none wasted. Even before I began to ask questions that were on my mind, I knew this was a man of unique character and attractive confidence. He knew what genuine leadership is about, and I knew he would be a great role model for me to emulate as well. I was excited as I drove the two-hour trip back home. Within a week, Mr. Cassels called and offered me the job as Senior Vice President of Operations. This was the equivalent title I then had at Carolina Freight.

Once Lynette and I prayed, we realized God was orchestrating every bit of this; I tendered my resignation to Ken Younger, whom I reported to at Carolina. He appeared to be somewhat shocked that I would leave Carolina, which was at that time a much larger company than Southeastern Freight. In fact, Carolina Freight was four times the size of Southeastern Freight. Carolina was also listed on the New York Stock Exchange and publicly traded.

Mr. Younger was a Duke University graduate and a strong, successful leader. Previously, he had a very successful tenure with Roadway Express. He also helped develop Sealand Services as an early leader in the container industry. Both of our top officers at Carolina Freight had gotten to know Ken over the years as a very capable trucking executive. They were both aging, and they recognized a need to strengthen the Carolina Freight Leadership team. Thus, Ken was employed, and he and I had a very solid relationship. I am unaware of what he may have expected to find in me, a local guy, as Sr. Vice President of Operations. At any rate, I knew the best thing anyone can do is to work hard, be a good example for others, and strive continuously to please your leaders.

There is no question in my mind that my role had now become demonstrating leadership that would be easy for others to follow. Maturing as a Christian, my Creator had opened my eyes to the great need to be an encourager of others without compromising the accomplishment of the objective. I knew that could be done, and I could now see that my commitment to Christ and to the ethics of Christ was simply the best way to demonstrate leadership. I had worked diligently to be a desirable asset for Carolina Freight and a respectful friend of my immediate leader. After all, I now had the greatest Guide and Helper possible who was preparing me for even greater challenges.

God's consummate plan for me was now becoming more and more evident. It had included my starting at the very bottom, learning a business step by step, in order to ultimately be in a place to encourage the hard-working people who make up a trucking company. Trucking is a "people" business, and to produce best results, the associates need and deserve encouragement. How well I knew that by my own experience.

I did not have a sponsor at the beginning, but now I had the help of the only One who had ever overcome death. I deserved none of what had been given to me, but the wonderful grace of God is so absolutely marvelous. That word *grace* means the undeserved favor of God. I love to just meditate on that beautiful word *grace* and how much-underserved favor God has given me.

When I tendered my resignation, Mr. Younger indicated he would "get back to me." I did not know what to expect, but he did get back with me the next morning and said, "Paul, we are going to make you Executive V.P. on Monday morning." I replied, "Ken, this is not about a promotional ploy. This is about life purpose. I have been praying about this for a while, and this is God's will for my life." Ken replied, "Well, I will start praying with you about staying." It became clear Ken had taken on the responsibility of keeping me at Carolina. I sincerely believe that. Truth is, I never really wanted to leave that great company if Carolina was where my Lord wanted me to be. When I had gotten on my knees that Saturday morning and told Him wherever you want me to go, or whatever you want me to do, show me, and I will go there, I really meant it even if it just meant staying in the great company that Carolina Freight had become.

A few days later, word about my attempted resignation began to be known, and if you have ever lived in a small town, you know, news travels fast. As it became common knowledge, I began to receive phone calls and visits from friends and co-workers, whom I had labored with in the early days. As I listened to what they had to say, asking me to stay and thanking me for my interest in them, etc., I became uncertain about what God's perfect will for me, His grateful servant, was.

As various people questioned my decision, I tried my best to keep flattery and false praise out of my mind. Many of them made this statement, "You are the only one who understands and will listen to working people." I knew that I was not the only one, but it did make me feel good to know those encouraging things were being felt and spoken. Truly, I did understand and care for them, the working people. God had given me a heart for laboring people since I had been where they were. Also, I continually heard from working people in most of the states we serviced. As you can imagine, it was a very challenging time, a period when guilt crept in about leaving a company that had been so very good to me.

At the time I tendered my resignation, Mr. Beam, the chairman of the board and founder, was on a tour in Russia with a group of other businessmen from North Carolina. On the Saturday he returned from Russia, he called me and began the conversation with "Paul, what's this I'm hearing about you, son?" (If you'll recall how we met—the sign painting encounter—you'll realize now how much things had obviously changed between us as he had just referred to me as "son.") It would be dangerous for me to take credit for what only an all-knowing God can do, so I will say no more. Mr. Beam and I had developed a wonderful relationship of mutual respect and admiration. Years earlier, we had come to an agreement as to how we would work together. It had come about in an unusual way. He was known for his ability to chew people up to the point that whatever they, or I, had done, we would certainly never do it again. Mr. Beam had founded the company during really hard times economically, and it was just his way of trying to keep everyone on their toes.

My encounter with Mr. Beam's frankness and very candid, almost blistering conversation happened in one of the very first meetings which I attended as the newly appointed Director of Operations, and I never forgot it. In that meeting, he personally eviscerated me. The verbal assault went on for a good ten minutes. It would not have been so bad if there had not been four other attendees in that meeting. After that meeting, I returned to my office, sat down at my desk, and began to examine myself. My initial purpose was to determine if I was bleeding anywhere. As I considered what had just happened, this thought occurred to me—no job is worth what I just went through. Therefore, I promptly called Mr. Beam's secretary to see if I could have a few minutes with him. She checked and responded positively. I then went to his office, not mad but critically wounded. When I opened the door, he greeted me as if nothing had happened. It was unbelievable to me that he was so nice and composed while I was a confused, wounded mess. I could not help but remember back to our first meeting in the trailer shop when painting the sign.

I knew Mr. Beam had the reputation for blistering the paint off the wall when he was upset about something, but never did I expect to be the wall. I began the conversation with, "Mr. Beam, I would like to talk with you about the meeting we were just in. Please know I fully understand you were just trying to make a point that would never be forgotten. However, your approach hurt my feelings and frankly just made me mad. My purpose for asking for your time is just to see if we could have a man-to-man conversation." He replied, "Well, I reckon we can." He used the folksy language often because it possibly caused some people to underestimate his tremendous mental acuity. I began with, "It is important for you to know I am here with a primary purpose to please you. I am fully aware you have built a great company. If you will simply and calmly tell me what you want me to do or not do, my promise to you is I will make certain it gets accomplished. If it doesn't, I will come back and explain the hindrance and get your advice on how to proceed. I am here to satisfy you and to follow your wise advice. Do you think we can go forward in that way?" He smiled and said, "Well, I don't see why not." My relieved response was, "Good, because I'm pretty sure I can't go forward if the future is going to be like that past meeting." Mr. Beam never was disrespectful or personally critical of me again. He still said to me what I needed to hear, but he was always a true gentleman, and we developed a mutually respectful relationship. That relationship was evidenced by the fact that whenever we would be having a customer event nearby, he would inquire to see if I was planning to attend. Then if so, in such a gentlemanly manner, he would ask, "Do you mind if I ride with you?" Entrepreneurship in those early days was a real challenge, and he had developed the tenacity and resolve to succeed where many others failed. Beneath it all, he was a man to be greatly admired and respected. I appreciated his calls to ride with me so very much since we had worked through some difficult times together.

Nonetheless, here I was at Carolina Freight, having been lifted out of a probably very limited environment into an excellent job among people who knew of my great respect for those who labored hard day after day. Instead, I, as a laborer, had been given the wonderful opportunity to learn, grow, and benefit from the advancement of a truly successful company. It was not an easy place to be—planning to leave this company—as I remembered how good the company had been to me.

As I tried to listen to all the input, little did I know, the enemy of God was doing all he could (not through the assistance of these people, however) to prevent me from being in the perfect will of my Lord and Savior. Finally, I yielded to the voices and pleas and decided to stay at Carolina Freight. My rationale was, "If God wants me at Southeastern Freight, He will show me clearly."

I called Mr. Cassels, all the while feeling terrible about going back on my word to such a gentleman. The conversation was very limited. I said, "Mr. Cassels, this is not as easy as I thought it would be. I need more time to think and pray about this. But please, if you need someone now, you go ahead and feel free to hire them." His reply was unexpected but indicative of the character of this unique man. He said, "Paul, you take all the time you need." That is the way we left it. I believe it was in April 1984.

With a new enthusiasm, I approached my work at Carolina because I wanted to be loyal to so many who had expressed their appreciation of me and who had been a part of influencing me to stay. It is comforting to be able to know and say that I did not have divided loyalties. My Heavenly Father knew that I was open to whatever He chose to reveal as His will for me. But I was persuaded to stay, and I devoted myself fully to my duties there at Carolina in Cherryville.

A few years earlier, a new pastor, Dr. Mike Minnix, had been called to the church we attended. He was a preacher's preacher, and every Sunday, he challenged us with the truth of God's Word. I could hardly wait from Sunday to Sunday to hear him expound God's Word with such clarity and confidence. Truly he was an anointed one, a dynamic and genuine presence in the pulpit, blessing his congregation with the profound truth of God's Word. His sermons always made me want to be more and do more for my Lord and Savior.

It was a normal practice for several of us as deacons to meet with Dr. Minnix in his study before he preached and to pray with him and for him. It was a special time I looked forward to every Sunday.

On this particular Sunday in early August, after praying with Dr. Minnix, we stepped out into a hallway that had an entry door into our large sanctuary. In that hallway, in my spirit, I heard this message: "I am not the One making you feel guilty." It was not audible, but it was absolutely clear. Please know that I cannot explain it, but God's Holy Spirit delivered this message loud and clear without any doubt whatsoever.

It is important for me to say I had not been debating the previous decision to stay in my present job. I had been totally giving my very best at Carolina Freight out of gratitude for the way people had helped influence my previous decision to remain there. Everyone had been so very helpful and kind to me since I had decided to stay. And then *this* experience on that Sunday in early August was like a lightning bolt. There was no doubt in my mind that God's Holy Spirit was speaking to me and had made it clear to me when I heard, "I am not the One making you feel guilty." It was not imagined. I am certain of it. His Holy Spirit had spoken directly to me. That was a liberating proclamation. I cannot describe the uniqueness of this event. It was supernatural, and maybe I should have known that God knew all along Lynette and I wanted only to do the right thing, whatever it was. He had given us our answer that Sunday morning. Never before had anything become so clear in such an unusual manner.

I could hardly wait until Monday morning to call Mr. Cassels. When I told him if he still needed someone, I was ready to come, he then surprised me. He replied similarly to my response to his initial call, "I've been waiting for your call." After that, Satan and all his demons could not have prevented this wonderful response to the enlightenment of God's will. It had been months and months, and Mr. Cassels had kept the door open, but never once whatsoever had he tried to influence me. I believe he knew that if we let our Lord handle it, then it would, by divine providence, work out as it was supposed to.

It was awkward, but I then wrote out a second resignation letter. Mr. Younger's response was rather cool, and I really regretted that I had disappointed him by leaving. He had been more than nice to me, and so had Mr. Beam. It was evident they both believed in me and really were counting on me to help move Carolina forward in the years ahead. All three of us had worked diligently to develop meaningful relationships over the many months since I had submitted that first letter of resignation. Now, I was uncertain if I would even be considered as a friend in view of my leaving.

Let me share a story about a previous event with Mr. Younger to shed light on our relationship. When Mr. Younger was initially employed, a few years earlier, there was an officers meeting on a Saturday morning for the purpose of his introduction. Mr. Younger spoke and made this statement to the various officers. He said, "I believe in open communication lines, and if I ever do anything that is a problem for you, or if you have a problem with me, call me and let's sit down and talk it out." It was a welcome beginning to our relationship, and I took him seriously.

The following event transpired a couple of years after Mr. Younger came on board. We had just made some substantial improvements in our on-time delivery results. I had shared those with Mr. Younger several weeks earlier.

He seemed pleased with the results, and I certainly felt good about the substantial progress. A few weeks later, I had been traveling Monday through Wednesday and got back into my office on Thursday morning. As usual, there was an ample stack of paperwork and on the very top was a letter from a sales representative to Mr. Younger. That letter pointed out a one-day delay on a single shipment. Mr. Younger had written a note on the letter and forwarded it to me. It read, *Taylor, thought you told me our service had been substantially improved. Apparently, you are mistaken. Younger.*

For some reason, I never liked to be called by my last name, especially by a friend. As I thought about the note, it brought back the memory of his statement at the introductory meeting. "Let's talk about it." So, I called his secretary, and she indicated he was available to me. When I walked in, he greeted me with, "How are you doing, pard?" It was a favorite greeting term that Mr. Younger used with fellow associates. I responded with, "I was doing fine until I got your note." And before I could continue, he said, "I'm the d—n president of this company, and I will write anything I please."

By this time, I knew it was one of those times when we must affirm ourselves, and I responded with, "Oh, I am very sorry I bothered you. I fully understand executive privilege, but when you came here, you told every one of us, 'If you ever have a problem with me, come and let's talk it out.' I didn't know you really didn't mean that." With that, I picked up the note and started out the door. His response was very conciliatory: "Hold on, my secretary will get us some coffee." We then sat down and had a surprisingly productive conversation. That communication was a solidifying event, a building point in our relationship. He saw I would stand my ground for myself, as well as for my company. His honor was at stake, and he knew it, and he did the right thing.

In every relationship, there will be a time to stand up and be counted. That was the only time we ever needed coffee in his office. He never overreacted with me again, and now, I seriously did not want to injure the relationship with a resignation. However, I did follow through and accept the Southeastern Freight Lines position.

As just a bit of an aside, Sybil Setzer had been my secretary until Mr. Younger came. He needed the best secretary in that new position. She was indescribable in every way—so competent, so loyal, so helpful to everyone. She was in a class by herself. If ever a secretary needed to be cloned, she did. I had offered her for this more important job, as his secretary, and missed her as my own, but I was glad for our president to have such competent help. She will always be remembered as one of my most respected and appreciated co-workers.

A few years after I had been at Southeastern Freight, I received a call from Mr. Younger. It was brief. "Paul, this is Ken Younger, I am retiring today, and I am calling all the people who helped me along the way. You are one of those people. Thank you." I thanked him for the call and felt so good about our relationship. I was honored that he had called. Several years later, Ken called again. He did not tell me he was terminally ill, but he did say this: "I'm just calling to tell you that you made the right decision when you left Carolina and went to Southeastern." Ken was a proud man, and I know that he seriously wanted me to know what he had just said was from his heart. I respected him highly for his willingness to verify what God had already made perfectly clear. The point to be made here is simple. There is a time to stand up and be counted, without shouting, screaming, cursing, or even being angry. That is God's way to settle matters. In my early days, I had an older executive tell me, "You can't be big and little at the same time." I needed to hear it, and it has been very helpful, straightforward guidance for me ever since. In the end, it was a wonderful thing to know the coolness I felt when I tendered the second resignation had now been replaced with a relationship of mutual respect.

On my last day at Carolina Freight, I received an unexpected phone call. (I had mentioned in another part of the book some events which were occurring when I inherited as my responsibility the Maspeth Service Center in Brooklyn, New York.) The Union steward for that service center was a fairly young man named Tom Hogan. At some point in time, previous management had allowed the steward position to become a non-working, plus twenty hours of paid overtime each week position. Once "past practices" are established in a union company, even if unreasonable, it is very difficult to end them no matter how irrational they may seem to be. But it was very difficult for me to accept. We had our share of differences until I finally realized I could not change this excessive unjustifiable expense. In the meantime, Tom and I had some seriously tedious conversations and exchanges. Anyway, my secretary indicated the person calling was a Mr. Tom Hogan from Brooklyn. My most immediate thoughts were, "Here's his final shot at me," and I answered with apprehension. Immediately he said, "Tom Hogan here, I understand you will be leaving us," I answered affirmatively. He said, "I expect it is to a non-union company," and I simply let him know that it was. It then shocked me when he said, "The reason for my call is to say thank you for all you did to make Carolina a better company and to wish you best of luck as you go." I was almost speechless, but I could have never had a more encouraging event occur. It caused me to know that even my toughest challengers recognized my heart and soul. It encouraged me to know they recognized my intent was to help the diligent, hard-working people who did the heavy lifting, to help them have the dignity they deserved as we built together a strong and successful company. Tom Hogan's timely call gave me a fulfilling peace about leaving a place and people who had been so very good to me. It was a company that had given me opportunity to become a day-laborer initially, and to leave as the Senior Vice President of Operations.

I owe so much to so many, but my Lord and Savior is at the top of my list.

# CHAPTER 12

# The Optimal Discovery—A Win/Win/Win

If I may step back in time for a moment, please permit me to discuss something that profoundly affected my leadership philosophy while at Carolina Freight Carriers. Over the course of many years in a business leadership position, I was aware of discussions about various business arrangements or scenarios. The two scenarios most often talked about were win/lose and win/win. The win/lose scenario usually ended in the loser withdrawing rather promptly once they realized they were on the wrong end of the arrangement. The win/win is a much more desirable situation to be in with both parties, the customer as well as the company, gaining benefits from the arrangements. Simple logic told me that was where every business person wants to be.

An example of a win/win would be a customer/business relationship with the customer receiving an acceptable product or service the great majority of the time. On the other side of that arrangement, the business owners would be receiving the benefit of profits as income in order to perpetuate the business.

Both of those arrangements made perfect sense to me, and I had never thought beyond the win/win choice. However, in the early 1980s, while I was responsible for Carolina Freight Carriers' physical operation, a significant event happened. It opened my eyes and mind to an optimum business scenario—a win/win/win. Wow! I was awed by what I was exposed to.

One of our larger and more valued customers at Carolina Freight, 3M Corp., headquartered in St. Paul, Minn., invited their top five hundred suppliers to an important meeting. It was not mandatory, but it was evident to me our attendance was important. Its purpose was to make certain we, as suppliers, maintained the same effort to serve both 3M and our mutual customers, as well, with consistent excellence.

3M Corp was and still is one of the most respected and successful companies in the world. I was very interested in what had triggered such a significant event, and I knew it would be beneficial and well worth listening to. Afterward, we could be aware of what their expectations of their suppliers might be. We could then carefully make certain we met those expectations. Little did I know how transformational that meeting would be for me.

Dr. W. Edwards Deming, the world-renowned expert in Quality Improvement Process (QIP) systems, had literally helped resuscitate Japanese industry after the devastation of World War II. Dr. Deming had said, "Most people are not aware they are imprisoned by current practices of management, and these management practices are the cause of decline as they prevent companies from functioning efficiently as a system." He is credited with turning around major companies and whole nations. He had done so by teaching them how to examine every detail, in every process, and then to work willingly together consistently, incrementally, and constantly toward improving same.

A needy Japanese industry had accepted his guidance enthusiastically, and Japan began to produce more and more quality (defect-free) products, especially automobiles and electronics. He had simply taught them how to educate, train, and enlist every associate in constantly seeking ways to improve the results they were responsible for.

The systems there that he introduced in Japan resulted in the following results:

- » Lesser cost to produce, resulting in lower prices for the customer and/or higher profit for the provider.
- » More reliable and dependable products.
- » More marketable products due to greater customer satisfaction.
- » Less waste which resulted in monies to invest in better tools for use in continued progress.

» From waste reduction, there was more money to increase wages and benefits for the workers from top to bottom.

» The attraction of superior associates who wanted to be a part of something so different, special, and better. (Remember: Different, Special and Better.)

The end result was a greater value for the customers and substantial benefits to the provider.

All people, deep down, want to be a part of something different, special, and better. Who doesn't want to be a winner, even in the workplace? Even those with the worst attitudes really want to be winners.

Those were wonderful results from the QIP processes, but there is one more that was and is far more remarkable: This business approach birthed a much more loyal, enthusiastic, excited, and competent workforce. The associates (every person) came to work every day to make consistent improvement in the processes they were involved in. Their workplace became a place of positive expectancy, consistent progress, and personal fulfillment.

In summary, morale skyrocketed.

As I listened carefully, it became very clear: there was now another option for a business on the table. The possibilities or choices for an enterprise were no longer just win/lose or win/win. What I had encountered now was a win/win/win. Wow! The customer was clearly winning with a better product and with fewer defects, which made it a better value. The company, even though doing well before, was now winning with greater profits and much more loyal and satisfied customers. This resulted in even greater market share. The associates, who all too often were previously taken for granted, were now clearly energized with the appreciation for their valuable input. This consequently resulted in greater compensation, and the associates were now winning also. This process was not just hoped for or imagined—it was *real*.

These companies had now tapped into the greatest resources possible. What is that? It is the ingenuity and enthusiasm that every person has been created to possess and be the steward of. The Quality Improvement Process approach had so revitalized the associates they did not need to be urged on. They brought their own enthusiasm for improvement in quality advancement to work every day. Why so? Because they had finally been recognized for their potential, they now exhibited a newly respected (and well-deserved) standing of true importance in their company.

There is a fascinating word I like to think about. That word is *inclusion*. Their companies had now fully recognized how important these people were to optimum corporate success.

At the 3M meeting, I listened intently, and as I did, I began to think back to my early days as a day laborer. I had always known there is a great reservoir of detailed knowledge out there in the heads of hard-working, loyal people who make up a large part of so many companies. Consequently, I had now decided this very day, I would spend the rest of my working life doing my best to give hard-working, loyal people the dignity that they deserved. *Inclusion* is one of the most important ways that can be done. Who doesn't want to be included? I was now beyond motivated—I was driven by the thoughts of this great opportunity.

Sometimes it is difficult for us to understand why some people who are laboring at hard jobs year after year, with no real defined clear path forward, are not excited about the future. However, what is heartwarming and inspiring is to see what happens to people at all levels when they realize leadership associates honestly desire and value what each of them can contribute to a quality improvement process environment. Many laborers have excellent ideas about how to make things better, easier, and more cost-efficient. The employees possess detailed knowledge gained over many years through their on-the-job experience. No one else knows the intimate details like these people. But there is one primary condition for their continued optimum participation. They must know their organization is seriously committed to valuing their input, implementing, and acting to change improvable situations. They must also know it is not just some passing fad or manipulative program that will fade away and that it is a permanent business practice to create a better way of life for all stakeholders. (A true win/win/win.)

I left St. Paul that day as excited as I have ever been about any workplace issue, for I knew the things I had heard there had the potential to align all our associates' individual efforts toward achieving excellence at Carolina Freight. The thought of *alignment* of all a company's human resources (associates) filled my head. It was so clear to me—true alignment would create a workforce that would be almost impossible to be outperformed. *Alignment,* by definition, means to be "arrayed (standing together) on the side of a cause."[1] The result would be to create a best-in-class organization where every individual would enjoy the wonderful benefits of same.

It was not easy for me personally to fully and completely grasp a vision so exciting. However, I knew alignment was the opposite of that destructive "D" word, *division*. I also knew that division is an evil destroyer, just as God's Word clearly portrays it (Matthew 12:25–26, KJV). Division has destroyed much. It is presently today destroying much in our great country.

I believed if we could properly introduce, educate, and train our people in a Quality Improvement Process, we could create a super positive work environment and a much more desirable future for every associate. There is a simple truism—If everyone is committed to and headed toward the same objective, they can continuously help each other along the way, and all parties ultimately win.

The more I thought about this approach, the more it became evident such a corporate-wide implementation of a QIP would be a profound *encouragement* to so many loyal people who wanted to see their company become increasingly successful. I also realized one of the best things I could do was to invest more time, energy, and thought in determining how we could develop more and better ways to consistently encourage our hard-working force of loyal people. After all, they labored day after day at hard jobs and were deserving of more sincere recognition than they normally received. That word encouragement

---

1    *Webster's Collegiate Dictionary*, 10th Edition

would not leave me as I thought about the potential of quality improvement via process improvement. There is no question competent, wise business leadership will never regret investing time, money, and energy in determining how to create realistic and sincere ways to continuously encourage all of their associates. I knew in my heart that I had just been introduced to such a positive opportunity. I had just observed a presentation that revealed a great approach to a better and more prosperous future for everyone, one that I would not forget about and that would prove useful in time at Southeastern Freight Lines. Rarely does such a profound opportunity present itself. I thank my God for the provision of such a wonderful revelation, which ultimately encouraged so many.

These hard-working people are so vitally important, and yet they can so easily be taken for granted. It is a very logical conclusion that it's utterly senseless to have people in your organization who are not important. What is even more senseless is to take them for granted and to treat them (who are important enough to receive a paycheck) by neglect, as if they are not important.

My Heavenly Father, by Divine providence, had led me to St. Paul to hear about an exciting strategic business approach in some detail. That approach allowed a company to tap into all the great resources their people possessed. I was, to say the least, impressed and excited about its potential for my company. Perhaps one reason it so resonated with me is I had been where many of these people who would be affected presently were. I could relate. I remembered rather vividly what it felt like to be at a lower level on the proverbial totem pole. I also remembered how infrequently we were informed about the progress of our company. It was easy for us to conclude, whether correctly or not, what we did every day was not very important. It costs to spend money in sharing important info about your business but allowing ignorance from neglect is far more expensive.

It was clearly evident to me now, however, any company that would wholeheartedly invest in this exciting business approach would be able to clearly differentiate or set themselves apart from at least their competitors who did not also follow suit and do the same. This approach clearly had the great potential to distinguish our company.

An important conclusion I drew was with having a real quality improvement process in place, in short order, every person would become a leader. Yes, you just read correctly—a leader. Every associate would be leading the way in their own role to find better, quicker, less complicated, and more economical ways to get the work accomplished and to thereby satisfy every customer, whether they be internal or external customers.

In the simplest of terms, I firmly believed that every day, every associate would be seeking ways to make improvements in the thousands of processes that make up our services. There would be a high level of recognition as well as frequent recognition for those valuable efforts. Then, morale would soar to unbelievable levels because working people would now be recognized as the valuable assets they are and always have been. The end result would be the opportunity to become a genuine world-class quality provider for the customers. There is no question that every one of those who made up such a successful organization would be the beneficiary of the organization's greater success.

I knew this could not be the traditional campaign of the month or a campaign for improvement by edict. Neither could it be orders from headquarters to tighten up, or "we will miss our earnings per share expectations." Those are not very motivational approaches, especially for people who are already working hard. When you are doing a hard job every day and working as hard as you can, you don't get excited about a work harder edict.

But now, this created a great awareness. This introduced to me a whole new way of educating, equipping, and developing every associate with one purpose in mind—to create excellence for the customers. The key would be for every associate to be a part of that creation and to share in the worthy rewards that excellence produces long-term, both in personal recognition and personal compensation.

Truett Cathy, the wise founder of Chick-Fil-A, said often, "There will always be a market for the best." It brings a whole new excitement in the workplace when a real QIP is transforming and allowing your company to be truly competitive for that honor to be the best. Colossians 3:23a (NIV) states, "Whatever you do, work at it with all your heart." That work ethic pleases our Creator. He created us in His image to be able to excel. And it is He who makes the difference in our lives.

I could hardly wait to get home from St. Paul and into the office the next morning. I was excited and knew in my heart and mind this was the very best way any company could ensure a successful future.

At the first opportunity back in Cherryville, I met with Ken Younger, our President, and shared what I had been exposed to. My recommendation was that we seek outside assistance to help train all our leadership and to prepare us for launching a first-rate Quality Improvement Process.

Mr. Younger listened to me patiently and without interruption. I am sure he could see how convinced I was that this would allow us to become a much stronger, more aligned, and more competitive company than ever before. Already we were recognized as a very successful entity, but the future is always about making improvement.

As we sat there, I awaited his response. As you may know, sometimes in boardrooms, pride prevents executives from acknowledging the need to become better. Then he looked me squarely in the eye and said, "Paul, I have been looking for something that will move us to the next level." And then added, excitedly, "This is it. Let's get the Quality Improvement Process started." And that we did.

This was a special time for me.

Quickly, we began to plan and train our people in preparation for effective implementation of the Q.I. Process. Then something happened rather suddenly. God, in His omniscience, called me to do something that substantially changed my life, a move to another wonderful company.

CHAPTER 13

# Full-Timers Only

When I began my working career as a temporary day laborer, I had no business knowledge, no skills, no influence, and no mentor. By definition, I was an unskilled laborer. No one could have been, at that time, less qualified for a successful business career than I was. All I had was a strong body, a willingness to consistently work hard, and a great need for income.

Little did I know then what I profoundly know now—the way we start out is not nearly as important as how we finish.

I had started my business career as a spiritually lost church member, not knowing nor truthfully caring that I was not in the kingdom of God. However, along the way, God's Holy Spirit convicted me of my lostness and my need for change. At that point, I began to try my best, with His help, to learn how to honor and serve my trustworthy Savior. I was so blessed and grateful to be free of me.

I seriously needed to earn as much money as I could honorably and yet, not compromise the important truth that was being revealed consistently in the best leadership and human relations book ever written. I was reading and being challenged and encouraged in exciting ways from God's Holy Word.

I knew business was a serious matter, and as it appeared, almost stood alone from the standpoint of ethics in the minds of at least a portion of the business owners. Have you ever heard that aged phrase, "Now, business is business"? I never really liked the thought that there was a different set of practices and ethics that dictated how shrewd businesses were to be operated. It was not universal, but at least a portion of the business world believed it and practiced it, and perhaps still does.

What bothered me about it was it gave the impression that our Christian character can be compartmentalized and set aside from certain more challenging business activities. I knew that statement had been around a long time and more than likely warned others with the phrase *caveat emptor* (let the buyer beware). At best, the attitude that "business is business" or "let the buyer beware" is a warning of some kind that people might not be as kind in the workplace on Monday in their business dealings as they were in the pew on Sunday. It seemed somehow that was to be expected and understood and even acceptable.

What is wrong with that picture? Well, there are several things. The most important thing is that our Creator's plan for us in conducting business stresses for us to honor Him first in ALL our activity. He tells us in Romans 12:2a (NKJV), "Do not be conformed to this world, but be transformed by the renewing of your mind."

Here, He is telling us, and I will use a broad, very broad, paraphrase, "I have saved you, not as a 'part-timer,' but as a 'full-timer,' to represent or re-present me in a very important place, the marketplace." In other words, your conduct in business, with My help, should show clearly that you can be trusted and believed because you are under divine leadership. In other words, He was saying my ways of doing business can absolutely be trusted for best results.

Allow me to ask you this question now. Don't you always feel somewhat better after doing business with a company that has professing, practicing Christian owners and associates? Don't you enjoy doing business with people who are on record as saying I am a follower of Jesus and who also demonstrate it twenty-four-seven?

Let me be clear. You don't have to have a prayer meeting every morning on-premises. You simply bring the same person to work every morning who worshipped God on Sunday in the church, who gave thanks to the Lord before eating breakfast this morning, who reads a portion of God's Word every day, and for whom prayer is an essential privilege every day, all because you want to honor and obey God for His precious gift of forgiveness, salvation, and liberty.

You also should look forward to encouraging and helping any and everyone you encounter in the workplace. That everyone includes customers and associates. It sounds almost too idealistic to be true, even possible. But this is where there is much too often a disconnect. God saved us as full-timers to be as Christian or Christ-like in the workplace as we are in the pew on Sundays. The evidence of our Christianity is substantially more highlighted when we reflect Him in the marketplace consistently.

Jesus preached a wonderful sermon, as recorded in the book of Matthew (5:13–14, 16, NKJV). He told the crowd and tells you and me, "You are the salt of the earth" and "you are the light of the world." "Let your light so shine before men, that they may see your good works and glorify your Father." It is important that we recognize the truth. He did not say where and when we are to "be" and "do" because it was clearly understood—*everywhere*. We have been transformed into full-timers. God saved us to be full-timers in a world that is darkening every day, with a culture that has turned its back on God. One of the certain reasons our world is darkening is because of the confusion part-time Christians bring to nonbelievers. Nonbelievers do not see the connection between what part-timers say they believe and its application in the marketplace. God desires you and me to be full-timers.

There is a simple truth for every believer to remember: the same Holy Spirit who convicted us of sin and brought us to Jesus goes to work with us every day—within us! He is available to help us live consistently, faithfully, and obediently in the marketplace.

The Holy Spirit indwells us to empower us to stay focused on our mission and our calling, yes, even in the workplace.

That is God's will and provision for every believer—as full-timers.

# CHAPTER 14

# Lasting Success

Isn't it a natural thing to desire to be successful?

What is real, lasting success?

Were some people created to be successful and others left to become failures?

What is the perfect will of God for every person He has given life to?

These are questions most of us have at least thought about at some time.

We live in a world enamored with and fixated on success. It is a natural thing for mankind to desire success. That is not an undesirable objective to have. There are, however, extremely varied ideas about the true definitions of success. Still, we should be certain we do not let pursuit of worldly success interfere with God's real purpose for us.

The most common worldly definition of "success" is substantiated by the dictionary definition, which reads, "A favorable or desired outcome: the attainment of wealth, favor or eminence."[1] If we are really honest, we know this is the world's definition, and most people think about success in these terms. Most of us could admit we grew up with that definition in our minds. Additionally, it is a natural thing to desire success for our children, friends, and people we love, even for ourselves. That definition includes finances, education, status, an enjoyable job, popularity, excellence in sports, and so on. With that said, we know it is not possible for all of God's children to achieve all, or perhaps any, of those worldly things. Besides that, there is another important question that needs to be answered about that definition. Do wealth, fame, and status truly bring success to people? Achieving these things has heavy requirements and expectations (and oftentimes causes major stress as well) while we pursue them. That leaves us asking, "What was man really created for? What is my real purpose?"

---

1    *Webster's Collegiate Dictionary*, 10th Edition

I am convinced there is actually a second definition of real success. I am equally convinced this is the success that God stands ready for every one of us to enjoy, and it is available to every single one of us. What is that second definition? It is simple and uncomplicated: "To be at peace with God, our Creator, and satisfied with ourselves." A beautiful truth about this definition is when we live for this to be reality in our lives, we are guaranteed success for all eternity. It is far different than the fleeting here-today-gone-tomorrow success that our world embraces.

More than a few times, I have been asked this question: What is the most important truth you have learned over your forty-plus-year career in business? Without hesitation, my answer is, "People can be successful, and most of them desire to do so."

It may seem overly simplistic, but it is so easy to overlook the tremendous potential with which our Creator has gifted mankind. We can be obedient, and God has given us the Difference–Maker to help us.

Why do I say that? If we go back to the origin of man, we find out several truths:

» We are made in God's image (Genesis 1:26, NKJV).

» We are fearfully and wonderfully made (Psalm 139:14, NKJV).

» God, Himself, breathed divine breath into man. In essence, we have His DNA. (Genesis 2:7, NKJV).

» God created man to be the steward of all His creation (Genesis 2:15, NKJV).

» God also created man in His likeness for fellowship with Him (Genesis 1:26, 28, NKJV).

There is an equally important reason I can attest to the truth—people can! It is because I have observed hundreds and thousands who have excelled, sometimes much beyond their own expectations. They succeeded when they discovered, with their Creator's help, they could "do exceedingly abundantly above all we can think or ask according to the Power that works in us" (Ephesians 3:20, NKJV). In essence, God created man to be successful. It is God's will and desire that every person be successful, and He also equipped man for success from the beginning. Simple reasoning tells us that a God who loves mankind would never create His most cherished creation to fail. He even gave us an Owner's Manual (His divine Word), which, if studied, revered, and applied, guarantees success.

There are two passages of scripture in God's Book of Truth which speaks clearly to God's personal intention in our lives: "For you formed my inward parts; you covered me in my mother's womb. I will praise you for I am fearfully and wonderfully made; marvelous are your works, and that my soul knows really well. My frame was not hidden from you when I was made in secret and skillfully wrought in the lowest part of the earth. Your eyes saw my substance being yet unformed, and in your book, they were all written, *the days fashioned for me* when as yet there were none of them" (Psalm 139:13–16, NKJV). God's Spirit first gave David these words of truth. Yet, they apply to every human being already born or yet to be born. The second passage speaks of God's will for every person: "The Lord is not willing for any to perish, but for all to come to repentance" (2 Peter 3:9, NASV).

It is inconceivable that a God who loves us enough to become sin and die for us would create people for any reason other than to be successful, especially when He loves us as if we are each His only child. We are never out of His thoughts. He knows the future and what it can be for each of us. That is beyond our full comprehension but is true nonetheless. *God made each and every one of us to be successful, but our choices determine if we will or not.*

After decades in the business world, I have come to believe that God's will for people to be successful is simple yet profound. Success is available to everyone, whether you are a stay-at-home-mom, an astronaut, a world-renowned athlete, a garbage collector, or a company CEO. Real success is available to everyone who 1) made or will make peace with God, through the only acceptable source, Jesus Christ, and 2) to whoever is able or willing to be pleased (satisfied) with themselves, by way of simple obedience to our Lord, by loving God and loving others.

You may now be thinking, "Paul, that's way too simplistic." But it isn't, because all the while God is saying, (as in His word), to every one of those who are diligently striving to meet those qualifications: "I will hear what God the Lord will speak, *for He will speak peace to His people*" (Psalm 85:8, NKJV). Show me a person who has confessed their sins and been forgiven of their sins, who is then set free, who is nurturing that relationship and is being obedient to God (i.e., someone who is fulfilled in their Christian walk), and that is someone I will show you who is absolutely successful, now and for eternity.

Jesus validates these words in John 14:6 (ASV): "I am the way, the truth, and the life; no one cometh unto the Father but by Me." Thus, Jesus is the absolute only way to real and eternal success. I have this note written, from some unknown source, in my Bible: "Our compelling purpose as God's children is to help people Know The Truth, Find The Way, and Experience True Life in Christ Jesus." Those words "the Way, the Truth and the Life" are found in John 14:6 (ASV), and they were spoken by Jesus Himself.

We are all successful when we are who we were made to be, forgiven, contented, obedient, and blessed worshipers of the living God by way of our precious Savior and a cruel cross.

You see, we could not keep the moral law, which is absolutely necessary for mankind to live in a stable world, but Jesus did keep the law. Jesus also, in His indescribable compassion for you and me, paid our sin debt when no one else could do so. He was and still is the perfect sacrifice. He has taken our sins upon Himself, as we accept His gift, and He reconciles us to God the Father. He died the promised death for you and me and paid a sin debt you and I could not pay as He took mine and your sins to the grave.

I loved the positions of leadership God gave me, unqualified as I was. That love was not for my prominence or elevation. Undoubtedly, He gave me an undeserved position that I might, only with His help, encourage thousands of people in the workplace and represent Him in the process. Representing Him is part of what we were created for. Man was created:

» For fellowship with God.

» To live free from enslavement (sin)—forgiven.

» To be fully developed (fearfully and wonderfully made).

» To excel, at whatever we do, since we are created in His image to represent Christ to desperate people on this earth.

We can know that our Creator has these expectations of His people. We can also know He will and does provide all the means necessary to do and to be these things. Therefore, He has provided the precious words He gave the prophet Jeremiah (Jeremiah 29:11, NIV), which are just as applicable today as they were long ago: "For I know the plans I have for you, declares the Lord, plans to prosper you and not to harm you; plans to give you a hope and a future." That is such a beautiful reassurance.

Finally, there is (in my opinion) a single most important element in success, which mankind must contribute. It is not wanting to, planning to, or wishing to, it is *deciding* to, once and for all. And each of us must decide to and do our part to make a committed effort to live up to our God-given potential. Success is a partnership. God has already done more than His part when He sent Jesus to set us free and the Holy Spirit to empower us to live victoriously. Therefore, I have found that my part has been to *yield* to my Creator as my Savior, Helper, Advocate, Counselor, Truth-Guide, and Leader because I was made for real success. God provides His children His help in order that we may effectively represent Him well. "The world crowns success by its definition, but God crowns *Faithfulness*."[2] This is so true. *Faithfulness* is real success. And real success results in freedom from guilt, worry, depression,

---

2       *The Speakers Quote Book* by Roy B. Zuck. Copyright © 1997 by Roy B. Zuck. Published by Kregel Publications, a division of Kregel, Inc., P.O. Box 2607, Grand Rapids, MI 49501.

and fear. "Where the Spirit of the Lord is, there is liberty" (2 Corinthians 3:17, KJV). He has done His wonderful part. We must do ours.

Which crown will last and satisfy? The world's? Or God's?

Our time on earth is but a tiny little rehearsal for the real thing in the vastness of eternity—and eternity is that destination where *true success* is recognized and celebrated.

Each one of us is an only child to God. In the marketplace, rarity always increases value. We are each uniquely a limited edition of one, and therefore very valuable to our gracious Savior and Lord. Since God created each of us for Himself, we can know He created each one to be successful eternally. That is His perfect will for you and me, and yet He leaves the choice to you and me.

The Lord has shown me over many years the profound truth that, with the power of the Difference-Maker, people *can* excel. We were created to excel, not fail, and that is a wonderful capability. Our Heavenly Father is about excellence and helping each one of us do the very best we can. We, by His help, can be our best. As we strive in partnership with God and empowered by the Holy Spirit, we then do not have to live with regret, which is without a doubt one of the hardest things ever to live with.

David and Renee Crane have excelled on their obedient journey. They are lifetime missionaries with decades spent in Africa. They grew up in our hometown and are two of our most admired and respected friends. Unfortunately, they have encountered hardships in spades. Over a decade ago—in fact, on February 4, 2007—David said this in his prayer: "God, I pray that we never 'feel good' about who we are until we are doing what you created and then saved us to do." All of us, as saved sinners, need to be praying that same prayer out of sheer gratitude for God's grace.

Satan always lies and creates doubt in unsaved people about what it will really be like to be a Christian. But one of the most important truths about being saved by Christ is (that Satan absolutely wants no one to know) that Jesus makes it possible for us to think less about ourselves yet still be very contented as we think more about others, which is exactly what Jesus did. He profoundly demonstrated that truth when He gave Himself for you and me.

Satan wants us to believe a Christian cannot enjoy life, but Jesus said it all in John 10:10 (NKJV), "I have come that they may have life and that they may have it more abundantly."

Could Jesus exaggerate? Absolutely not!

When anyone argues against Christianity, unless they have been reborn by God's Holy Spirit with faith in Jesus Christ, that person argues as an *uninformed, unenlightened* bystander. When I have been touched by the mercy and grace of God and am still a "critic and dissatisfied user," then I could possibly be a credible critic. But rest assured, it will never happen. God doesn't have any dissatisfied users.

I share this not as an expert on the Holy Spirit but as an awed, satisfied beneficiary of this most special gift sent from the Father. And that great gift, the Holy Spirit, empowers His children to obey Him and to do great things much beyond their natural capability. Yes, what a blessing God has created and prepared us for so that *people can excel through the power of the Difference-Maker.*

People can choose to accept His will—and His peace. They always go together. That is lasting success. What a powerful and compelling truth—the Creator of the universe has come to make His dwelling both with and within us. It is astonishing that the Creator God, who created by simply speaking our world in place, lives in us and reveals His wonderful message to us. Success is there for the taking if you open your heart to Christ Jesus. Then, it is a partnership with God empowered by the Holy Spirit that drives the achievement and the peace.

We could never have more purpose than to represent Him faithfully and know that He is pleased that we have chosen true success His way, not the world's very deceptive and very temporary way.

# CHAPTER 15

# Deliverance: The Precious Gift

This chapter describes what happened to me the evening so many years ago when I was overcome with guilt caused by my worldly living. I confessed my sins and asked Jesus to forgive me. Immediately the Holy Spirit came into my life and set me free, even though I did not know this overwhelming power was the Holy Spirit at that time. I had been severely habit-bound for many years and was too weak to overcome sinful, destructive habits on my own. I recognized on that same evening when I returned to the chapel that God had set me free and given me His power to live in victory.

One of the greatest truths that Satan wants all of us to not be aware of or to ignore is the tremendous emphasis the Bible puts on the words deliver, deliverance, delivered, deliveredst, deliverer, deliverest, delivereth, delivering. *Strong's Exhaustive Concordance of the English Bible* contains these words in various verses more than six hundred times. The only logical conclusion you can reach from this is *deliverance* is seriously important to our Lord. That deliverance is from the enslaving power of harmful, sinful behavior to the absolute freedom and liberty that only God's Holy Spirit can provide. I needed to understand this truth. When I was bound by the enslaving habit of smoking cigarettes that I could not quit (but I denied that truth), I was then enslaved by Satan. And if I, or anyone else, is still bound by a habit, I am really enslaved by Satan rather than free in Christ.

I, personally, realized one of God's greatest attributes is as a *deliverer*. I recognized this when I gave my life to Christ to cleanse me  and when the Holy Spirit became resident in me. The Word of God verifies that important truth: "Where the Spirit of the Lord is, there is liberty" (2 Corinthians 3:17, KJV). God will deliver you (set you free) and, at the same time, take away your desire for any previously enslaving habit. First Corinthians 6:19 (ASV) raises a serious question for every believer: "Know you not that your body is the temple of the Holy Spirit?"

Each of us must decide whom will I listen to—a clever Satan who continually tells me my enslaving habits are my business and no one else's, or the God who gave me physical life and spiritual freedom and promises me a peace that passes all understanding (Philippians 4:7, KJV)?

Personally, I have experienced the truth of deliverance, made known only as the Holy Spirit opened the door of my heart for *deliverance*. At the time the Holy Spirit entered, I was bathed in a divine flow of unexplainable peace. It now is a wonderful thing to be experiencing God's peace continuously. Meanwhile, I see people chasing futilely after things that will not satisfy them. They are seeking after something they will never be able to have in this world apart from God's gift of "peace that passes all understanding" (Philippians 4:7, KJV). His promise is completely validated by His sinless comforting presence.

Someone wisely said, "The chains of habit are too weak to be felt until they are too strong to be broken." But the amazing truth is that there is a deliverer, and His name is Jesus, and His continuing resident helper is the Holy Spirit.

I am completely convinced there are many, many people who withhold becoming Christians because they are concerned with what they may have to give up. Yet they have been blinded, as I was, and kept from the truth. And in that deceptive blindness, they haven't the slightest awareness about what they will receive—freedom, power, and genuine peace if they give over that habit to Him.

This is what I have personally experienced and what I have learned about our Creator over the last fifty years—if He doesn't give me what I want, it is because He wants to give me something better. Better yet, if He doesn't give me something better, He knows it is not best for me, and He will give me the capacity to become satisfied with what I have. Actually, to be satisfied with His comforting presence is more than okay. Besides, Jesus promised in John 10:10 (KJV) that "He came so that you might have life, and have it more abundantly." That is a profound, solid truth.

One of the most comforting verses in the Bible is Psalm 85:8 (NKJV): "I will hear what God the Lord will speak, for He will speak peace to His people." What a beautiful promise, experienced by every born again, delivered Christian.

Why did Jesus, Son of God, with God in heaven, come to earth? God had given us (mankind) the law, but we had continued in sin. Man could not keep the law. We had turned the law into religion—religious rituals, without lives to back up our pretentious actions.

Jesus came to clean-slate us. God sent us a willing Deliverer and the only One who could take on and bear our sin and made an acceptable way back to a right relationship with Him. We were lost, which meant separated from God and our creation purpose, as well as separated from the wonderful life God created us for.

God sent the only Gift that could overcome our lost condition. That Gift is His sinless Son who brought the gifts of forgiveness and restoration. But it's really not a precious personal gift to me, you, or anyone else until we accept Him. Then we know by experience how wonderful He is!

We must decide something, though. Are my desires greater and more important to me than the Deliverer's presence in my life? Christ came to bring abundant life and reserve for us a place in heaven. What a precious gift from the One who died for me in order that I can live eternally in an indescribable state of peace.

God sent a *deliverer*. The Bible is clear. Jesus died once for all, as written in Romans 6. Then, when I allow Him to deliver me from the power of sin, He not only does so but also, He sends the mighty power of the Holy Spirit to help me represent the Lord faithfully until He calls me home.

During a lifetime, each of us has a few friends that somehow are truly special. It has been one of God's best blessings for me to have known Andy Torrence for fifteen years. He wanted nothing from me but genuine friendship. Now he is in heaven.

When I think of deliverance, Andy comes to my mind. I never knew the *old* Andy, who for decades was a determined alcoholic. His carryings-on are legendary. Yet, to be a role model for his three-year-old son, he recognized his addiction was too overpowering for him to overcome. But thank God, Andy knew God could deliver him. He fell to his knees, repented, and asked for deliverance. Instantly, God honored Andy's prayer and set him free.

Not only did God meet his need, God's Holy Spirit gave him a great love and a tender heart for his fellow man, especially other struggling alcoholics. Andy was transformed. I have never known anyone to be more grateful for Jesus' forgiveness and restoration. It was never about Andy. Rather, it was about his new nature that made him so special, a new nature that empowered Andy to put other people before himself. Every Sunday, you could expect Andy to be on his knees at the altar, interceding, not for himself, but for others. He had a heart of great love and respect for all of God's most special creation—people. I am certain that is why his life was so very attractive and magnetic to so many people. Andy obeyed Micah 6:8 (NKJV) and did what God said is good and what God requires: "Do justly, to love mercy and to walk humbly with your God." Andy loved the mercy God showed him. By God's Holy Spirit in his life, he was always merciful in dealing with others. Andy cared about the outcasts, the downtrodden, and the forgotten. He exuded humility. His gratitude for deliverance and grace permeated his life with humility. That gratitude and love for the Lord still inspire me. They always will.

It is difficult for me to describe how gently, humbly, and gratefully Andy allowed the Holy Spirit to mold him into being. His appreciation for his deliverance and salvation motivated him to allow Jesus to not only be Savior but to be Lord and Master of his life. He never let circumstances kill his joy. Andy was so thankful for the miraculous grace of God. Even when there might have been injustice in regard to his son's criminal trial, or his own terminal cancer, Andy never let it change what God had molded him into over those last thirty years. Andy's life is a reminder that God has a far better and more rewarding plan for our lives than we do. What a wonderful gift God makes available to every one of His born-again children.

Indeed, Andy was a role model for all of us. It is an unforgettable memory as I recall how proud he was of the thirty-year Alcoholics Anonymous Sobriety

Chip he would pull out of his pocket so often. But the most memorable thing about my special friend was the way he always gave our precious Savior all the credit. Thanks be to God for the new reborn Andy. He accepted the gift of deliverance here and has now gone home to heaven. Without a doubt, when he stepped into glory, he heard from the lips of the Lord there, "Well done thou good and faithful servant." Andy wore the mantle of deliverance so very well.

Another story of deliverance also comes to mind. Many years ago, when we lived in North Carolina, on a very cold windy January evening, we were leaving home to attend our Sunday evening Bible study and worship service. The wind had blown open the door to our screened porch, and as I walked out, I realized when the door had closed, a very small bird had become enclosed within the porch. With darkness approaching, the small bird was fluttering wildly to find a way to escape. I propped the door open and tried for several minutes, with a broom, to guide it to the open door to no avail. Then I realized the only thing to do was catch it in my hands, carry it out and release it. It took a little while, but I finally succeeded in catching this small black-capped chickadee. However, when I walked outside and opened my hand, the little bird just lay there with its eyes closed. It did not take the opportunity to be free. Perhaps it thought it was too good to be true. I then turned my palm down, and as the little one began to fall, apparently, instinct took over. It extended its little wings and flew off into the dark—free. It was delivered from the captivity of the porch and my hand.

I have often thought of that bird analogy like the deliverance God offers to mankind. Unless it has happened to you, it seems almost too good to be true. God, in many cases, had to do the same thing to show us we were free. But we can be certain of our deliverance. Jesus Christ can and will do what we cannot if we will only trust Him. God's truth guarantees it: "Therefore if the Son makes you free, you shall be free indeed" (John 8:36, NKJV).

I thank God for the bold, authentic, prepared preachers I have heard over the years following my deliverance. Every preacher at our church who followed

Dr. Charles Carter (my wonderful pastor at the time of my deliverance and several years thereafter) blessed and challenged me. During those early years of my deliverance, every time I attended church, I sat as close to the pulpit as I could to be sure I missed nothing. I owe every one of those preachers a debt for their faithfulness to God's Word.

The Evangelism Conferences, where preachers preach primarily to other preachers, were held annually in North and South Carolina. They were programmed with John the Baptist preachers, who were clearly called and anointed to preach the Word of God. They lived this scripture: "He must increase, but I must decrease" (John 3:30, KJV). These preachers were fearless, faithful, and had never heard of, or much less been influenced by political correctness. Lynette and I never missed one of the conferences over many years because they fed our souls and challenged our faithfulness to more determined levels.

Those faithful preachers revealed, without apology, God's expectations of His children. During that time, a powerful truth was proclaimed over and over—there is brokenness in the beginning when deliverance is at work. They explained that God is not going to help us build a life that really matters unless sin has been absolutely regretted and dealt with—with willpower. It takes man's determined and decided will and God's astounding power.

When I repented and turned my life over to Christ Jesus, I was delivered and no longer under the satanic influence of the enemy of God and man. Even though I did not deserve deliverance, it had been given to me by a Savior who is not about deserving but only about grace (the unmerited favor of God).

People can live powerful, fulfilling lives (but unbelievably much more so) when God's Holy Spirit is our promised indwelling Helper! Jesus tells us in John 16:14 (KJV) that the Holy Spirit "will glorify Me." What exactly does that mean? The Holy Spirit will keep you and me focused on the wonderful deliverance we enjoy at the great price provided only by our sinless Savior. The Holy Spirit is so central to faith that I will focus on Him in the next several chapters.

# CHAPTER 16

# Enter the Holy Spirit

Previously in this book, I have made numerous references to the Holy Spirit, but I feel there is a need to define in greater depth just why the Holy Spirit is so important to a born-again believer. In these next three chapters, we will examine the Holy Spirit, which all too often is not well understood. I say this because experience has taught me many do not understand it. That is unfortunate because this subject is so important in our conversion as Christians, and then in the empowerment, we all need to live victoriously for Christ.

The first chapter describes the personal revelation I encountered when He, the Holy Spirit, so focused my attention on and then glorified Christ, the One who paid my ugly sin debt. The other two chapters have been written to help clarify biblically the tremendous role the Holy Spirit plays in every Christian's conversion and spiritual growth and development. These words delineate the most important and impactful occurrence in my own life. They also reiterate the truth about the tremendous power that changed Peter from a denying cowardly disciple into a fearless, powerfully effective preacher and most faithful follower of Jesus.

Let me again speak briefly to the revolutionary experience that occurred in my life, then later, I will address Peter's experience.

In 1969, my Heavenly Father put a man in my life, Joe Alexander. As I shared in a previous chapter and think worthwhile to repeat, he was uniquely different and possessed a peace that was indeed rare. Joe invited me to attend an upcoming revival at our church. Because of how much I respected him, I reluctantly agreed. Unenthusiastically, I went to the church and seated myself near the back. I attended simply as an effort to keep my promise to Joe, my respected workplace friend. The visiting preacher preached, and then the choir sang. I remember looking at my watch during the hymn and thinking,

163

*I'll be out of here soon.* But God had a better plan for me. As noted previously, I have thankfully discovered He always does.

As a youngster, I had heard preachers occasionally mention the Holy Ghost, which is the term sometimes used in other versions of the Bible. However, I could not imagine a *ghost* being *holy,* and I had no comprehension of the role of God's Holy Spirit in every believer's initial conviction or ultimately in His empowerment to live their Christian life. Wow, was I in for a new and wonderful experience as He filled my life as a born-again Christian. I then realized the Holy Ghost and the Holy Spirit were terms that were interchangeably used within God's Word.

You may recall as the choir sang, I began to uncontrollably weep because the burden of my sins had overcome me with conviction and guilt. God's Holy Spirit had overwhelmed me and caused me to see myself as I really was. The Holy Spirit had shown me how desperately I needed to repent and become a true child of God, not just be a pretender or uninvolved take-it-or-leave-it church member who was listed on the church membership roll. Beforehand, I was a lost, worldly, uninterested church member. I wasn't even a good part-timer. In fact, if no one had done any more to obey the Lord and support the church up to that point in time than me, that church would have no longer existed.

In essence, what I now know happened is... the Holy Spirit of God is the One who awakened my soul from a destiny of eternal separation from God and God's saved people. He, the Holy Spirit, overwhelmed me, shook my foundation with sorrow and guilt for sin, and He became my lasting foundation on which to build a new life, as Jesus promised, "abundant life" (John 10:10, ESV) built on the solid rock of Jesus. The Holy Spirit, who was now resident in me, began to keep me focused on Jesus and the precious gifts of forgiveness and regeneration that only He could have brought to sinful man, and I certainly had been one of those sinful men.

I really began to live that night when I responded, not to words, or music, or emotion, but to the powerful Holy Spirit of God. The Holy Spirit brought conviction and regeneration and led me into the wonderful kingdom of God, which Jesus had made possible. The Holy Spirit had made me aware it was my personal sin that had put Jesus on the cross.

I had come unknowingly in my spiritual ignorance as a visitor with no intention to do anything, but I left as a grateful, forgiven child of the Living God. Thanks be to the Living God and thanks to the sacrifice of the Risen Savior (now my Savior) and the powerful conviction of the Holy Spirit who had so focused me on Jesus' grace that evening. Our God has made awesome provision in order that people can "hear what God the Lord will speak, for He will speak peace to His people" (Psalm 85:8, ESV). God alone provides the wonderfully empowering Holy Spirit, the Difference-Maker, to enable us to live obediently and victoriously with His power as the born-again children of God.

I knew with certainty that night this great truth: "Greater is He that is in you than He that is in the world" (1 John 4:4, KJV). I sensed this was truth even though I had never read this promise at that time.

God's Word has a multitude of absolutes. This is one: "So then those who are in the flesh" (without the indwelling empowering Holy Spirit) "cannot please God, But you are not in the flesh, but in the Spirit, if indeed the Spirit dwells in you. Now, if anyone does not have the Spirit of Christ he is not His" (Romans 8:8–9, NKJV).

This is an absolute truth—God has given us this truth in order that we can know for certain we have repented, been forgiven, and now are for certain in the kingdom of God.

No one before had ever asked me if God's Holy Spirit was resident in me, and that is an eternally important question for each of us. It is the Litmus test for anyone who wants to be certain about their personal salvation. Having the Holy Spirit resident within us is a certain and powerful reality when we are truly saved. The Holy Spirit at work in our lives validates our spiritual rebirth in God's family. People can—through the power of the Difference-Maker— achieve in abundance, live obediently, and enjoy His precious presence and guidance in the process. When we face our old and ever-present enemy, sin, and then allow our will to be empowered and guided by God's powerful Holy Spirit, we will always have victory over evil.

As I think back to how close I came to the worst decision I could ever have made, it is frightening! I stood waiting for the church service to be over so I could leave and continue to do my own thing, but, suddenly, a great wave of conviction and guilt came over me. It was like nothing I had ever experienced before. I experienced God's Holy Spirit power for the first time in my life, and He had unexpectedly become real, convicting, and overwhelming to me. He began to show me how much I truly needed to be regenerated (created anew).

Here I was, a church member for twenty-one years, but without the Holy Spirit in my life to help me grow and develop by allowing Jesus to truly be my Lord. God's Holy Spirit had brought conviction and repentance that evening in a profound earth-shaking way. The Holy Spirit is indeed a powerful, powerful One to enable God's people to grow strong and stand against the wiles of Satan. I had for so long been without this amazing Helper, Counselor, Advocate, and Comforter as described in God's Word. I did not even realize how precious His presence would quickly become as my enabler to live joyfully as a truly born-again Spirit-led forgiven Christian. I had been a lost church member for decades, but now I was truly a member of God's family.

I am so thankful for Joe's obedience to God's call on his life to "go and make disciples." His faithfulness led to my realization of how much I needed to be forgiven and simply accept God's gift of forgiveness and indescribable peace... as God's Holy Spirit opened my previously blind eyes to a whole new wonderful life. Without the Holy Spirit, I could never have written this book. He is my motivator, co-author, and life changer. What my friend Joe has done consistently for decades is what every child of God has been saved to do. That is to be a faithful exemplary witness and make disciples as we are going about our lives daily.

# CHAPTER 17

# God's Gracious Gift of Heavenly Power

The Holy Bible is not an easily understood book. In fact, it is almost impossible to fully understand without the assistance of the One, who gave the sixty-six books to the forty authors who then wrote them down. That One is the Holy Spirit of God.

Second Timothy 3:16 (NKJV) helps us know more about this fascinating book. It reads, "All scripture is given by inspiration of God, and is profitable for doctrine, for reproof, for correction, for instruction in righteousness." Verse 17 goes on to tell us what the result of application will be: "That the man of God may be complete, thoroughly equipped for every good work" (God's will). God's Word is given to enlighten and prepare us for the purpose God created us to live out while here on earth and thereby re-present Him faithfully.

Inspiration means "God-breathed." The Holy Spirit of God gave each of the writers of scripture exactly what they were to record. That is how it was God-breathed. Since this power was given from God by the Holy Spirit, it makes perfect sense that we need the Holy Spirit, not just to understand it as our interpreter, but to help us apply it in our lives as well. The Holy Spirit, then, is our powerful enabler to live faithfully, obediently, and victoriously for our Savior. What a great blessing God has provided for His children. His Word reveals to us the way we, as Christians, are to live, and the Holy Spirit empowers us to faithfully follow that way.

One of the most important things we need to understand is the truth of the Trinity and the importance in our life of each one of these members of the Godhead. There are three persons in the Godhead. They are Father, Son, and Holy Spirit. The Holy Spirit is the One who we know the least about. In fact, as a youngster and while attending church somewhat irregularly, I heard the pastor refer to the "Holy Ghost," and I did not have a clue what that meant. I now understand he was referring to the Holy Spirit.

On that night many years ago, when I was overcome with guilt for my personal sin, I had no idea it was the Holy Spirit who had so overwhelmed and convicted me. He, over the many, many years since then, through the Bible, has helped me understand that the three persons of the Godhead (Father, Son, and Holy Spirit) have all played a critical role in my true salvation. All three also continue to play a role in my development to become a faithful and grateful disciple of Jesus. It had become clear that on the evening when I was convicted, the Holy Spirit ensured in my life the same result Jesus promised His disciples. In John 16:14a (KJV), it says, "He shall glorify Me." That is exactly what the Holy Spirit did in my life. He caused me to realize it was my personal sin that put Jesus on that cruel cross. That is how the Holy Spirit glorified Christ to me as my Savior, as I realized what a tremendous sacrifice Jesus made for me! It is amazing. The Holy Spirit did what no one else could do! He so focused me on the wondrous gift of forgiveness and salvation Jesus had made possible for me—Christ was and continues to be glorified!

At the time, I did not know what had happened. I did know this—I had been spiritually impacted in an indescribable and never before experienced way. What I had not realized yet, (when I was so broken and sorrowful) was that I now had a Resident Translator in the Holy Spirit to help me understand God's Word for practical, consistent application in my life. But I also did not know yet how powerful the Holy Spirit would be as my Resident Power to obey and live out God's Word in my life. What a precious gift had been given to me, a forgiven repentant sinner.

As I began to value and read God's precious Word, I learned this—all three members of the Godhead were present at creation.

» God, the Father, simply spoke and created (Genesis 1).

» The Holy Spirit of God "moved upon the face of the waters" at that same time (Genesis 1:26, KJV).

» When it came to creating man, God said in Genesis 1:2b (KJV):

"Let *Us* make man in *Our* Image, after *Our* likeness." This was God and the Holy Spirit.

That explains where two members of the Godhead were, but where was Jesus? John 1:1 (KJV) tells us, "In the beginning was the Word, and the Word was with God, and the Word was God." "The Word" is a profound title of the Lord Jesus Christ. John 1:14 (KJV) takes us farther in understanding: "And the Word was made flesh, (came from God), and dwelt among us and we beheld His glory, the glory as of the only begotten of the Father, full of grace and truth." What a fitting description of Jesus, my Savior.

You may be like I was before I was truly born again. I wondered why there were three different persons mentioned as God in the Bible. It was a mystery, but I never lost sleep over it because I was not very interested in religion or the church. At that time, I did not realize how desperately I needed a spiritual rebirth.

Then my life was turned upside-down. I had been overwhelmed by an unexplainable silent power, of which I knew nothing. Upon my salvation, I now wanted to know more because of the wonderful, indescribable peace this power had brought into my life instantaneously.

I did not have much biblical knowledge, but I did know Adam as the first man had disobeyed God in the garden and was then removed from the garden as a sinful presence and not allowed to stay in the presence of a Holy God. But at that time, I did not understand God had created man for fellowship with Himself, and God still loved mankind even though he had become sinful. God had warned Adam of the penalty of sin (disobedience), which would result in separation for eternity and ultimately death. But Adam was tempted and gave in to Satan's wiles. Adam sinned and then was shamefully dismissed from the presence of the sinless Holy God.

God missed fellowship with man, but He had a plan. Since God is just, judgment will always be certain. God had warned Adam beforehand, if you eat of the forbidden fruit, "you will surely die." A Holy God was bound by

His Word, and therefore, Adam was condemned to death. God's plan was for someone (a person) who was without sin to become sin for Adam and pay Adam's sin debt. This would set Adam free from the sentence God had pronounced, and it was the only recourse.

Before we go any farther, we need to better understand the power of God manifested in the power of the Holy Spirit. Just how powerful is the Holy Spirit? We have all read about the birth of Jesus Christ, man's only remedy to sin, from the womb of a virgin named Mary. God's Word provides our answer. Luke 1:35, 37 (KJV) describes what happened. "And the angel answered and said to her, The Holy Spirit will come upon you and the power of the Highest will overshadow you; therefore also, that Holy One who is to be born will be called the Son of God." Verse 37 (KJV) proclaims, "For with God nothing shall be impossible." The Holy Spirit was the agent of God who placed baby Jesus in the womb of the Virgin Mary. How's that for indescribable power?

In the "fullness of time," God sent forth His Son to redeem mankind. It gives me real joy to think about what God the Father did at that time, that perfect time—God sent the perfect Son to provide salvation. Jesus came to redeem them that were born under the law which man had so often broken, "that we might receive the adoption as sons" (Galatians 4:4, ESV). God had a plan for lost, sinful mankind to be restored and forgiven—but at an extremely great price— for Jesus, who was absolutely sinless to become sin for us. What tremendous grace God demonstrated for mankind! Grace is the free, unmerited, undeserved, and impossible to earn favor of God.

Can any of us imagine how horrible it was for Jesus, the perfect, sinless Son of God, to take on all the sins of the world and become sin for you and me? Nonetheless, He was faithful to His calling, and that is exactly what He did. We praise His name today and forever for His faithfulness!

Jesus was cruelly tortured, crucified, and then died. He was profoundly dead as determined by the Roman soldiers who thrust a spear into His side to be certain. Jesus' body was then placed in a borrowed tomb. But, on the third day, He arose and was made victorious over death for you and me. Jesus had thereby provided a way for all of mankind to accept Jesus as Savior and to have victory over death.

The only One who could absolutely pay Adam's sin debt was God's only perfect Son, Jesus Christ. There was no other sinless man who could become a worthy Sacrifice for Adam or for you and me. Jesus came to earth as a baby, grew into manhood, though sinless, and was crucified because of man's sin. Thereby, God's judgment for sin was paid. What a gracious plan our Heavenly Father has for all of us who are unworthy in ourselves. All mankind needed to do now was to, one by one, accept Jesus' wonderful gift of forgiveness and accept Him as our Savior.

However, if Jesus was dead, just how did He overcome death? That is where the third powerful member of the Trinity (Godhead) comes in once again. The Holy Spirit entered the tomb and gave Jesus life anew, raised a dead Christ completely to new life. That is a powerful miraculous accomplishment!

During the thirty-three years Jesus had been on earth, He had selected and developed disciples to carry on the work He had begun with them over the three years they were together. During those years with Him, the Disciples had watched Jesus restore sight to the blind, heal the lepers, feed the multitude with only five loaves and two fish, raise a dead Lazarus, and many more miracles as He also taught them about the future. He defined and prepared them for this role—to "go and make disciples" and to take the gospel around the world. How many of them were there? There were only twelve. That seems like a mighty huge task for twelve ordinary men. How on earth could they accomplish such an enormous task in a world that literally hated Christianity? For clarity, Christianity was so hated because it interfered with their worldly pleasure. It is still rejected today by many for the same reason.

Before Jesus was crucified, He began to tell His disciples He would be going back to the Father. You can imagine how this troubled them to think that they would now be without their profound and beloved source of inspiration. Not only that, with Him leaving them, where would they obtain confidence for such a challenge which He had now put before them? That challenge was to go and make disciples in an intensely dangerous carnal world.

It is amazing to hear how Jesus responded to them, "Nevertheless, I tell you the truth: It is to your advantage that I go away: for if I go not away, the Helper will not come unto you: but if I depart, *I will send Him to you*" (John 16:7, NKJV). Jesus said His leaving would be to their advantage.

We are about to read of the Holy Spirit coming into the world for the important purpose of calling exceptional attention to Jesus Christ and to what Christ has done to restore mankind's only opportunity for forgiveness. The Holy Spirit would also provide the power to be faithful to their assigned responsibility: "Go and make disciples."

Jesus responded to His disciples' concerns with this truth about the Holy Spirit: "He shall glorify Me, for He shall receive of mine and shall show it unto you" (John 16:14, KJV). In other words, Jesus was saying the Holy Spirit will keep a profound focus on what I, Jesus, have done, that you and/or anyone else who wants to be saved might have abundant everlasting life.

We have now seen at least a portion of the primary roles of the three persons in the Godhead. They are Father, Son, and Holy Spirit. I had not thought about it in this way, but the Holy Spirit is the least known or possibly the least understood. However, the Holy Spirit plays an indescribably important part and is intimately involved in our initial conversion and birth into the family of God. The Holy Spirit is also closely involved in our continuous development as Christians. I can tell you without a doubt before I ever knew anything about His role, He overwhelmed me! It was the Holy Spirit who pointed out the high price Jesus paid with His being crucified for my very personal sins. The Holy Spirit put a divine spotlight on how much Jesus had done for me and how much He loved me in spite of my guilt. I will forever be indebted! He shook my carnal foundation. Awakened, I wanted to know more and more about this wonderful unexplainable event that had occurred in my life. Many faithful prayer warriors over the long period of time had literally prayed me into the kingdom of God as the Holy Spirit had so glorified Jesus that evening.

As I began to read and study my Bible, the activity of the Holy Spirit became more and more important to me. After all, I had been radically transformed by this powerful One. We have already learned that the Holy Spirit is the One who inspired the scriptures to be written by forty different writers. He is also the One who helps us understand this unique book of truth for our application. In addition, He (the Holy Spirit) also counsels, comforts, and prays for me. He keeps me focused on what Jesus has done for me (John 16:14, NASV). He helps my weakness and gives me supernatural power to represent Jesus faithfully as an obedient disciple (Acts 1:8, ESV). He leads me into all truth (John 16:13, NASV).

Moreover, after I had learned all the wonderful things above, I was delighted to learn I now had resident in me, the One who would lead me in a life now potentially filled with the "fruit of the Spirit —love, joy, peace, patience, kindness, goodness, faithfulness, gentleness, and self-control" (Galatians 5:22–23, ESV). All I had to do was follow. It was truly a great joy to learn that as soon as I had trusted Jesus as my Lord and Savior that wonderful evening, He "sealed me" (Ephesians 1:13, NKJV) by the Holy Spirit. I was secured for eternity! Amazing! I was now beginning to realize what had so miraculously happened to me.

Just like the disciples at Pentecost, every repentant believer is filled with the spirit. This "filling" is to be a repeated process as we study God's Word and commune with Him in prayer. Why does He continually fill us? One reason, without question, is that we are then able to represent Jesus well. And He fills us in order that Jesus is glorified in our lives. He gives us joy and peace as we think about His gracious gift of salvation. When we request and seek the continual filling of the Holy Spirit, He provides the power for us to be obedient and faithful in every area of our lives. Then we will continuously hear Him speaking peace to us, His forgiven children. "I will hear what God the LORD will speak; for He will speak peace unto His people and to His saints" (Psalm 85:8, KJV).

Every church member needs to be very careful here. Let me repeat, I was a lost church member for twenty-one years. I knew nothing about the absolute necessity of the Holy Spirit dwelling in my life. Romans 8:9 (NASV) is very clear, but I did not know the verse or care about it. It declares: "If anyone does not have the Spirit of Christ, he does not belong to Him." That is as conclusively as it can be said! Why would that be? It is simple. Without truly surrendering to Christ, we would not have the Holy Spirit and thereby then have no power to represent Him in the manner He deserves and expects.

There is another equally unequivocal truth stated in Romans 8:14 (KJV). "As many as are led by the Spirit of God, these are the children of God." God's children have a distinct identity. Can it be any more plain than this? There is no more challenging work to be done than to try to live for Christ or do the work of the church in the flesh. God will never bless carnal efforts, but He will always bless obedience and responsiveness to the leadership of His wonderful Holy Spirit.

We need to be reminded daily of the powerful truth revealed by God's messenger in Zechariah 4:6 (ESV): "Not by might, nor by power, but by My Spirit; says the Lord of Hosts." This was given to God's people, who were about to begin the enormous task of rebuilding God's temple. We now have the greatest gift anyone could ever want. We have the same tremendous power of the Holy Spirit, always seeking to empower, guide, and bless our lives that we might glorify Jesus—continuously!

I had to be honest and see how immoral I was as a flagrant sinner before I could acknowledge and appreciate how wonderful and perfect Jesus is. It took the power of God's Holy Spirit convicting me to cause me to be honest about my need for forgiveness and need for a new, powerfully fresh start as His born-again child. It is called "regeneration," and it is beyond description. Satan is clever and wants us to compare our lives with others. We can then rationalize: "I am not as bad as so and so." But Jesus wants us to stay focused on Him and let the Holy Spirit grow us to be more and more like the Christ who died and set us free. Jesus will always be our pattern, not other people.

The Holy Spirit helped me see it was my ugly, sinful life that put Jesus on a torturous cross, and for that, He exchanged His perfect life. The Holy Spirit had now focused on an exchange in my life, as described in Ephesians 3:20a (NKJV), "Now unto Him who is able to do exceeding abundantly above all that we can ask or think, according to the power that works in us!" Before, I had but a piece of paper, a church membership. But now, miraculously, I had the tremendous strengthening power of God to help me resist our evil, jealous, destructive enemy Satan.

The Holy Spirit's power is needed to live the Christian life, to grow in grace, to obey God's Word, and to develop into full maturity. That necessity is the work of the Holy Spirit, the Difference-Maker. The strength of God's church is determined by the members obediently being filled continuously with God's Holy Spirit power.

Charles H. Spurgeon is known as the Prince of Preachers. He is a preacher of centuries ago who often preached to ten thousand or more persons regularly. In his excellent book *Spurgeon on the Holy Spirit*, he writes this: "God's people are a Holy people. God's Spirit works by love and purifies the soul. Once His Spirit comes into our hearts, He will have no rest until He has turned every sin out. God's Holy Spirit and man's sin cannot live together peacefully. In due time, the Spirit will drive out all sin and will present us blameless before the throne of His Majesty with exceeding great joy. Friend, if you do not have the Spirit, then you are nothing better—no matter who you are or what you may be—than the fall of Adam left you."

I do now know this, that the powerful Holy Spirit is the One who so convicted me of my worldliness and sin. It was the Holy Spirit who pointed me to Jesus for forgiveness that evening so many years ago. Jesus was the only remedy for my wrecked, broken life.

The awful thing that was wrong with me—I was fully into my humanity as Adam's poster child.

I have since learned I can never have what Jesus promised in John 10:10 (KJV): "I am come that they might have life, and have it more abundantly" unless I have God's Holy Spirit, through the forgiveness of Christ, untethered and unhindered (unquenched) in my life, guiding, correcting, and encouraging me every day.

Charles Spurgeon also makes this profound statement: "Christ's dying is nothing to you unless you have a living Spirit within you. Christ brings you no advantage saving, personal and lasting, unless the Spirit of God has baptized you in the fountain filled with His blood and washed you from head to foot."

Perhaps, one, if not the very best example of what the empowerment of what the Holy Spirit does in the life of believers is Jesus sending out His disciples. You are probably familiar with His last words and command given to them immediately before He ascended back to heaven. He said, "All authority has been given to Me in heaven and on earth. Go therefore and make disciples of all the nations, baptizing them in the name of the Father and of the Son and of the Holy Spirit, teaching them to observe all things that I have commanded you; and lo, I am with you always even to the end of the age" (Matthew 28:18–20, NKJV).

Get this picture—they had seen Jesus humbly and horribly crucified for doing what He is now commanding them to do! Would you or I be uneasy and apprehensive in their place?

- » They have no money.
- » They have no building.
- » They have no prestige.

Wow!

What did they have? They had unshakable faith in the mighty power of God's Holy Spirit given them at Pentecost. God's Holy Spirit will always be enough! They absolutely proved it!

You and I have the entire gospel and a home in glory because they, the empowered ones, were faithful. We also have God's Holy Spirit to enable us to live faithfully and obey Him, not just for ourselves but for the sake of others who need to hear the gospel and to be born again to a life of peace and purpose.

The Holy Spirit was the ever-present indwelling Power that enabled that small group to get the gospel to the world. There is a great lesson here for every true believer!

We need God's Holy Spirit, now more evidently and more fully at work than ever before, as we represent our Savior. He is that same Holy Spirit that so glorified Christ at Pentecost when three thousand people were saved! See Acts 2:41.

There is a command in God's Word relative to the Holy Spirit that we have not spoken to. First Thessalonians 5:19 (NKJV) states a warning: "Do not quench the Spirit." What does this mean? We quench the Spirit when we blatantly sin. But we also quench the Spirit when we resist His influence and when we say *no* to God. When the Spirit urges us to spend more time in prayer or read the Bible more regularly, and we don't, we quench the Spirit. Or when we fail to share the gospel with someone we know needs to be set free, we say, "No, not now, maybe at a more convenient time," we quench the Spirit.

The real danger here, the quenching of the Spirit, is one of the primary reasons for decline in our churches today. God gave us His Spirit to enable us to be more faithful, not less so. We will not see this change, churches growing and thriving again, until God's people become more determined to obey the leading of God's Holy Spirit. He is the power of the successful church, and there is no other substitute, including—and especially—worship style. That has now been proven.

I am convinced God is far more interested in what we do after we leave the church building than what we do inside it. Our response to our worship is of utmost importance. Our world desperately needs to often encounter Spirit-filled and Spirit-led obedient Christians. Where? In the marketplace, grocery store, stadium, workplaces, schools and universities, and neighborhoods. After all, if we are truly saved, we are saved to "go and make disciples" (Matthew

28:19a, NIV). It takes a disciple to "go and make disciples." A true disciple is an empowered, equipped, obedient follower of Jesus. Someone wisely said, "We are going to have only two things when we die—our love for God and our love for each other," demonstrated by our willingness to obey Him and proclaim the gospel.

Can we ever honor and worship God any more than when we gratefully obey Him and allow the Holy Spirit to participate in every decision we make? Of course not!

The beauty of God's grace is He not only gave us His profound guide for life—the Holy Bible—but also gave us His powerful Holy Spirit. And by enabling us with His Holy Spirit, we might not just "Know the Way," but we can also "Go the Way" and represent Him with God-confidence as Spirit-filled believers.

What a blessed privilege to be an eternal light in an ever-darkening world!

# CHAPTER 18

# The Difference-Maker

From everything we read about Peter, we learn he was a rugged fisherman who was quick to speak, and like too many of us, sometimes spoke when he should have remained silent and listening.

As a fisherman, he was his own boss and probably answered to no one. I am convinced he was the kind of person who did his own thing and spoke his own mind. It appears he had much confidence in himself.

Why, then, did Jesus select such an unexemplary one to become one of His first disciples? Well, we know now what Jesus knew then: there would be a radical transformation in Peter, one almost unbelievable to you and me. And yet, that same radical transformation is available to anyone today who desires a life of profound purpose and wonderful peace. What happened to Peter is neither a secret nor a mystery. It is clearly written in God's Word!

First Corinthians 1:27 (NKJV) tells us clearly why Jesus chose Peter: "But God has chosen the foolish things of the world to put to shame the wise, and God has chosen the weak things of the world to put to shame the things which are mighty."

Jesus called Peter, knowing when the crisis came, Peter would deny that he was His disciple. Peter and Jesus had a conversation about that specific thing during which Peter swore that he would never deny his Master. The problem, however, was Peter would be trusting in his own strength to help him be courageous and stand when the difficult challenge came. Jesus, however, knew Peter would not have the spiritual power initially to stand as boldly as Peter thought he would be able to stand.

The Bible now clearly delineates when that testing did come, Peter failed miserably. He failed so miserably he was intimidated by a servant girl in the courtyard of the high priest on the night of Jesus' arrest.

Peter was trusting in his own strong willpower and physical strength. What he needed, what all believers need, is God's power to stand faithfully as followers of Jesus, and to gain this, we need Holy Spirit's power in us. Jesus saved us to represent him faithfully and powerfully to a lost world. This being said, it troubles me that we do not hear nearly as much as we should about this astounding power of the Holy Spirit. The Holy Spirit actually comes into the lives of every repentant, forgiven follower of Jesus as Lord and Savior. In fact, He is the essential power for anyone to live faithfully for our Savior. Several passages in Romans verify this: "For as many as are led by the Spirit of God, these are the sons of God" (Romans 8:14, NKJV). This verse says that every born-again child of God will be indwelt with this essential power of God. In Romans 8:9 (NKJV), another truth is verified: "But you are not in the flesh, but in the Spirit, if indeed the Spirit of God dwells in you. Now, if anyone does not have the Spirit of Christ, he is not His." This verse is repeated here because it is vitally important in helping us know the essentiality of having this power of God in our lives as His children.

It is inconceivable that God would call us to do His work on earth and not provide the strong power needed to do so. It requires the power of God's Spirit for Christians to stand against the wiles of Satan.

The first fourteen verses of John chapter sixteen are enlightening as to God's Holy Spirit's purpose in our life. He is our constant Holy Guide and Helper.

In my own case, I would never have imagined when I repented on my knees and asked Jesus to save me that God's powerful Holy Spirit could have ever entered into my life in order to transform my life with such power as He did. I did not know that important truth beforehand because I had no interest in learning what the Bible teaches.

The Godhead teaches us an important truth that we should know and be grateful for. There are three members of the Godhead, three persons in one. They are God, the Father; God, the Son; and God, the Holy Spirit. Each of these was present when the world was created, and each serves a critically important purpose in the lives of Christians. In another chapter, we have addressed the roles of each of these three, but for now, let's look at, for the sake of a better definitive term, what we will identify as the Difference-Maker. Why such an identity? Holy Spirit, the Difference-Maker, did just that in Peter's life. He made the difference, and He certainly did it in my own life as well, and I will never be the same. It is important for me to say, without question, when I knew nothing about the Holy Spirit of God, I still was overpowered with guilt and conviction by Him.

The Holy Spirit has more than one basic role:

- » Conviction first: I am made acutely aware of my sinfulness (Sorrow).

- » Then enlightenment: I realize God is resident and providing the help I need (Awareness).

- » Then empowerment: I begin to experience deliverance from my temptations (Deliverance).

When no person could keep God's law, His commandments, Jesus did! He kept the law, never sinned, and because He was sinless, He became the only worthy, sinless sacrifice for everyone who wants a better life. He paid a debt we could not pay, and He was crucified, died, and was raised from the tomb. He is now sitting at the right hand of the Father, interceding for you and me. Believe me. The Father hears His obedient Son!

Immediately after Jesus was baptized by John the Baptist, He was led by the Spirit into the wilderness to be tempted by Satan. He then fasted for forty days and, as you can imagine, was exceedingly hungry. Satan came and tempted Jesus to turn stones into bread. Jesus answered Satan with this Word of God: "It is written, man shall not live by bread alone, but by every word that proceedeth out of the mouth of God" (Matthew 4:4, KJV).

While Jesus was in the wilderness, Satan continued to tempt Him in various ways. Jesus always responded to him with the Word of God. That is a sure-fire way for all of God's children to deal with Satan also. "Thy Word have I hid in mine heart that I might not sin against thee" (Psalm 109:1, KJV). That fact is a verifier that we can effectively defeat Satan with God's truth.

It is interesting to note after that forty-day period of extreme hunger and temptation, God's Word tells us Jesus dismissed Satan with these words: "Get thee behind me, Satan, for it is written, Thou shalt worship the Lord thy God, and Him only shalt thou serve" (Luke 4:8, KJV).

You might be wondering why the Holy Spirit, once He was resident in Jesus, led Him up to be tempted. I am convinced this was to be certain Jesus knew (with God's Spirit as His helper, John 14:16, NKJV) that He (Jesus) would be able to withstand Satan's efforts to keep Jesus from being faithful to His mission. Thank God, Jesus was faithful and faithfully endured not only the temptation but the torture on the cross for you and me.

Did you also notice Jesus, who was holy and undefiled, was baptized to identify with lost humanity?

Perhaps the most important point to be made is that everything Jesus did in His earthly ministry was done by the power of the Holy Spirit because initially, He had come to earth as a man just like you and me.

To be saved, we must recognize that we have to be identified with Christ, and that is accomplished only by the Holy Spirit (conviction). The Holy Spirit is the One who brings us to conviction of our sin and points us to Jesus as the only One who can provide forgiveness. He reminds each of us that it was our personal sins that put Jesus on the cross.

We have also seen here a manifestation of the Trinity. As the Lord Jesus is coming out of the baptismal water, the Spirit of God descends upon Him like a dove, and the Father also speaks from heaven. The Lord Jesus is now identified with His people and empowered by God's Holy Spirit to resist any temptation of the enemy to thwart God's plan of salvation for all people (including you and me).

Jesus then began to call His disciples, as we see in Matthew 4:18–20 (KJV). First, He called two rugged fishermen named Simon (called Peter) and Andrew, his brother. Please note He did not call "religious ones." These were ordinary people just like you and me. These two fishermen were casting nets when He called them. Verse 20 tells us, "they straightway left their nets and followed Him." They did not hesitate. This says something about the wonderful, powerful presence of our Savior. Obviously, Jesus had a positive, compelling nature for these men to instantly give up their vocation and, in faith, follow Him.

Jesus continued to call out other disciples, all the while teaching, preaching, healing lepers and cripples, even raising a dead Lazarus. Jesus was clearly preparing His carefully (divinely) selected disciples that they might carry on the work after His crucifixion and His return to being seated at the right hand of the Father. Jesus is now there, interceding constantly with the Father for you and me. All of the gospels detail the events that took place with His disciples over the next three years.

Peter's love, confidence in, and admiration of Jesus are each clearly recorded in the gospels of Matthew, Mark, Luke and John. As Jesus began to prepare the disciples for His crucifixion, it was difficult for them to believe what would follow. After all the miracles they had observed which Jesus had performed, why would Jesus not be received and welcomed as the long-awaited Messiah?

In chapter 26 of Matthew's gospel (NKJV), Jesus is telling His disciples: "All of you will be made to stumble (fall away) because of me this very night" (verse 31). Peter answered and said (verse 33), "If all are made to stumble because of you, I will never be made to stumble." That was Peter speaking "in the flesh" before he received Holy Spirit power at Pentecost. That is when Jesus told Peter (verse 34), "Before the rooster crows, you will deny me three times." Then Peter responded (verse 35), "Even if I have to die with you, I will not deny you!"

Jesus was later arrested, and "then all the disciples forsook Him and fled" (verse 56).

Verse 57 of Matthew 26 is straightforward: "And those who had laid hold of Jesus led Him away to Caiaphas, the high priest, where the scribes and elders were assembled, but Peter followed Him at a distance to the high priest's courtyard." What does this say to you and me about following Jesus in a half-hearted manner at a distance? While the crowd spat in Jesus' face and beat Him, Peter sat outside in the courtyard, and as a servant girl accused him, he said, "I do not know what you are saying" (verse 70). Another girl saw him and said, "This fellow also was with Jesus of Nazareth" (verse 71). But Peter denied it with an oath, "I do not know the man" (verse 72). A third time a group accused Peter because they could identify him by his Galilean speech dialect, "And your speech betrays you" (verse 73). Then Peter began to curse and swear, saying, "I do not know the man" (verse 74). Immediately the rooster crowed, "So Peter went out and wept bitterly" (verse 75).

There is great truth here about following Jesus at a distance (actually, it's called desiring Jesus as Savior to be a security blanket, perhaps, but not as Lord).

Thank God, this is not the end of the biblical account of God's empowering of the original disciples, who, given a second chance to be loyal and faithful, began to change the world with the gospel. And they did it fearlessly!

Every believer knows the truth that Jesus was raised from the tomb and made various appearances over a forty-day period. On one occasion, more than five hundred people witnessed the risen Christ. The twenty-fourth chapter of Luke is a wonderful account of one of those appearances. Several disciples were walking on the road to Emmaus, which was seven miles from Jerusalem. In verses 15 and 16, we read, "Jesus, Himself drew near and went with them, but their eyes were restrained, and they did not know Him," but when they stopped for the evening meal, "He took bread, blessed it, and broke it and gave it to them, then their eyes were opened and they knew Him."

The words found in Luke 24:46–52 are among the most encouraging verses in the entire Word of God. In the New King James version, they read as follows: "Then He said to them, 'Thus it is written, and thus it was necessary for the Christ to suffer and rise from the dead the third day, and the repentance should be preached in His name to all nations, beginning in Jerusalem. And you are witnesses of these things. Behold, I send the Promise of My Father upon you [the Holy Spirit]; but tarry in the city of Jerusalem until you are endued with power from on High.' He then led them out as far as Bethany, and He lifted up His hands and blessed them. Now, it came to pass, while He blessed them, that He was parted from them and carried up into heaven, and they worshipped Him, and returned to Jerusalem with great joy, and were continually in the Temple praising and blessing God. Amen!" They obeyed Him!

Now the disciples would await the promise, no longer with sadness, but with joy!

Luke's account is continued in the book of Acts, chapter 2:1–4 (NKJV), "When the Day of Pentecost had fully come, they were all of One Accord [unified] in one place (as instructed by Jesus on the Emmaus Road). Suddenly there came a sound from heaven as a mighty rushing wind, and it filled the whole house (or place) where they were sitting. Then there appeared to them divided tongues, as of fire, and one sat upon each of them, and they were all filled with the Holy Spirit and began to speak with other tongues, as the Spirit gave them utterance." These physical signs made certain the disciples knew they had Holy Spirit power to enable obedience to what Jesus had commanded.

In verses 5–11, we read that the assembled were from many different places and speaking languages that were all different, and yet they heard the Galileans speaking, not in Galilean, but in all the different languages of the countries they were from. The scripture says, "We hear them speaking in our own tongues the wonderful works of God." They were amazed and perplexed, saying to one another, "Whatever could this mean?" (verse 12) Others mockingly said, "They are full of new wine" (verse 13).

Then a miraculous thing occurred. The cowardly Peter, thrice the denier of Jesus, stood up and raised his voice (by the way, there are times when we as God's saved people need to *stand up* and raise our voices, sometimes in praise and sometimes in proclamation!). Peter then preached the first sermon in the church (verse 14). "When they heard this, they were cut to the heart and said to Peter and the rest of the apostles and brethren, what shall we do?" (verse 37) Verse 38 follows: Then Peter said to them, "Repent and let every one of you be baptized in the name of Jesus Christ, for the remission of sins, and you shall receive the gift of the Holy Spirit, for the promise is to you and your children and to all who are afar off, as many as the Lord our God will call" throughout all ages.

What was the result of the denier's sermon, now that he was filled with God's Holy Spirit? "Then those who gladly received His Word were baptized and that day, about three thousand souls were added to them" (verse 41).

"The disciples continued steadfastly in the apostles' doctrine and fellowship, in the breaking of bread and in prayers" (verse 42). (Obviously, they had more than religion). "Then fear came upon every soul and many wonders and signs were done through the apostles who were filled with the Holy Spirit. All who believed were now together and had all things in common and sold their possessions and goods and divided them among all as had needs" (verses 43–45).

Is there any question these were transformed and empowered people?

Verse 46 says, "So, continuing daily with one accord in the temple, and breaking bread from house to house, they ate with gladness and simplicity of heart, Praising God and having favor with all people and the Lord added to the church daily those who were being saved." (There is no question about the marvelous impact the Holy Spirit had on the disciples and the people's lives by Holy Spirit power.)

There are two profound things we need to see here:

1. The matchless grace of God—agreeable to forgive the denying Peter and raise him (the one who denied Jesus three times and then wept bitterly) and give him the great honor, to preach the first sermon in the church.

2. The undeniable power of the Holy Spirit, promised to every true believer, to bring about spiritual results that can be brought into being no other way.

No one will ever be able to be faithful to go and do God's work effectively apart from the indescribable power of God's Holy Spirit.

There is a description of such a condition in God's Word in 2 Timothy 3:5b (KJV) which is "having a form of Godliness but denying the power thereof" (i.e., religious activity that is not connected to a living relationship with Jesus Christ). What a wonderful picture of God's will it is for all who accept His gift of forgiveness through Jesus and possess the wonderful accompanying indwelling Holy Spirit (a wonderful equipping and strengthening).

There is absolutely no question God's Holy Spirit was a profound *Difference-Maker* in the life of Peter and the disciples. He wants to do the same for all who may not realize they have that same power available. And He will provide the excitement, courage, and the power to represent Him in a world that so desperately needs what only He can provide.

We must all ask, is God's powerful Holy Spirit really present and empowering me today? If not, why not? He is the Difference-Maker!

Please know I would not be so personally enamored with the Holy Spirit had I not been overwhelmed with guilt when He convicted me of my sins. I now realize also, the Holy Spirit is the One who has empowered me to live for Christ, to love and better understand the Word of God, and also to be quick to glorify (point to) Our Lord for any success in my own life. I am in no way boasting about myself but about God's provision of the Holy Spirit.

Trying to live for Christ in the flesh is futile. That is why God provides the enabling power of the Holy Spirit to make it possible for you to not only live for Christ but to live victoriously!

It is vitally important for us to understand God has saved us for much more than heaven. He has saved us to be disciples just like the original ones. We have the gospel today because ordinary people were filled by the Holy Spirit at Pentecost. Once they were empowered, they became faithful and fearless. They powerfully represented Jesus. They left His Word for us to know that each of us forgiven ones could know we have been saved to become "difference-makers." It is only by the blood of Jesus who cleansed us—and by the Holy Spirit's power within us—that we can make a difference.

In order to honor our Creator and Redeemer, we must have the Holy Spirit resident and leading us.

Yes, people can become what Jesus saved us to become—*difference-makers.*

What a precious privilege—the Difference-Maker!

We, the forgiven people of God, can truly become difference-makers because the heavenly Difference-Maker dwells in us and empowers and inspires every born again child of God to live out our faith consistently and thereby make a significant difference in our ever-darkening world.

# CHAPTER 19

## Does It Really Matter? No Question About It!

"What I do with my life is my business, and as long as I don't hurt anyone else, it is none of anyone else's business." We have all probably heard this said by someone.

That might sound reasonable, and it's true. God does allow each of us the choice of how we will live our lives. But God created us for Himself, and He has a wonderful, fulfilling plan for each of our lives. As previously mentioned, each one of us is an only child to Him. No one has our DNA, fingerprints, voice prints, or the unique pattern of the iris of our eye. We were each uniquely planned and created.

Throughout our lives, there are many people whom we will interact with. It is God's plan for us to always share the positive difference He can make in anyone's life, so we need to do so. It is just like the incredible difference He has made in our own lives, so it should not be hard to share with others this most wonderful thing that has ever happened to us.

Once anyone becomes saved, we all have the same expectations from God: we are to carry on the most important work in the world. After all, we have God's Holy Spirit to help us do this. What is that work? It's representing and sharing Christ Jesus. Also, once we lead someone else to Christ, they will have that same gratifying role of helping others find real meaning and purpose in their lives and consequently enjoying the peace of God.

God created every person for fellowship with Him. There is nothing else in the entire world that can come even close to that contentment. And there is no greater fulfillment than to influence someone who is without lasting purpose and fulfilling peace so that they may be made whole by faith in Jesus Christ. A person can only have those two wonderful conditions—fellowship with Him and completeness with new purpose and peace when they have been made whole by faith in Jesus Christ.

Yet, there is a serious question we all need to think about. Would God make the most important work in the world an optional matter for us? We all know the answer to that question. Heaven is real, and so is hell. As forgiven believers in Jesus, who will never know the eternal punishment of hell, we have the obligation to care about our fellow man, just like someone cared about us enough to lead us to Christ.

The Holy Spirit of God will strengthen every one of us to help our fellow man by sharing the gospel. That is one of the things that the third member of the Trinity, the Holy Spirit, does. The Holy Spirit always glorifies and points to Jesus and exalts what He has done for us. He died once for all, but we have to claim that gift of forgiveness one by one. God expects each one of us to love Him enough to share Christ with the lost who have not found their way home yet. It's really not hard if we truly know and love Jesus, plus we have the powerful Helper empowering us.

There is one other question that should challenge every single Christian. If I am unwilling to obey Christ and share the great transformation of my own life, who then will be there to share that truth with the generations to come?

Does it really matter? You better believe so because God has transformed us and empowered us. Hence, I am without excuse, and so is every other Believer. "Go and make Disciples."

Here are Jesus' very last words on this earth: "Go and make disciples."

Thank God those who preceded me obediently did so, and today I stand free and forgiven because they were faithful to that sacred instruction to share the wonderful gospel.

I cannot emphasize it enough. You can rest assured it matters for eternity whether we take seriously what our Savior has instructed us to do. But are we grateful enough to Him for his suffering on our behalf to obey? Yes, it really matters, no question about it!

Our Lord expects each of us to share that most wonderful truth and the most important thing that has happened to us—being saved from sin by Jesus Christ. Here are a few examples where sharing Christ made the difference.

Many, many more examples will be covered in another chapter.

Many years ago, a friend asked me if I would help him work with older boys at John G. Richards. It is a boy's prison and confines boys up to age eighteen. It is located in the state prison complex on Broad River Road in Columbia, South Carolina. I had told the Lord on the night I was truly born again that if there was something I could do for the cause of Christ, that I would do it. In spite of not knowing anything about prison ministry except that there was a great need, I willingly agreed to help.

Thus, the two of us would go every Wednesday evening and conduct a Bible study with usually twelve-to-fifteen young men. Most were in their mid-to-late teens. If I remember correctly, when a prisoner turned eighteen, he was then transferred to the men's prison to complete their sentence. It was a heartbreaking thing to see so many incarcerated during some of the best years of their life. Also painful was seeing how sin had caused such consequences for these youth, knowing many of these delinquencies could have been avoided had only someone shared Christ with them earlier in their life and helped disciple them. Some of these young men were really repentant and experienced the new birth in Christ Jesus. The repentant ones always listened attentively to the good news God's Word brought, and they were very respectful.

I remember a very hot period of days in August. In fact, it was so hot inside that we were allowed to have the Bible study outside the dorm and under a picnic shelter; however, there was no risk of escape. It was a little cooler outside with a slight breeze, but still extremely hot and uncomfortable.

It was interesting and encouraging to see that the ones who volunteered to attend the study were always courteous and interested. They were contrite and regretful about their crimes, while still having to endure sin's consequences. It was truly tragic to see the regret many of these young men had for their wrong behavior. On this Wednesday evening, we finished our study and started walking back into the dorm. As we slowed down going through the security process, there was a backup awaiting clearance at the door. In that line, I was right behind James, a tall, muscular African American and a well-spoken and well-mannered lad who always listened raptly when God's Word was shared. He was facing the door, and I was immediately behind him. I placed my hand on his shoulder, and he turned to see who had done that. When he did, I asked, "James, how are you doing?" With a broad and pleasant smile, he answered, "Mr. Paul, I am doing so good since I became a Christian. I made the honor roll this time, and I am going to get to go on an outing to the zoo tomorrow." I congratulated him for his good choices, and I could see in his eyes a "prodigal who had come home" who was now being rewarded.

The zoo outing was to occur the following day, Thursday. When I picked up the State newspaper on that following Friday, the headline read "Youth dies on outing to the zoo." I really did not want to read further, but I did, and I was devastated to read his name. James, the young man who had been so full of life (as we can have only through Christ), at the age of seventeen, had tragically drowned.

As I read further, the paper indicated that because it was so very hot, the group (obviously without permission, but innocently) had gotten into the rapids which flow by the zoo; it's really refreshing water because it is released from the bottom of Lake Murray Dam. When additional water is released, the rapids in the river rise quickly and become very turbulent. There is a warning siren, but somehow some of these young men stayed in the water, and James' foot had gotten caught between two boulders. He could not get free and drowned.

I was so terribly sad on the one hand that this fine reformed teenager had lost his life. However, I was encouraged by his testimony of the wonderful things Jesus had done and was continuing to do in his life.

I do not know the details of his conversion from guilty sinner to forgiven saint, but this I do know. The fact that people took the wonderful gospel into that place of incarceration mattered. It does matter, for eternity, that we obey Jesus' last command. It mattered to James and his soul. That command is to those of us who have already been set free to share the good news of the Gospel and Jesus' love. All who are saved today are saved because someone was faithful to share.

Is there a "James" in your life whose eternal life depends on your obedience to the great commission?

*People can be obedient* to His commission because the Lord has prepared us to do so. He has given us the Holy Spirit, the Difference-Maker, to enable us and thereby glorify Jesus. We never know when it will be someone's last chance to be set free and prepared for heaven as our young friend here was.

There is a saddening truth that we now know. According to the North American Mission Board, ninety-five percent of Southern Baptists never share a verbal gospel witness. They never tell anyone about Jesus. I do not know about other denominations but doubt the number is any better. A real love for Christ will compel us to have a love for the lost. We must never forget, "but for the grace of God, there go I."[1]

Wouldn't God's churches be growing and prospering today if we all took seriously Jesus' last command to each of us before He went to the Father? How could our society be degenerating in such a disastrous way if God's redeemed people, bought back by the blood of Christ, took His claim on our life seriously? Said another way, would our society be so deteriorating if we obeyed Jesus' last instruction to us? That instruction includes every true Christian being obedient to His command to share the gospel.

Again, Joe Alexander was such a man who took that command to heart. You may recall his persistence in inviting me to church and his following up on getting me there and what happened. What Joe did by inviting me to revival service mattered. How Joe lived so exemplarily before me mattered. What every person does matters. It matters *eternally* that we follow Christ, obey Him, and share The Gospel.

Over the last fifty-plus years, there have been so very many people that I have encountered who have lived victoriously. They realized it does matter how they live for Christ. It would be impossible to speak and write about all those who have so helped inspire me on my journey. They have shown me

---

1    Quotes, STANDS4 Network, John Bradford, 1553.

by their example how important obedience to Jesus' last command really is! There is another example, however, that I can never forget and need to share.

In 1975, all the churches in my hometown, or almost all, came together and planned a city-wide crusade. This was about five years after I was born again. Dr. Clyde Dupin, a widely respected non-denominational evangelist, was the evangelist for this event. Dr. Dupin, in plainest terms, is a very effective small-town Billy Graham. His integrity, effectiveness of ministry, and commitment are "cut of the same cloth." His life has inspired and impacted my life.

Anyway, the Crusade was to be a seven-day event held in the high school stadium. Apparently, the field of others was limited, so I was asked to be the local chairman. Once again, I recalled that I had promised my Lord the night he forgave me and saved me that I would do whatever I felt, with His help, that I could do or was asked to do. So, I accepted.

An interesting incident occurred related to the crusade. Several days before the crusade was to begin, a lady called me with a request. She said in essence, "I am a believer, but my husband is not." Will you and the team pray for him because he has agreed to attend? I assured her we would do so and that we did. If she had not cared enough about his salvation, she would never have called.

As the general chairman, I sat on the platform with the musicians, evangelists, and prayer leaders. I looked into the stands, spotting that couple on the very first night. On the second night, they were there again, and when the invitation was given, her husband made his way down the stadium steps to one of the awaiting counselors and then to one of the counseling tents. I must tell you, when this happened, there was a wonderful feeling of peace that came over me. It was indescribable, as I knew he was giving his life to Christ. I knew this man was about to begin to enjoy true life at its best, just like God planned for all mankind.

That is not the end of the story. Several nights later, as the invitation hymn was given, it surprised me to see his wife descend the stairs to the counselor and then to the counseling tent. After the benediction, I went to the counselor because I had been directly involved with this couple, feeling some responsibility to see if, somehow, I could help them. When I inquired of the counselor as to what God was doing in that family, I learned that the wife said, "I want what my husband has." It was apparent the transformation that had occurred in the life of her husband caused her to realize she had never really yielded her own life fully to our Savior. She perhaps had become a church member in times past but now needed to crown Jesus as Lord. God's Holy Spirit had led her to now make Jesus not just Savior, but Lord as well. The dramatic change in her husband had impacted her in a compelling way.

So what is the point? It is this—a life fully yielded to Christ does matter because it is so attractive. If we are consistently led by God's indwelling Holy Spirit, others are attracted to such a peaceful and fulfilling Savior.

The way every person lives their life really does matter. A life striving to honor God is profoundly impactful. And it matters to those who observe the peaceful presence of Lordship and ultimately desire the same. Psalm 85:8 (NKJV) is a promise to anyone who will allow Jesus to be not just Savior, but Lord as well. That verse says, "I will hear what God the Lord will speak, for He will speak peace to His people."

God doesn't save us just for our own benefit, but for the benefit of others equally as well. Yes, I am "to be my brother's keeper" as I live my faith. With His Power, God equips me to live faithfully as an example for my brother to follow.

Let's address this viewpoint again: What I do with my life, as long as I'm not hurting someone else, is my business. This is usually expressed when someone is not willing to change their behavior. In the fourth chapter of Genesis (NKJV), the Lord confronts Cain. "Where is Abel your brother?" (verse 9) Cain replied with an impudent answer, "I know not: Am I my brother's keeper?" (verse 9). Perhaps that is a question we should give much more thought to, and then act upon.

God has a plan for all of humanity, and that plan is for each one of us to be concerned for, and to care for, others. He made us to represent Him in our fallen world and to help others find the way of repentance, forgiveness, and God's peace, *real peace* "that passeth all understanding" (Philippians 4:7, KJV).

When God created man, He created us in "His own image," and He made us "fearfully and wonderfully." Why? He made us for Himself and to rule over His created universe. He made us to be used in a positive and wonderfully fulfilling way. He gave us real momentous purpose—to represent Him!

God has not called all of us to go to some terribly dangerous mission field and represent Him there, but He has called and equipped some to do just that. They then go, not with self-confidence, but God-confidence. He has also not called all of us to go to seminary and become preachers, but He has called and equipped some to do just that. They then faithfully do that, all the while knowing God's Holy Spirit will sustain and help them. God has not called all of us to teach His Holy Word as Bible teachers, but He has called some to do just that. And they faithfully do that, knowing they are within the perfect will of God.

There are many other full-time Christian vocations that people are called to and equipped for. But there is a real question we need to ask ourselves when you or I become a transformed believer and ask Jesus to be Our Lord and Savior, *What does he expect of you and me?* He has saved us for—and calls us to—represent Him faithfully and consistently, as we rely on His Holy Spirit Power (at work within us) to help us do so in our fallen world.

God has called every one of us to demonstrate Christianity by letting our lives and actions clearly reflect His ownership and influence in our lives. In a harsh world, there is nothing more attractive than the life of an obedient Holy Spirit-filled Christian. A Christian filled with the Holy Spirit loves their Savior and their fellow man enough to live for Christ and share Christ confidently, happily, and naturally.

Just like we love to see our favorite athletes fanatical about playing their best and winning consistently, so does our Heavenly Father love to see us determined to be faithful to His call upon our lives. That call is to go and unashamedly represent Him full time regardless of where we are.

One of the reasons I am a believer is because of a few people in my workplace who lived out their faith every day, not because they wanted to be seen, but because they wanted their Savior's influence to be seen and desired. They wanted others to know about the most important thing that had ever happened to them. They were grateful enough for God's forgiveness that they desired that same wonderful blessing for others.

When Jesus went back to the Father, He left crystal clear instructions for His disciples. Those instructions were given to the twelve disciples who were there in the upper room, and also those instructions were given to all of us who would become disciples over the ages to come. This is what He said straightforwardly, "All authority in Heaven and on earth has been given to me, therefore, go and make disciples, baptizing them in the name of the Father, Son, and Holy Spirit, and teaching them to obey everything I have commanded you. And surely I am with you always, to the very end of the age" (Matthew 28:18–20, NIV).

When the disciples expressed fear and uncertainty about Jesus telling them He would be going "back to the Father," Jesus had already assured them. Jesus promised them He would send a Helper, Advocate, Counselor, and Guide to empower them to be faithful to that command. Jesus has never withdrawn that command to "go make disciples" and hasn't withdrawn the promise of equipping with His Spirit. Yet, how easy it is for us to ignore our responsibility of sharing Christ. And by doing that, we ignore giving other people's lives real meaning. We also fail to offer them the means to avoid eternity in a place of torment.

Think about it this way—My own obedience to go and make disciples is depended upon by others. If I never respond, *I become their broken lifeline to eternity with God.* It has never been just about me and my Christian life, but those other people God intends for me to reach. That is a sobering and serious thought.

When I walked the aisle in Bible School, I had religion without transformation. I had "religious legitimacy." I had become a member of the church, and I was well-intended. Then the best thing that could have happened to me did happen: the Lord shook me out of my religious pretense, and Jesus Christ became real to me.

We can never represent our Savior better than when we obey Him and unashamedly share the liberating truth of the gospel. My cherished friend and brother in Christ did that for me. We, too, are to bless others by doing likewise. Joe not only shared, but he was also an example before me of a consistent well-lived life, committed to Christ Jesus. It is not a burden or difficult chore to share about Christ as we realize we have been blessed with the wonderful truth of the gospel. People can live above the fray. With God's help. And each of us can be a great influence and example for others, just as God had planned it all.

Does it really matter? Without question. It matters to someone who needs to be set free. We are God's saved people, and God has prepared us and is sending us because He knows people can do the most important work in this world. There are people today that God is depending on you and me to share the gospel with. It is an awesome responsibility, but so much more a precious privilege!

For anyone who is anxious or fearful about sharing the gospel, we simply need to claim God's promise: "For God has not given us a spirit of fear, but of power and love and of sound mind" (2 Timothy 1:7, NKJV). God's people can then conclude that fear is from the enemy of God. God's Word then settles the fear matter with this truth: "He that is in you is greater than he that is in the world" (1 John 4:4b, NKJV).

People Can be faithful! And yes, it matters for eternity! We are to go and make disciples. We are saved to benefit others and help the lost. God equips us, gives us the tools, and provides the courage. Yes, it really does matter! It matters to a lost soul that needs to be set free.

God has done His part. He has sent His powerful Holy Spirit to empower, guide, and give us God-confidence as we obey His last words on earth.

People can—and should—be obedient, honor God, demonstrate Christianity, and unashamedly share Christ often and gratefully.

# CHAPTER 20

# The Most Essential Role

After Jesus graciously forgave me and saved me, there was a word that came up repeatedly as I began to attend church. The word was *disciple*. As I began to read my Bible expectantly, it became clear that Jesus had very carefully selected each of the twelve Disciples that followed Him.

To be perfectly honest, I had never given much thought to these ancient ones. In fact, I had no idea how important these disciples were. Neither did I realize that if they had not been faithful to Jesus' last commandant, I would still be lost and without any meaningful purpose, and hell would be awaiting my arrival because I was born of Adam with a sinful nature.

There has now been an awakening on my part, and it began when I first realized these truths:

» Discipleship is vitally important because it determines the influence of the Christian Church.

» The Christian Church, then by its faithfulness and influence, determines the condition of our world. This is great truth!

Those two statements represent profound realities. How many times have you heard parents and especially grandparents express real concern about the declining condition of our world and our country? That concern is in regard to grandchildren and great-grandchildren. What kind of spiritual environment will there be for them? What kind of country will they face? Why is it true so many are concerned for future generations? It's true because of the accelerating moral and spiritual degeneration in process across our country today.

Truthfully, as I began at a very elementary level to grow spiritually, the importance of discipleship became more and more obvious. In fact, if Joe

Alexander had not been a devoted disciple of Jesus, his influence on my life would probably have been uneventful.

I learned that when Jesus began His earthly ministry, the first thing He did after baptism (when the Holy Spirit descended symbolically as a dove) was to choose His disciples, a diverse but rather ordinary group of men. Among them was one of the most hated people who existed at that time, a tax collector named Levi, also called Matthew. Matthew was Jewish but collected taxes for the occupying Roman government and was hated by the Jews. He often collected more than Rome required, and he then pocketed the rest for personal wealth. At best, Matthew was a less-than-respected person to be chosen as a disciple of Christ. But Matthew's ultimate transformation offers hope for all the rest of us as disciples of our Master.

Jesus took these twelve ordinary men, perhaps, just like you and me, and taught them daily for three years. He poured His life into them, preparing them for carrying on the work of God when He would no longer be with them. Jesus demonstrated mighty power that could come only from a divine source. His disciples saw miracle after miracle, including raising a dead Lazarus.

Jesus knew He would be leaving the fate of all mankind to these twelve men. Actually, Judas, the betrayer, hanged himself, and only eleven were left to keep the gospel truth alive and spreading. This was now their whole purpose for living, but they were so few in number. Nevertheless, they were so very committed as disciples that they persevered, most of them even to martyrdom. Yet even their martyrdom accelerated the growth of Christianity. People were awed when they saw that these disciples were willing to die for what they believed, observed, and, more importantly, experienced!

The gospels give various accounts of Jesus being seen alive on numerous occasions after the crucifixion. On one occasion, more than five hundred people saw the risen Christ at the same time.

In the book of Luke, chapter 24 (NKJV), we read of Jesus appearing to His disciples after He had risen. One of the instructions He gave was in verse 49: "Behold I send the promise of My Father upon you; tarry (wait) in the city of Jerusalem until you are endued from on High." Verse 52 tells us they were obedient, and they worshiped Him, and they returned to Jerusalem with great *joy* and were continually in the temple, praising and blessing God. They knew that one day they would be reunited with their wonderful Savior! They knew His promises would always be kept.

Jesus later gave these disciples (as well as you and me) these final instructions. As previously mentioned, they are recorded in Matthew 28:18–20 (NKJV): "All authority in heaven and on earth has been given to Me. Go therefore, and make disciples of all the nations, baptizing them in the name of the Father, Son, and Holy Spirit, teaching them to observe all things that I have commanded you, and lo, I am with you always even to the end of the age."

Jesus had told them to wait until they received the Holy Spirit's power and *then* to take the gospel to the entire world. We should all thank God for their faithfulness! It was really a revelation to me when I realized that every generation of believers has that same command: "Go and make disciples," even if it is just going across the street. He has called you and me as His disciples to do the very same thing. Jesus has empowered every one of us, His born-again children, with that same powerful Holy Spirit. He has done so that the wonderful gospel might be received and welcomed by those He has put in our path, especially our family. The spread of the gospel (our only hope for a lost world) now rests with every grateful follower of Jesus. That, without question, includes you and me as His grateful disciples. As I think back to that period of my spiritual history when realizing how critical being a faithful disciple is, I recognize it is one of most significance. How is the gospel going to be shared throughout the entire world, generation after generation, if His saved followers are not faithful? As all of God's people (disciples), we must realize God has saved us for far more than just eternity in His wonderful presence. He has also saved us to represent Him as His empowered, sent disciples. Our challenge is unconditional *obedience*. We have the wonderful truth of the gospel, and Holy Spirit will empower us and guide us as we gratefully obey sharing it. We have experienced an undeserved transformation and an accompanying "peace that passeth all understanding" (Philippians 4:7a, KJV).

Moving forward in time after I had retired, a former Pastor and respected friend of mine, Dr. Rob White, invited me to participate in a mission endeavor in India. Out of respect for him and because I owe Christ a debt I can never repay, I was happy to accept! It was always a blessing to be in his and his wife Sandy's company.

*Lynette and Paul headed to India with Sandy and Dr. Rob White*

Rob explained to me that Christian pastors were being trained in India through the efforts of RHEMA, a ministry headquartered in America. This was happening because there were no Christian seminaries in India. There were three subjects available to be taught by Dr. White, a fellow Christian that Dr. White had known for many years, and me. Missions, Evangelism, and Discipleship were the subjects to be taught. Rob allowed me to select the one I would feel best about teaching for the six days we would be teaching. On subsequent trips to India, he also gave me that choice. It was a great blessing to participate in this teaching for six years. The material we used was provided by Luther Rice College & Seminary. We each enhanced the material with personal insights and experiences.

As I gave the choice some thought, discipleship became my selection. When I reasoned about the choice, it became clear that both missions and evangelism were performed by disciples. Plus, I was more comfortable with discipleship since I am a disciple. And I wanted to learn all I could about my role as a disciple.

It was a wonderful blessing to me to be able to encourage these Indian brothers in Christ. Especially, I felt inclined to help them because they are always swimming upstream to faithfully serve our wonderful Savior and Lord in a less than receptive place. They pay a high price to live for Christ on this earth. As I studied the material, one thing I learned was that a true disciple of Christ is expected to always be in the process of maturation. For certain, this truth and this challenge would help in the process of my own spiritual growth. I knew that I would have to rely on God's power and leading to teach discipleship well to these devoted fellow disciples.

Studying the prepared material, the Lord increased my passion for discipleship. I began to fully understand what God's plan was originally, and still is, for every generation of disciples! That is for each generation to faithfully fulfill the role as grateful disciples and to develop the next generation of disciples. If we do this, God's church will always be growing in numbers and influence. But it cannot be optional, or the results will be disastrous. God's people must grow, must be disciples, and must do what disciples do.

As I have thought back about the whole matter of discipleship, I have reached a conclusion: we too often relate discipleship with the original group of disciples, and it is so easy to overlook the role of every saved believer (you and me)! Jesus has saved you and me to do the same thing the original disciples did—to share the great blessings of salvation and liberty and to obediently demonstrate Christ-like behavior twenty-four-seven. In other words, every believer is to be a disciple and is to share the gospel and thereby grow and strengthen the church.

With that thought in mind, I will share a portion of the information prepared by Luther Rice College & Seminary. Before I do so, I will share this truth from the material. It so grabbed me when I read it for the first time. "Discipleship is not an option for the church; it is the main work of the church! The neglect of genuine discipleship throughout church history has contributed greatly to the nonfulfillment of the Great Commission!" Amen and Amen!

Below are some more of the biblical truths and principles of discipleship that I had the blessed privilege to share with hungry Christian pastors.

The command from Jesus Himself for the church to make disciples is crystal clear in the New Testament. In fact, the action commanded in the Great Commission in Matthew 28:18–20 (NIV) is to "make disciples of all nations by going, baptizing, and teaching them to obey scripture."

I noticed here that Jesus did not say go and make converts or even church members. To convert involves a decision, whereas being a true disciple involves a lifelong developmental process of "conforming to the image of His Son" (Romans 8:29, KJV). Discipleship is a process of humbling and seeking His Will consistently rather than being content with minimal believer effort.

I am convinced one of the worst things that can happen to anyone is:

» To know about Jesus but to not know Him personally.

» And to not realize their still lost condition.

» And to not have His Holy Spirit to empower them.

If I do know Him, then I need to ask honestly this most important question: Is He truly my Lord? *Will I follow Him unconditionally?*

The New Testament church did obey the Great Commission, and the results were phenomenal. The church expanded, and believers were established and encouraged in their faith. How often did God add to the church? "And the Lord added to the church *daily* those who were being saved" (Acts 2:47b, NKJV). How sobering and sad it is to know that today in America, the great majority of our churches are in decline. The future of every church depends on the body of believers *owning discipleship*. That is an absolute truth. The operating orders of Christ to the church are clear. The challenge is for us to respond in committed obedience. Hopefully, we will heartily agree with what St. Ignatius said hundreds of years ago: "It is not hard to obey when we love the One whom we obey." The Bible also tells us, "To obey is better than sacrifice" (1 Samuel 15:22, KJV).

Just what is a disciple by definition?

"A disciple is a *committed follower, submitted servant*, and a *student learner of Jesus Christ*. A true disciple is one who has come to Jesus as <u>Savior</u> and come to Jesus as *Lord* and *Master to follow Christ in obedience and learn from Christ, his teacher*."[2] Even more accurately, a disciple is defined as "one who has committed himself to become like Christ in character and conduct."[3] The question is, "How so, and by what means?" John 3:30 (ESV) holds our answer: "He, Jesus, must increase, but I must decrease."

"When you and I yield to the leading of the Holy Spirit, He will always point toward and glorify Jesus with our lives" (John 16:14, NKJV). Just as a drunken person acts foolishly, a Spirit-filled person will always reflect Christ.

"Discipleship is a way or direction of life. Jesus taught His disciples by sharing principles with them, practicing those principles before them by example, and having them personally participate. He expected something from them."[4] And I will add to that He expects no less from you and me today. This is *absolute truth*!

Jesus has called us to a life of consistency as His disciples, His representatives. He is the model for us: "Jesus Christ is the same yesterday, today and forever" (Hebrews, 13:8 NKJV). He has done His part well! Now, we must decide individually if we will now do ours. We have been saved for *faithful* discipleship. We have been given the Holy Spirit power to enable us to represent Jesus well. Remember, the Holy Spirit is the One powerful enough to raise a dead Christ. No one else can do what He has saved each of

2    Educational material produced by Luther Rice College & Seminary, 3038 Evans Mill Road, Lithonia, GA 30038
3    Luther Rice College & Seminary material
4    Luther Rice College & Seminary material

us personally to do, to do our part. There are people near each of us who may well miss heaven, and the joy of salvation, if we do not accept our responsibility as a forgiven, empowered, obedient disciple.

You may well be thinking that we can never live up to the life Jesus lived before man on earth. We must not forget the precious gift He sends to every born-again believer. Why does He send the promised Holy Spirit? He sends Him that we might live with God's Power and produce the promised fruit of the Spirit: love, joy, peace, patience, kindness, goodness, faithfulness, gentleness, and self-control. We will then display a life that clearly points to our Savior. He has empowered anyone who desires to obey and represent Christ to do so with the mighty power of God's Holy Spirit. These attributes displayed in a life open doors for that obedient person to share the gospel confidently.

Charles Stanley, one of Americas most faithful and respected preachers, in the September 2017 issue of *From the Pastor's Heart*, wrote, "Disciples are Christians, but not everyone who attends church is a disciple. It is important enough to repeat! Those who simply listen to sermons without applying what they learn or sharing their faith are not disciples. A true disciple hungers for Christ and His Word, and as a result, grows in his or her Christian life." He goes on to say, "Although Jesus doesn't call us to literally give up everything we own, we must recognize that God is the owner of all we possess, and we are just the caretakers. Therefore, we should hold everything loosely. A true disciple of Christ walks through life with a detachment from the things of this world in order to become fully attached to Christ as a practicing disciple."

Nobody said becoming a faithful, effective disciple of our blessed Savior is easy. The world, with all its allurement, pulls hard on every one of us. However, the success of the church is determined by those who are willing to crown Jesus as Lord and follow Him in complete active faith, just like the original disciples. Is the success of the church important enough for you and me to obey the One who gave His very life to set us free?

I am convinced the enemies of God and God's people become enraged and terrified when that Christian convert begins to move from their salvation experience on an increasing quest (or journey) of *obedience* as a fully committed disciple of the Master. "That convert will have learned there is a resident power of God in their life, and they have begun a life with that power by glorifying God through perfect obedience. Then joy and peace will be the overflow from the intimacy that follows worship, submission, and obedience in *discipleship*."[5] Every disciple can and will then know God's perfect will carried out in obedience, which will produce perfect peace in our lives. What a great blessing awaits God's obedient disciples.

One of the greatest failings of the American Church today is failing to effectively *disciple new believers with passion and a great sense of urgency.* Why is that true? Probably because we are too interested and distracted by worldly things. I believe God is nudging at the church to align with His word and make a greater impact through discipleship. Discipleship requires undeniably irreversibly yielding our lives to Him because we want to serve Him more than we want to serve ourselves. Is discipling new believers really that important? What would our country and our world look like today if every believer became a practicing disciple as well as a proclaiming disciple? Wow! As goes Christianity, so goes the world.

Jesus made certain that man would always be able to sustain and grow His church. It is called faithful discipleship. Anyone who really wants to and decides to, can. We are made in the image of our Creator and empowered by the same Holy Spirit. That Holy Spirit so filled the original disciples that they were willing to give their lives in order that you and I today might enjoy true life in the care of our Savior and follow their exemplary discipleship. And every generation of believers is called to go and make disciples.

In John, Chapter 17, as Jesus neared the horrible crucifixion and separation from the Father, Jesus reveals how much He loves his disciples. He prayed earnestly for them, and praise God, He also prayed for you and me! He said in that prayer, "Neither pray I for these alone [the original disciples] but for them also which shall believe on me through their word" (John 17:20, KJV).

5        Educational material produced by Luther Rice College & Seminary, 3038 Evans Mill Road, Lithonia, GA 30038

Here He is praying for you and me and every other Christian. Do you believe God the Father heard his obedient sinless Son's prayer? No question about it!

Jesus put prayer on deposit as recorded above for us (you and me) to be faithful and unified until we are with Him in glory. What a wonderful blessing—with expectations! He has certainly done more than His part. The real penetrating question is, am I grateful enough to become an empowered disciple, faithfully doing the most important work in the world? That important work is representing Jesus well, as full-time grateful disciples, confidently making Him known at every opportunity and consistently seeking those opportunities.

Yes, people can be obedient and do what Jesus saved us to do on this earth before we go to our heavenly home—go and make disciples! People can do just that because Jesus prayed for God the Father, through the Holy Spirit's power, to help us do so! The most reassuring truth we can know is our gracious God would never call us to this most significant work to fail. God supplies the supernatural power, the Difference-Maker, to allow us to know that people can go and make disciples, and His powerful Holy Spirit leads the way. What a precious privilege to be the voice and see captives set free!

One of my most favorite Bible promises is, "Where the Spirit of the Lord is, there is liberty" (2 Corinthians 3:17, KJV). We are protected from Satan's influence, loosened from his captivity, and we are empowered to powerfully and effectively: "*Go* and *make disciples.*"

Discipleship involves obedience, worship, prayer, Bible study, participation in mission efforts, and constantly looking for opportunities to share the gospel with lost and hurting people. It requires some committed time, and we must decide if we are grateful enough to give the time He deserves.

Another important reason sharing the gospel regularly is so important is that as we do so, it keeps awareness of God's amazing grace ever before us. As this occurs, our desire to honor and obey Him is ever increasing.

Sometimes, perhaps when fatigued, we might wonder, "Am I not already doing my part?" But the real question we need to be asking is, "Lord, are You pleased with the part I am doing?"

If our gospel will change the world, and we know it will, it must first awaken and change us. That awakening and change will bring a greater sense of urgency to the point of determined Lordship. We will be determined to crown Jesus Lord and follow Him, up close like Peter after Pentecost, as a faithful empowered disciple!

Faithful, Spirit-filled disciples who share the gospel truth make converts who will become, over time, faithful disciples themselves. They then, out of gratitude for God's grace, salvation, and resultant peace, will go and repeat the process!

God has saved us for much more than going to church and going to heaven. God has saved us for going to make disciples, but...

The first place we must go is to the cross.

# CHAPTER 21

# Wisdom's Value

When you hear the word *wise*, what do you most often think about? In my own case, I think about someone who, when asked, can always give sound, trustworthy advice. Also, a wise person is someone we can look to for assistance in decision-making. It's someone in whom we can have confidence.

Generally, most wise people have accumulated their wisdom through numerous observations and experiences over a long period of time, though not always. Remember, God is the provider of perfect wisdom. That, God being the provider, then may provoke a question on the part of the reader. Do you mean wisdom can be given by God just for the asking? Yes, I firmly believe God's Word provides the answers to all our questions. So let's see what it says about this one, wisdom!

King David had a son, Solomon, who became King when he was very young. It is speculated that he was between fourteen and sixteen years of age. He was inexperienced but intelligent enough to know that he within himself was not capable of ruling over such a great people.

Hear the sincere and wise prayer as recorded in 1 Kings 4:29 (KJV), which Solomon prayed,

*And now, O Lord my God, thou hast made thy servant king instead of David my father: and I am but a little child: I know not how to go out or come in. And Thy servant is in the midst of thy people which thou hast chosen, a great people, that cannot be numbered or counted for the multitude. Give therefore, Thy servant an understanding heart to judge thy people, that I may discern between good and bad: for who is able to judge thy people, this thy so great a people?*

What Solomon said pleased the Lord:

*And God said unto him, Because thou hast asked this thing, and hast not asked for thyself long life; neither hast thou asked for riches for thyself, nor hast thou asked for the life of thine enemies; but hast asked for thyself understanding to discern judgment; Behold, I have done according to thy words: lo, I have given thee a wise and understanding heart; so that there was none like thee before thee, neither after thee, shall any arise like unto thee. And I have also given thee that which thou hast not asked, both riches, and honor: so that there shall not be any among the kings like unto thee all thy days.*

Solomon awoke, and God had spoken to him through a dream. God speaks to us today through His Word, which Solomon did not have completely, as you and I have today. The New Testament had not been written because Christ had not come to earth yet.

God honored Solomon's request for wisdom to judge the people well, and he ruled at a time of great peace and prosperity. My, how we need our elected officials to learn from this, to seek wisdom, and do likewise. If they did so, many more would be recognized as statesmen rather than vacillating politicians.

"And God gave Solomon wisdom and understanding exceeding much, and largeness of heart, even as the sand that is on the seashore" (1 Kings 4:39, KJV). "And there came of all peoples to hear the wisdom of Solomon, from all kings of the earth which had heard of his wisdom" (1 Kings 4:34, KJV).

God can always be trusted. Solomon lacked wisdom but knew he needed wisdom to benefit his people, and God graciously provided. His wish was granted by an all-knowing Father.

During that period of time, Solomon searched the world to determine what was important and what was not important under the sun. "Under the sun" was the term he used for the things of the world. Solomon had a wonderful mind, and he loved learning and understanding more and more about God's creation. As a result of all of his seeking to know truth and to know as much as he could about our universe, he reached some clear conclusions which are valuable for you and me. They are recorded in the book of Ecclesiastes.

In Ecclesiastes 12:8 (KJV), we read, "Vanity of vanities, saith the preacher, all is vanity." What does this say to you and me? It says life is without purpose, meaningless, and empty if we are just living for the here and now!

He also speaks to perspective on education. "And further by these, my son be admonished: of making many books, there is no end, and much study is a weariness of the flesh" (Ecclesiastes 12:12, KJV). Solomon certainly was not against education, but he knew learning alone was not the answer to life. Real education occurs as we study and have the illumination by God's Holy Spirit to assist our understanding and application of what we learn.

Solomon speaks so profoundly to our youth: "Remember now thy Creator in the days of thy youth, while the evil days come not, nor the years draw nigh, when thou shalt say I have no pleasure in them" (Ecclesiastes 12:1, KJV). He knew the consequences of sin are always to be lived with and how difficult that could be. He also knew "regret" for sin is one of the most difficult things to live with as well. There is another reason He speaks to young people because they still have a lifetime in which to honor God in service. They can avoid wasted years. Oh, how I personally wish I could relive the wasted spiritual years before I surrendered to His forgiveness! I cannot help but think about how many more people I could have helped know "The Way, The Truth, and The Life" (John 14:6b, KJV), if I had surrendered my life earlier. Solomon also knew that the longer a person lives in sin, the harder it becomes to humble oneself and repent.

What else did this most wise one have to say of benefit to you and me? After a lifetime of study and experimentation, he recorded this invaluable conclusion and clear directive! "Let us hear the conclusion of the whole matter, fear God, and keep His Commandments, for this is the whole duty of man" (Ecclesiastes 12:13, KJV). He is saying, hear the most important thing for you and me. It is to worship, revere, and obey God. Solomon expressed this word from God as an absolute! "And keep His commandments" (verse 13). However, in order to keep them, we must know them (read His word), and we must have a determined desire (out of gratitude for His grace) to keep them. We must ask God to give us a craving desire to know, love, and keep His Word. Note: "*Godliness,*" which is worshipping and revering and obeying God, is in direct opposition to "*selfishness,*" which is often demonstrated by uncaringly living to satisfy one's own desires and simply to please oneself. The less Godly one is, the more selfish, and vice versa; the Godlier someone is, the less selfish that person will be.

How much are people willing to pay professional counselors, psychologists, and experts in return for advice today? They often spend a great deal of money. Why? People are looking for answers and solutions, but often times looking for them from the wrong sources.

God, by way of Solomon, has given us the absolute best answers we could ever possibly receive, and they are free. These answers lead to a life of peace, fulfillment, and contentment. And an eternity in the presence of our Blessed Savior.

We read about Solomon's wisdom, that ancient figure in biblical history. No question, he was wise, but how about you and me? Don't we need wisdom to navigate through the treacherous waters of a sinful world? Of course, we do, and our Lord knew that long ago. That is why He promises in the book of James 1:5 (KJV), "If any of you lack wisdom, let him ask of God, that gives to all men liberally and upbraideth not; and it shall be given him." (God won't put you down for asking.) "But let him ask in faith, nothing wavering. He that wavereth is like a wave of the sea driven with the wind and tossed" (James 1:5–6, KJV). Faith has the right answers. And wisdom is free to everyone.

You may, however, be saying that obeying those commandments is far more difficult and challenging than you can handle. I understand this. It is an honest response. The great news is our Savior has taken care of that! Philippians 4:19 (KJV) has our answer. He will provide all we need: "But my God shall supply all your needs according to His riches in glory by Christ Jesus!" He has kept that promise. All we have to do is desire and claim His blessings as we apply His wise teachings in our lives. It is *through our obedience* that God shows and teaches us to discern good and evil—then we can, with His help, live wisely and righteously.

# CHAPTER 22

# Prayer: Essential or Optional?

If we trust God's Word as a book of absolute truth, let's look at what it reveals to us about the question above.

Jesus, the perfect, sinless Son of God, has said over and over in the gospels, "I have come down from heaven not to do my own will, but the will of Him who sent me" (John 6:38 KJV). Jesus realized fully if He was going to be able to do God's perfect will that He must stay in prayer with the Father. He had to stay connected!

Before we go any farther, let's look at the parallel in the lives of every believer. In 1 Thessalonians 5:17–18 (NAS), God's Spirit gave the apostle Paul this critical truth for every believer: "Pray without ceasing. In everything give thanks, for this is the will of God for you in Christ Jesus." This doctrine does not mean praying twenty-four-seven, but being faithful, persistent, and consistent in believing prayer. If I am going to honor God faithfully, my prayer life must be without interruption. In view of the busyness of our world today, it appears that prayer has been relegated to a last resort rather than a wonderful first opportunity. All too often, creature comforts, pleasurable events, and other worldly attractions can leave us wearied to the point prayer is neglected.

What does prayer always say? "Lord, I believe in you and your will and direction for my life!" What does not praying consistently say? "Perhaps that prayer is not all that important."

God's Word promises in Psalm 37:23 (KJV) that "The steps of a good man (righteous by the blood of Christ) are ordered by the Lord." All we have to do is to rely on God's Spirit, as we spend time in prayer to reveal to us day by day God's plan for us. However, without prayer, we will struggle to honor our Lord.

As we may remember from the Bible, in the time of the temple worship, only the High Priest could make sacrifices for the people. No person could appeal to God on their own.

But Jesus came, and He was tempted by Satan, yet He resisted that enemy of God and man. Jesus lived as a man, just like you and I, in order to know what man faces and in order for Him to become our great High Priest.

Please read this slowly, carefully, and gratefully: Now our Savior sits at the right hand of the Father. He has finished His work on earth. Jesus makes intersession continuously for us, God's saved children. He is the only sinless One who is worthy and acceptable to intercede for us. But if I do not have a personal relationship with Jesus, based on confession of my sin and His forgiveness, my prayers will never be heard by God the Father. The Bible is absolutely clear on that. Jesus is the voice that God, the Father, hears when we pray.

Let me take this one step farther. It is impossible to imagine that anyone could think that when Jesus, the obedient Son, intercedes for us, that God the Father does not hear us, and consequently, responds and answers our prayers in whatever way is best for us. We must not forget God knows the future and we do not.

When Jesus walked on this earth, He showed us clearly how important prayer is. Luke 6:12 (NKJV) is just one example: "Now it came to pass in those days that He went out to the mountain to pray and continued all night in prayer to God." That night He was praying about which disciples to choose. Did He not choose well? We now know why He chose well! But can you conceive of praying all night? What a great One to be interceding as your High Priest and mine and what a reminder, also, that we have such a Great High Priest always waiting to hear from us, the grateful children of God.

John 17 (NKJV) gives us the details of what Jesus prayed for His disciples (including you and me) the night before His bloody crucifixion. His concern was more about others than about Himself, and He talked with the Father on our behalf. He specifically prayed that God, the Father, by the Holy Spirit "not take them out of the world, but that He should keep them from the evil one" (see verse 15). Jesus thereby literally put prayer "on deposit" for you and me.

Have you ever thought we could do the same for others? Just suppose someone is terminally ill and they are aware they are going to pass away. That sick person could store up prayers for their loved ones. Suppose also that "someone" is the parent of a wayward, lost, rebellious child. That parent, if they are a Christian, can pray in Jesus' name for God's Spirit to work on that child even after that parent has passed away. That parent can pray for God's Spirit, in His convicting way, to work in the life of the lost child every day until the child is hopefully saved. What a blessed privilege our great High Priest makes available to us.

Again, we see in John chapter 17 Jesus praying for the unity of His disciples, and for you and me, as well as believers. He prayed that we would be unified. We have the Holy Spirit resident in us to strengthen and ensure that we stay unified as His obedient disciples.

It should touch our hearts that when Jesus was facing the most horrific, shameful death known to man, that He had you and me on His mind. There is a beautiful song that reminds us of that most touching and sacred time in Jesus' life. The title of the song is "When He Was on the Cross, I was on His Mind." What a Savior!

I refer again to that passage in 1 Thessalonians 5:16–17 (KJV), which instructs us in regard to prayer. It says, "Rejoice always, *pray without ceasing*. In everything give thanks for this is the will of God." God always means what He says. It is convincing here that He meant for us to stay in a constant state of communication with our Savior. After all, once we are saved, we are to represent Him full time. Besides, it is hard to give in to sin when we have just gotten off our knees in touch with our redeemer! God always hears us when we pray sincerely in Jesus' name!

I realize we live in a very attractive, seductive, and consuming world, a place so tempting and enticing. Every day there is something new and tempting that we don't want to miss—the most current version of anything. Our minds are almost working overtime to keep up with every new fashion, tech feature or version, entertainment venue, and so on. But, how about time for the One who paid our sin debt and made a way back to God's original perfect plan for mankind? In the end, what really matters? In the end, all those attractions will be nothing more than wood, hay, and stubble. When we are desperately pleading for the continued life (healing) of a seriously ill loved one, can we confidently show up as a practiced prayer warrior or a half-committed follower "afar off" like Peter before Pentecost? That is a serious question Christians should often give serious consideration to.

We have access to the Father, through the Son, and only through the Son. Charles Stanley, in *Daily Devotion*, June 2015, said this so well. "Understanding our position (with Jesus as our High Priest) should give us confidence and boldness as we humbly ask and expectantly look for God's awesome answers." In other words, we can have absolute certainty when we pray in the only name that matters, the name of Jesus. We can know He has made a way for us to be heard.

Before reading the Bible, we should always pray, and our prayer should be for:

>> God by His Spirit to help me to understand what I am reading.

>> God's strength to apply His Word.

>> We be guided to pray for and to ask for what is God's will.

When I was privileged to be teaching discipleship to Christian pastors gathered from all of India, I had a very humbling experience. At the morning break, four or five pastors approached me, and one of them humbly asked, "Mr. Paul, can you teach us how to pray better?" I had never been asked this before, and it humbled me that these people who had risked literally everything, including their very lives, to make Jesus Lord, would be so determined to be obedient in prayer.

I thought about this serious question for several minutes. I then reassured them, "Because you want to *pray better*, the Holy Spirit within you will help you." Then I gave them the thoughts that the Lord had given me:

» Ask the Holy Spirit first to clear your mind of any other thoughts or distractions and the cares of the day, as your first prayer request. We all know Jesus deserves our full focus.

» Read your Bible first thing in the morning, if possible. It has always made my prayer life more fulfilling when I read the Book of Truth first.

» As you know, God loves "first fruits," not leftovers. If at all possible, pray right after you have read the Bible, and God can and will then guide your prayer and shape your day.

You will then, during the day, have many more opportunities to pray about many different but important matters.

Over a lifetime, I have come to realize one of the least understood things about prayer is while we are praying, we are *spending time completely focused on our Lord And Savior.* That in and of itself is enough reason for all of God's people to make prayer a necessity—and consequently, pray more!

When we really think about how much we each owe our Savior and how much our churches need renewal, it is clear there is indeed a real need for a prayer awakening. It is inspiring to think about what a great awakening would occur if all God's people chose to humble ourselves, pray and believe, and then expect the reality of God's promise in 2 Chronicles 7:14 (NKJV): "If My people, who are called by My name will humble themselves, and pray and seek My face and will turn from their wicked (worldly) ways, then will I hear from heaven and will forgive their sin and heal their land." Oh, how very much our country desperately needs healing! In essence, this is a promise that if we truly give Him first place, He will respond in a marvelous way!

There is great power in prayer, which I can attest to in many ways. Also, there is one occurrence that will always be prevalent in my mind, which is why I am a Christian today because:

» Someone I respected and admired invited me to church.

» Many older ladies, otherwise known as "prayer warriors," had been praying for me and others, by name, for months, and some had been praying for years.

» The Holy Spirit enabled and honored their prayers.

» The church believed in God's power and organized a revival, renewal efforts. The leaders in that church made time for God's business. After all, who gives each of us twenty-four hours a day?

Prayer is therapeutic. Never have I felt better or freer than when I have prayed with an uncluttered mind and spent time with my Savior. "Where the Spirit of the Lord is, there is liberty" (2 Corinthians 3:17, KJV).

Don't we always want to spend more and more time with our best friend? If He is not our best friend, He certainly is the One whom we are most indebted to, so He should be our best friend.

This is a certain truth—the more time we spend in His Word and especially in prayer, the better we will know Him, and the better we know Him, the more we will love Him, and the more we love Him, the more our lives will reflect Him, and others will want to know Him also.

Once again: "Pray without ceasing" (1 Thessalonians 5:17, KJV). That is a blessed instruction from God. In other words, be in a state of practicing His presence. That is a discipline every Christian should be determined to master. When we pray, we are in His presence, and we should, each and every one of us, desire prayer time each day to become the norm rather than the exception. Please know that Satan will fight us all the way. But the battle was won long ago and celebrated with an empty tomb.

When we are willing to be objective and honest about our prayer life, we need to look at Jesus as our role model. Luke chapter 22 tells us Jesus and His disciples had come to the Mount of Olives. Verses 40–45 (NKJV) give us the reality of that occurrence. "When He came to the place He said to them; pray that you may not enter into temptation." He was withdrawn from them about a stone's throw, and He knelt down and prayed, saying, "Father, if it is your will, take this cup away from Me; nevertheless, not My will, but yours be done. Then an angel appeared to Him from heaven, strengthening Him, and being in agony, He prayed more earnestly. Then His sweat became like great drops of blood falling down to the ground."

Here we see the fervency of Jesus' prayer. We also see the angelic ministry from the Father. Jesus so wanted to know His Father was there, just like you and I today want that precious sense of peace that only Jesus' presence can bring.

Know this. If Satan can continue to defeat us (God's people) in our prayer life, he can and will defeat us in intimacy and obedience to God's wonderful will for our life. However, a practiced, consistent prayer life will illuminate God's Word. Then God's resident Holy Spirit will enable us to be faithful and live not with self-confidence, but God-confidence—victoriously!

Here's the bottom line. Our Lord gives each of us twenty-four hours every single day. He has entrusted the stewardship of time to each of us. He also gives us complete freedom in choosing how we will spend that time. So, we are back to the title question, *Is prayer essential or optional?*

The answer depends upon what you or I want in life. If we can claim authentic identity as a child of God, we should desire more and more time in the presence of our Savior. We can then hear more profoundly the peace He promises in Psalm 85:8 (NKJV), "I will hear what God the Lord will speak, for He will speak peace to His people."

The stewardship of time is a challenge for all of us today in a frenzied, distressed, and demanding world. If we want more time with the One who has set us free, we simply need to ask Him to help us do so. In His Word, He tells us over and over to *bring our needs to Him.* That includes finding more time to spend with Him in prayer. We must never forget He loves each one of us like an only child, and He gives us, supernaturally, His undivided attention. All we have to do is ask in believing faith for Him to help us make prayer a lasting priority in our lives and to help us make ample time for same every day.

Oh yes, Satan will do his best to keep us occupied with worldly trivia, but we need to remember, "Greater is He that is in you, than he that is in the world" (1 John 4:4, KJV).

If we are to have the victory over Satan in our life that Jesus died for, we must desire, seek, and accept nothing less than more intimate time with our Savior in prayer. If our churches are ever to become powerful in influence again, God's people, individually, must spend much more time daily with Him in prayer.

*Prayer—essential or optional?*

*Essential, if Jesus is truly my lord!*

God's desire for every believer is that we look forward to our prayer time to become the most anticipated time of our day. That is God's perfect will for all of us, His children.

Over the years, I have learned how essential reading and the study of God's Word are. It is a worthy thing to become a faithful scholar of God's Word. However, becoming a prayer warrior is equally important! Every Christian in a world that has truly lost its way needs to be determined to draw aside. We need that quiet, serious time in touch with our Savior and Redeemer. Satan and the world want to interfere because "Be still and know that I am God" is a quiet time when we are *reassured* and *energized* as we spend calming time in His precious, powerful presence.

As God's children, we must never forget prayerlessness most often leads to powerlessness. Are we grateful enough for God's grace to spend more and more time in prayer with Him?

# CHAPTER 23

# Family—God's Watchcare

God has made this promise in His Word: "I know the thoughts I have toward you, to prosper you and not to harm you" (Jeremiah 29:11a, NKJV). A paraphrase for this scripture is that I want only the very best for you, my special one.

God essentially tells us in His word, even though you were born in sin (iniquity) and the price of sin is death, I still came to set you free from that penalty of death and sin. Because sin always results in death, I became your substitute, and I love you too much to not provide a way to life everlasting and peace for you. I want you to be with me! My plan and will for you are to live a life that produces love, joy, peace, patience, kindness, goodness, faithfulness, gentleness, and self-control (the fruits of My Spirit Galatians 5:22, NASV). You have never been out of My Thoughts. You have never been forgotten or left to your own devices. You have always been under My gracious watchcare. These are words God could even audibly speak to us since we already know they are true. He assures us countless times in His Word.

Until we all get to heaven and become glorified, we will never be aware of what all God has protected us from or has kept us from. I am convinced, once we have that awareness, we will worship our deliverer and protector as never before when we finally get home and are glorified! We may never know what all Satan would have done to torment and destroy us apart from the gracious watchcare of our Savior and Lord.

Life can be challenging and no more so than when lives of our loved ones teeter on the brink between life and death. I know this from personal experiences. Each story that follows from our family's history can teach some of these valuable truths. All that follow are unforgettable, some as if they only occurred yesterday. But God never promised that life would be easy. In fact, the Bible says in John 16:33a (NLTV), "Here on earth you will have many trials and sorrows." James 1:12 (BSB) also states, "Blessed is the man who perseveres under trial, because when he has stood the test, he will receive the crown of life that God has promised to those who love Him." It is not a question of "if we will face these challenges," but "when and how we will handle them when they come." Again, from personal experience, threatening events tax us to our limit but hopefully, by sharing some of my family's most challenging times, some important and helpful truths will emerge. Most certainly, God's watchcare enabled Lynette and me not only to get through them but to have our faith strengthened in the process.

Two of those severe challenges, Bo's threatening throat crisis and the dangerous Brooklyn trucking situation I survived, already have been shared with you in other chapters. We, to this day, believe Bo's experience was a miracle from God and answered prayers of so very many devoted believers in our great church. Other challenges that follow were just as threatening. That "it could have been so much worse" will always be the story when we reflect on "if not for God's grace and watchcare." What a blessing that our gracious Lord and Savior remarkably and almost miraculously watched over our family. It can be so easy to take for granted His tender care for us and our loved ones.

## Sandra's ARDS

Several years ago, our middle daughter, Sandra, who has now gone to be with the Lord, had pneumonia which developed into very serious lung disease, acute respiratory distress syndrome (ARDS). It had become very critical since fluid had actually leaked out into her chest cavity and was pressing on her lungs. She had been in the hospital for over three weeks, and she was becoming more critical each day while putting on forty pounds of fluid as well. Sandra's prognosis was not good, for she was also struggling with sepsis. In addition, she had been on a ventilator for almost three weeks, and now doctors were having discussions of a tracheotomy. As we understood it, this was almost a last resort to survival. With sepsis, ARDS, and pneumonia,

Sandra was very grave. A disease specialist was called in to grow cultures to try to determine a more targeted treatment.

We were in a praying church and a wonderful Sunday school class, and the support was extraordinary.

»   The deacons had come to the hospital, anointed her with oil, and laid hands on her.

»   More than forty members of our Sunday school class secured a room at the hospital in which to pray so that the large group could all pray together with our family.

»   Lynette was led to fast for an extended period, and our entire family was refocused and strengthened.

»   All of this was a powerful witness to others who were not of the faith.

»   One of our prayers was that this event would have great spiritual impact and that prayer was demonstrably answered.

Following these many efforts of prayer, something extraordinary happened. Sandra's doctor was going away for the weekend and gave final instructions relative to the setting of the ventilator. I do not understand all of this, but I do know Sandra was almost (in appearance) in a coma, and it was beyond heartbreaking! The relief doctor for the weekend reset the ventilator, and in a matter of hours, Sandra was sitting up in bed. It was almost miraculous. Do you think God intervened? You guessed it—He most certainly did. We were beyond grateful and excited. However, on Monday morning, her regular doctor returned and reset the ventilator to the previous settings. Fortunately, one of the nurses took Lynette aside and whispered, "You need to change doctors." I was not aware of this conversation, for I had not gone back to the hospital yet. But as I was on my way there, one of our dearest and most respected friends called on my cell phone and told me, "Paul, you need to change doctors, and you should request so-and-so." The recommended named doctor was the very same one the nurse had given Lynette. Wow, what a coincidence you may be thinking! No, it was not a coincidence! It was another instance of divine watchcare and answered prayer. As a result, we did indeed change doctors, and the turnaround in Sandra's condition almost seemed absolutely too good to be true. As the new doctor began to change the treatments, as well as the settings on the ventilator, her response was almost unbelievable. In just a short while, she was fully awake and asking for her breakfast. Sandra, miraculously, in a few days, was well enough to be dismissed.

It would be impossible to describe the effects our Christian friends and church brothers and sisters had on us. God's people prayed hard, and they so demonstrated the love of and faith in Christ by how they comforted us, and by so doing, they kept our faith strong, and God was greatly glorified. Often, I have thought how sad it is that people who do not have a church family who loves them enough to pray earnestly for God's divine watchcare are missing such a wonderful blessing. That wonderful Monday morning advice from two totally separate and unconnected sources was another example of "seldom early, but never late." How gracious and spectacular is the watchcare of our Lord!

## Please Call Our Preacher

One morning when our daughter, Edwina, was in her early twenties and headed to work, she began to feel very sick with her body not feeling normal, and she had an unusually bad stiff neck, so she headed to the doctor instead. Arriving at the doctor, he ran a urinalysis test and determined she had a kidney infection and prescribed an antibiotic. She went home and started taking the antibiotic as directed but continued to feel worse and worse. By that evening, her fever was very concerning/high. Lynette was at her home helping with the baby, so Lynette, Edwina, and Edwina's husband discussed her condition and decided perhaps the prescription just hadn't had an adequate amount of time yet to start helping. The following day Edwina continued to feel more and more sick as the day progressed, experiencing vomiting, diarrhea, and intense pain in her back, not to mention the fever climbing even higher. It had gotten late in the day, and doctors' offices were closed. They called a family nurse who suggested putting her in an ice bath which still didn't help the fever much. It was another sleepless night for all of them. By the following morning, Edwina was so sick she was asking her mom to please call the family preacher to come, fearing she was truly dying. At this point, they decided to go to the ER, and upon arrival, her temp was 106.7!

Without detailing all of the next steps, Edwina was transferred to a better and larger hospital and admitted. They did tests and determined she didn't just have a kidney infection but a kidney abscess as well. Consequently, she was put on a strong antibiotic IV and kept in the hospital on the IV for three weeks, getting all the infection cleared up and signifying how awfully sick she was.

As we later learned, a kidney abscess is much more dangerous, and quick care is critical. This is not to blame her doctor for misdiagnosing her condition as a kidney infection, for a kidney abscess can easily be missed without an X-ray or scan since the symptoms are similar to a kidney infection, plus kidney abscesses are not very common.

We are to this day very thankful God healed Edwina without permanent kidney damage requiring dialysis or worse. Once again, God healed and protected her in her serious sick condition with His precious watchcare.

## Lynette's Terrifying Diagnosis

In 2000 Lynette had a sudden drop in hemoglobin. After a significant number of doctor visits and tests, her doctor gave her the diagnosis.

As I was waiting for our pilot to hanger the plane at the airport in Columbia, South Carolina, after returning from a trip to Orlando, I called home to see how things were. That is when I was told by one of the children, "The doctor believes Mama has pancreatic cancer." Shocked, I never expected to hear the dreaded "C" word, but nevertheless, it was now a part of our lives.

At that time, I knew very little about pancreatic cancer, so my next step was to seek what info I could from WebMD and the internet. What I read was almost breathtaking! The articles read that the average life span of a pancreatic cancer patient from the time of diagnosis to death is approximately six months. I will never ever forget how my world was suddenly shattered by such horrific information. It was impossible for me to even conceive of this. My strong, wonderful helpmate, who had so protected our home while I endeavored diligently in the workplace, may now have cancer. How could she be terminally ill with six months or less to live? This was overwhelming. This also occurred at a time when I was considering early retirement in just a few months so that she and I might do the short-term missions work God had given us both a passion for.

Her doctor had mentioned a couple of surgery options, depending on what he might find when he got into the surgery, one being Whipple. We began to read and study to learn all we could about the Whipple operating procedure used often when the pancreas is operated on. The Whipple procedure consisted of taking a section of connecting tissue from all other organs to the adjacent pancreas and removing a portion. The section left would be reattached to the pancreas after it had been surgically repaired. Clearly, this was major surgery! While I truly knew God would watch over us, I was still grieved and terrified at what the outcome could be, as well as what my precious one would have to go through. We had prayed much, but this was huge.

Quickly, we began the search for a surgeon who was better experienced in doing these extremely complicated operations, but though we found one, for some reason, Lynette was not confident that this surgeon was God's will for her surgery. She constantly said, "I have confidence in my present doctor." When I had inquired of him as to how many surgeries of this kind he had performed, the answer was three! Oh, how I was becoming more and more anxious and trying every day to persuade my loved one to "let's keep looking" for a more experienced surgeon, but to no avail!

I remember this as if it was yesterday. The night before the surgery, she and I finally reached a compromise in which I had suggested that when your doctor gets into the surgery and if it requires the Whipple, let's don't proceed. And then let's find the very best Whipple surgeon in the country, wherever that doctor may be. After she had finally reluctantly agreed, we decided we would tell the doctor of our decision in the morning.

The next morning, we arrived ready for the procedure. The prepping began. And continued. The doctor arrived, and wouldn't you guess when it came time for us to communicate her wishes, Lynette was zonked, already out of it, so that lot fell to me. As you can suspect, you could feel the tension in the air because the surgeon did not love this plan. Nonetheless, I felt a little better about the operation with this decision.

After the surgery was performed, the doctor came out to share what he had found, and this is what he said, "When I got in and near the pancreas, there was a plane of separation, and the pancreas appears to be cancer-free." We will have it biopsied downstairs to know for certain, but I feel good about it." It took four or five days to get the biopsy report, but it was worth the wait—no cancer. God's amazing protection was demonstrated once again.

There is an old saying that "Nothing is wonderful when you get used to it," but I must say this still feels really wonderful as I recall it. When you constantly are aware of the watchcare of our risen Lord, you realize this is too sacred and too wonderful to ever "get used to" or taken for granted. My beloved life partner is still doing well twenty-plus years later. Thank you, Lord.

## The Head-on In Georgia

Many years ago, while I was still employed at Carolina Freight, Bob Austell and two of my other great friends had decided to drive to Atlanta on a Saturday morning to buy a few suits from Walton Manufacturing. This was a local manufacturing company, and their outlet store sold directly to customers there in Walton. You could buy well-made, nice suits for half-price or less than the retail prices in North Carolina.

231

Bob was the driver. I sat in the shotgun seat, and the two others were in the back seat. We were nearing Walton, traveling on a two-lane road, and it had just started to drizzle slightly. As we were approaching a curve, a car traveling toward us from the opposite direction rounded the curve, apparently too fast or with slick tires. At any rate, the driver lost control and was moving directly into our lane. I expect we were traveling between fifty or sixty miles per hour and reflex time was minimal. There were two choices: leave the road, which was on a slight embankment, or hit head-on.

Little did I know that my good friend, Bob, had the presence of mind, in just an instant, to see what, if anything, would prevent leaving the road and avoiding the head-on collision. When he glanced, he saw a large utility pole directly in the path of the car, and it definitely would have severely crushed my front seat position if he had chosen that path. So he chose head-on—and it was just that! We were all banged up, but nothing broken or cut, just sore. The driver of the other car had leg and perhaps some other non-life-threatening injuries.

Stuck there in the middle of nowhere, we made our way into Bradbury's Country Store, where our showing up had seriously interrupted the Saturday morning checker game that was underway. Never will I forget how those watching would cheer for their player with urgings like, "Jump him, Uncle Jim." We waited there for six hours for several of our wives to drive down and pick us up.

I did not know it when it happened that Bob had been alert enough to evaluate the best path forward. He later told me about it, and I will always be grateful to him. There is no doubt about it; He saved my life that Saturday morning, and I am certain it was God's watchcare provision that gave him that ability to instantaneously make the right decision.

I love the promise He first made to the Hebrews but has since made to all who will receive the precious gift of forgiveness through Jesus Christ: "I will never leave nor forsake you" (Hebrews 13:5, NKJV). That is why His watchcare will never be anything but a *certainty*.

## The Monetary Gift to Bo

When our only son, Bo, was approximately two years old, his two older sisters loved to play with him. He was still sleeping in his crib. When he took a nap, they could not wait for him to awaken so they could play. It was a blessing to know how much our children loved each other and loved to occupy themselves and play together. Always we valued how kind our children were to each other. Willingness to share was never a problem with them. They never developed selfish habits to a fault. Almost. Anyway, they were so kind to each other that they did not require their mother or me to be around all the time, and it was a good thing. I was consistently working ten-to-twelve-hour days away from our home and, on some occasions, worked even longer hours. Lynette, eventually, as the mother of six, was working even longer days in the home. But we were young, strong, and happy with our young family.

Our parents loved these precious little grandchildren. They loved to give little gifts of candy and bubble gum and often would give the older girls a little pocket change. Equally, our children loved the attention and looked forward eagerly to grandparents' visits. Late one afternoon, either Paula or Melinda came into the kitchen and announced, "We shared our money with Bo." It was so kind of their grandparents to give them change and such a good thing to the girls that his sisters wanted Bo to have some money as well.

Immediately it registered in our minds this could be dangerous, and we went to the crib where we found Bo sitting up in the crib with watering eyes. It was evident he was attempting to swallow something that was too large for his small throat. It was too late, since the coin was already wedged in his little throat. Panic set in within both of us! We grabbed the other children and left them with my parents while we headed with Bo across town to the closest hospital twenty minutes away in Shelby, North Carolina. As we started out of my parents' driveway, Bo began to labor even more in his breathing. When we had driven about another five miles, he began to gasp and turn blue. It was evident we could not keep him alive until we reached the hospital.

However, being an instinctive mother, Lynette had the presence of mind to quickly turn him upside down and slap him firmly across his small back. It seems like a long time ago, but I remember it as if it was yesterday when the coin was projected out of his little mouth. How wonderful it is to remember how the gracious watchcare of our Father instantaneously led his mother to save his life. Amazing!

## The Unplanned Nudge

All of my father's relatives lived in the mountains of North Carolina. They lived primarily in Boone and the smaller surrounding towns. Mae Richardson was one of my father's cousins, and we spent many vacation weeks with her family. She had three sons, Jerry, David, and Don, and my, how I loved our playtime with them as a growing boy!

When our daughter Melinda was very small, Lynette, Melinda, my sister Ruth, and I decided we would go to the mountains for a few days. We left just as the sun was setting, and it was about a two and a half to three-hour drive. There was a steep mountain that had to be climbed on the way. It is called Blowing Rock Mountain, and because it was so steep, the road was filled with S curves. Sixty-plus years ago, that was the only way such steep mountains could be traversed with roads. As we traveled, a fog began to roll in. The later it became, the more it thickened, and by the time we reached the base of Blowing Rock Mountain, it was literally pea soup. We had not been too skeptical of the fog on the straighter highway, but now it was a different story. At times, we could not see more than twenty-five or thirty feet in front of the car. As a result, to be completely honest, I was driving primarily from memory. Yes, it was extremely foolish, but we were still young and foolish, and God was watching over our young family.

Finally, near the top of that high mountain, as I was deliberating which way the road curved, an urge came over me just to stop. I did just that, and I sat there for a few minutes. Thankfully, while just sitting there, the fog opened up, and I could then see clearly the road and the direction of the curve. What became so obvious was that I was just about to curve our car off the road before I had been urged to stop. It almost took my breath when I realized, had I kept going, I would have caused all in our car to have been killed! We would have run over the edge of the mountain and plunged hundreds and perhaps thousands of feet to the base of the mountain below.

You see, I would have chosen the wrong road turn, even though I thought it was right. I'm so thankful to this day for God's nudge to pause and His amazing watchcare.

## The Backwards Flip Without a Net

When Bo was approximately six or seven years old, he was playing with several friends at a neighbor's house. Their home had a basement with a stairwell of about ten concrete steps leading down to the basement door. It was surrounded by a brick wall with a narrow ledge on top. As Bo was sitting on the ledge, he somehow fell backward onto the concrete landing at the bottom of the stairs. Immediately the other children ran to our house to make us aware of his accident.

When we arrived, he was groggy and bruised. Further, it was evident, or it appeared, that Bo had landed on his head, hitting that hard concrete landing. It left him dazed and us fearful, not knowing what bones might be broken and the condition of his brain relative to a concussion. We immediately rushed him to the hospital, where he was carefully examined and X-rayed. After a thorough exam, they indicated Bo had a mild concussion and did not admit him. They did advise us as to how to take care of him for the next several days.

As his mother and I think back, we realize how easily he could have become a quadriplegic from a broken neck or back. Amazingly, never in his growing years did he exhibit any symptoms of impairment from that brutal fall. Not only that, he became an awesome football player.

We can never be grateful enough for the wonderful, tender watchcare of our gracious God.

## Abundant Mercy and Restraint

One of our daughters, Paula, was working in a maximum security facility hospital which detained some ICE inmates. These ICE inmates would be held there awaiting the next step, whether it was deportation, awaiting trial for another crime, or something else.

Lynette and I were at the beach for a vacation, and we received a call from a sister that our Paula was in the hospital in serious condition. Needless to say, we gathered up necessities and rushed hurriedly home.

When we arrived at the hospital, we were ushered to her bedside only to find her with her face almost disfigured from bruising and battering. Also, she was semiconscious. This made our other children extremely upset and distraught, and we were absolutely crushed and devastated to see one of our precious children so horribly abused and suffering. Her face was already swollen and black and blue.

Then we were given more details about what had happened. This prisoner had been allowed out of his cell to roam the floor on which he was detained. Somehow, he knew our daughter's routine and had hidden behind a door to a room she regularly entered. When she entered, he grabbed her, placed his hand over her mouth, and began to rip her clothes away. He sexually assaulted her, and as she resisted, he beat her mercilessly with his fists and bashed her head on the concrete floor. It is clear he was empowered by Satan himself to inflict such damage so cruelly. Paula was in the hospital for four or five days. As you can imagine, even when she was released, she had to live with the horrific nightmare of his inhumane treatment of her. Later we learned from her attending doctor that she could have died in another fifteen to twenty *seconds*. As this inmate was choking her, if she had not been discovered by other prison employees at the time they did, she would not have survived. Seldom early, but never late. Thank you, God. We will forever be so grateful!

## No Permanent Heart Damage

In 2021, our daughter Eugenia was having a very stressful year, and she was not feeling well. She had already recently taken some time off from her job to deal with a couple of situations concerning loved ones. So, given the demands of work, she kept pressing herself to continue to go to the office. However, while driving there that morning, she began to feel pressure in her chest, and then as she got nearer her office, the pressure had also moved into her left arm. She went on inside and mentioned her discomfort to a coworker. She took a couple of phone calls but began to feel much worse, with much greater pain as well as nausea.

Her boss drove her to a nearby doctor's office, where they had her chew an aspirin and put three nitroglycerin tablets under her tongue. The doctor's office simultaneously called EMS to carry Eugenia to the hospital. The ER staff quickly put her on a Heparin IV drip and admitted her for a heart catheterization the following morning. Sure enough, during the catheterization, they found her three major arteries were eighty to ninety percent blocked, with the main one being ninety percent blocked. The doctor told us this was a blessing and the quick treatment prevented Eugenia from having a classic STEMI heart attack, normally causing permanent damage to the heart. Although she did have a (NSTEMI) heart attack, the swift treatment prevented any permanent damage and thankfully signaled the need for stints to prevent a more significant attack. We continue to Praise God for His watchcare over her.

Most of us are unaware of how many times we, and those we love, have been greatly endangered over our lifetime. We are aware of some of those times God has faithfully been merciful and protected us from the destroyer. Thus, there is no doubt our lives have been so richly blessed, even more than we will ever be aware of, by God's watchcare. Our hearts have been greatly touched by His goodness, and our trust in Him has deepened and grown because of His faithfulness and mercy. It is a blessed practice to be still and thank God. "I will give thanks to you, Lord, with all my heart; I will tell of all your wonderful deeds" (Psalm 9:1, NIV). And I take great comfort in God's promise: "I will never leave nor forsake you" (Hebrews 13:5, NKJV).

In 1975, I heard Jack Taylor, one of God's finest preachers, preach from Psalm 85 (a Revival Psalm). He shared the following great and comforting promise: "I will hear what God the Lord will speak, for He will speak peace to His people and His saints" (Psalm 85:8a, NKJV). What kind of peace? It is "The peace of God, which surpasses all understanding" which "will guard your hearts and minds through Christ Jesus" (Philippians. 4:7, NKJV).

We can be comforted in knowing no matter what the future brings, as His children, we will never cease to be under the watchcare of our precious Lord.

When life gets heavy, it is always good to stop and realize how He has blessed us so graciously.

"For I, the Lord your God, hold your right hand; it is I who say to you, Fear not, I am the one who helps you" (Isaiah 41:13, ESV). Our load is always lightened when we realize we continually have a Faithful Helper! What does He tell us about life's burdens? "When you pass through the waters, I will be with you; and through the rivers, they shall not overwhelm you; when you walk through fire you shall not be burned, and the flame shall not consume you" (Isaiah 43:2, ESV). Additionally, Matthew 11:28–30 (ESV) assures us, "Come to me, all who labor and are heavy laden, and I will give you rest. Take my yoke upon you, and learn from me, for I am gentle and lowly in heart, and you will find rest for your souls. For my yoke is easy, and my burden is light."

*Paul and Lynette's Adult Children from left to right;*
*Eugenia, Sandra, Bo, Melinda, Paula and Edwina*

# CHAPTER 24

# Gratitude for Grace

Grace is a word we do not hear much today, not nearly as much as we once did. Just what does that word mean? Grace is clearly defined as the "unmerited favor of God." In my own case, I would like to describe it as the *indescribable* unmerited favor of God. Why do I describe it as such? It is because I have been so impacted by His indescribable grace.

In Ephesians 2:8–9 (NKJV), we read this wonderful truth: "For by grace you have been saved through faith, and that not of yourselves, it is the gift of God, not of works, lest anyone should boast."

What absolutes do we learn from this?

»   Grace is a precious gift from God.

»   We, as mortals, cannot achieve or earn grace, but we can xtend it to others.

»   Neither can we boast about grace.

It is worthwhile to take a bit of time and just think about what God has done for mankind when we, in our Adamic nature, are born into sin and separated from a Holy God. Justice would call for us to be punished by leaving us in that awful place of separation.

However, it is because of the wonderful love and grace of God that no matter how horrible our sins, grace allows for our complete forgiveness. Unfortunately, we must still live with the earthly consequences of our ugly sins, but we know by God's grace, we are completely forgiven. How can that be? Because of Jesus. Jesus, in His sinlessness, took upon Himself our sins. He died the death that substituted for the punishment of our sins. We would have been eternally separated from God and God's people but for God's *indescribable* grace and favor.

Second Corinthians 5:21 (NKJV) says, "He made Him, Jesus, who knew no sin to be sin for us, that we might become the righteousness of God in Him." That is a remarkable thing—an exchange of man's sin for God's righteousness by way of God's precious son, Jesus. Man's sin debt has already been paid for. Hebrews 7:27b (NKJV) verifies this: "He died once for all when He offered up Himself." Christ took our guilt in order that we might take His place of acceptance. What a Savior!

Why do we not hear more about the wonderful grace of God? I believe it is somewhat because worldliness keeps us from meditating on this grace of God. Our busyness also keeps us from reflecting on the graciousness of so many who have blessed us with their influence and kindness. Gratitude is almost a forgotten word today, unfortunately. Why? We fail to be full of gratitude because there is such a focus on self and worldly things. Hedonism (self-indulgence, entertainment, and pleasure-seeking) has crowded out too many of our thoughts and our gratitude for grace and swallowed up our time.

God ultimately gave mankind His moral law. Moses received that law on Mt Sinai, where God gave him the Ten Commandments as recorded in Exodus 31:18 (NASV). The Ten Commandments were divided into two groups. One group of the commandments defines how man is to live together in a relationship with his fellow man. The other group defines how we are to live in a relationship with God.

God clearly gave us the Law for several reasons. These Ten Commandments, when kept, would guarantee a right relationship between God and man. Another reason for adherence is it would also provide the best guidance to create a stable and safe society.

They were also given for another reason. Over time this moral code (Ten Commandments) would show the people, us, how much we need a Savior, for we continue to disobey God's clear set of benevolent rules, no matter how hard we try not to do so.

It may sound ironic but thank God for clearly defining for us what He expects. Though He knows the frailties we have from birth, He ultimately sent Jesus to pay our sin debt as we broke God's Law.

Thank God for the Law, these Ten Commandments. If we did not have the law, we could never have known how much we needed the grace of God. Even though there is separation of church and state, no country could ever do better than have God's moral law to help guide us as a society. Honoring God's law as a guide would prevent us from degenerating into complete rebellion. Unfortunately, today we live in a society where more and more people resent the Ten Commandments. But if there was a decided, even reasonable, effort to keep these commandments, our earth would be so much a better place than it is.

No country can ultimately survive without a concerted effort to guide and protect the people with sound moral laws. God demonstrated that to us thousands of years ago. But enlightened alleged leaders have worked diligently to remove the influence of God from any public arena, as well as from the great majority of our higher learning institutions. The problem is that when we tire of and try to eliminate any of the focus on the God of the universe, we have undertaken a most calamitous adventure. In fact, God's Word tells us even nature reminds us of His glory: "The heavens declare the glory of God" (Psalm 19:1, KJV). Also, Isaiah wrote this from God as well (Isaiah 6:3, ESV), "Holy, Holy, Holy is the Lord of Hosts; the whole earth is full of His glory." Romans 1:18–20 (NKJV) is a warning to those who are attempting to discredit and eliminate God from the public square or from schools. It reads, "For the wrath of God is revealed from heaven against all ungodliness and unrighteousness of men, who suppress the truth in unrighteousness, because what may be known of God is manifest in them, for God has shown it to them. For since the creation of the world, His invisible attributes are clearly seen, being understood by the things that are made, even His eternal power and Godhead, so that they are without excuse." In essence, they refused to glorify God and "their hearts were darkened" (verse 21). "Professing to be wise, they became fools" (Romans 1:22, NKJV). If we want to see where all this vehement rejection of our gracious Creator God leads, read the remainder of Romans, Chapter 1. It is sobering when read.

In addition, when we read these devastating promises of God's certain judgment, it causes and compels us to be all the more grateful for the wonderful grace of God.

As we think of grace, obviously, the grace of God is foremost in our minds. However, it is important to realize we are surrounded by grace-givers right here on earth. I owe so many who have been so gracious to me and my family. It is a good thing to find a quiet place and let my Savior remind me of the many that have been gracious to us.

If I look at my life as a ledger, I must say my receiving side far outweighs my giving side. Before beginning to delineate my earthly grace-givers, it is important that I leave no question, the One I owe the most is my Lord and Savior, Jesus Christ.

I owe my dear mother, whose faith never wavered over her ninety-six years on this earth. She buried her first-born son, Edwin, at the age of twenty-nine, my precious sister, Ruth, at age forty-two, and my father, at fifty-nine. She never blamed God, and though she had dementia and Alzheimer's for the last twelve years of her life on earth, she could still recall the Word of God. She perhaps sometimes could not remember what she ate for breakfast a few hours before, but she could quote scripture for you. Even on the day she went home to glory, she quoted the entire twenty-third Psalm. Those were her last words here on earth. God knew I needed a special mother like her. He graciously provided her for me.

I would be remiss if I didn't say how much I owe my precious wife, Lynette, for the grace she always extended to me, gladly agreeing for me to work very extensive hours. Without complaint, she managed our home and our six children as I provided for our family and the Lord advanced my career.

Both sets of our parents were so gracious to help us and very generous to us and our large young family. We look back at them as angels. Surely tired from their own jobs, they still graciously frequently stopped by our home after work to offer a helping hand. A sweet memory for our children to this day is of their grandparents stopping by, often bringing them small treats of candy we could not afford to give them. On Sundays, when I had to work, and one or some of the children might be sick, and Lynette needed to stay home with them, her parents carried the other children to church. More than once, Lynette's parents assisted with purchasing a large ticket item we needed when our finances were tight. Both sets of parents were always seeking ways to extend grace to us, and we will forever be grateful for all their love and goodness. To this day, Lynette and I take comfort in knowing they are receiving their rewards in heaven for the kindness they sacrificially shared.

*Lynette's parents, Thelma and Jim Homesley*

I owe my exceptional preacher and pastor, Dr. Charles Carter. He gave me the most important advice anyone ever could on the night I was saved, literally born again. He was direct, and his direction was compelling. He was not the least concerned with what anyone, including myself, might think about such strong directives. He was so faithful to God's calling on his life. Political correctness was not yet a newfound identity for compromise. Thank God! I also owe the dedicated, fearless preachers, especially Dr. Mike Minnix, who followed Him and also who challenged and encouraged me with truth.

I owe the dear people in God's church who prayed me into a place of submission to His wonderful purpose for my life. They prayed for me by name, and I never knew they even cared.

I owe the church for never giving up on me. They, like Joe Alexander, extended grace and continued to reach out graciously. I owe the church because it was a discipling church. Worldly activities and things never crowded out time for Bible study and worship services twice on Sunday, morning and evening. Wednesday night was a night for extended earnest prayer. Revival events, which lasted a week, were scheduled at least twice a year. Every January, a different book of the Bible would be taught by a visiting preacher. It began on Monday night and ended on Friday night. God's people welcomed and made time for these important discipling events. But unfortunately, things have changed concerning the church. In far too many churches, the world dictates or overly influences its schedule and consequently its impact. It should actually be the other way, with the church influencing the world to follow God's book of truth and live with Godly priorities.

I'm grateful there was evangelism. Evangelism was taught and practiced. God's people were not so busy or intimidated that they would not seek out and share the gospel with people who needed to be set free.

How could I not be grateful for prayer and all the victories that are won in prayer? I most certainly am! Our victories in life are gained on our knees. When we bow before Almighty God, we acknowledge Him as our Maker, Defender, Redeemer, and Friend. As we yield ourselves, our plans, and our problems to Him, He intervenes for His Glory and our good. I have never ever prayed in the name of Jesus that I did not feel better when I turned it over to Him and said, "Amen."

Yes, I am even grateful for the law God gave to Moses. It has shown me how much I needed a Savior. Still, I have too often allowed the enemy of God and man to deceive me by not doing what I should.

I owe the saints God kept in front of me. They lived with such Godly consistency. I could not deny the empowering presence of God's great Holy

Spirit power in the lives of those transformed people. One of those saintly men, when he learned God had called us to a new place of service, came to our home to say goodbye (for a little while). He was a collector of knives. He brought me one from his collection and said, "This is for you, my brother." He hesitated and then continued, "This is my best and most favored one." How could I not be grateful for such a grace giver? He was not trying to say, "Look at my sacrifice," but "This is how much I love you."

How could Lynette and I, as young parents, not be grateful for God's wise saints? They not only prayed for my salvation (literally prayed me into the kingdom), but then they poured themselves into our spiritual growth with their Godly wisdom, advice, encouragement, and exemplary living before our watchful eyes. That remnant, the most faithful and consistent few (most of them much older than us), never got over the wonderful grace of God themselves. They lived so consistently in front of us that we knew we should hear and apply their wise counsel. They were the remnant that we could count on. God's perfect plan is that the wonderful remnant continues to increase in size and devotion. That would be a most glorious thing. Yes, that is what God intends for every church member to be—a grace-giver. Wow! God's church would then be so very irresistible.

I owe Dr. Fred Stephenson, a most respected and admired friend, a retired professor from the University of Georgia. He never became so educated, even though he earned his Ph.D., that he did not continue to learn the most important things about life. He never became so knowledgeable that he forgot his Creator and the source of his wonderful teaching ability. I am convinced he knew and embraced this truth: "My help cometh from the Lord" (Psalm 121:2a, KJV). I owe Dr. Fred for his encouragement and loyal friendship over the many years. He helped me grow as a businessperson and has been a consistent encouragement to me as a special friend. He also encouraged me to write this book.

I also owe the Cassels, the founders and owners of Southeastern Freight Lines, for the blessed opportunity they gave me to be a part of same. What is so special or unique about these people? Simply this—they are of a rare few who love God and people *more* than they love money and personal recognition. A precious rarity! I was so blessed to be a part of that company. I owe the faithful leaders who helped me in the workplace expand.

I also owe the warriors who have fought, many to their death, to defend and protect our great country. They are heroes, without discussion from the left. My gratitude for their sacrifices for our country was substantially increased by this example. When I toured the ship, *Constitution*, in Boston Harbor, it was a rainy day, and I was so touched as I viewed the sickbay. It consisted of canvas hammocks strung between upright posts between the mezzanine deck and the main deck. It was a breezy place. There were iron buckets hanging on each of the posts. There was also a blacksmith forge on the mezzanine deck nearby. That forge was for repairing damage done to any iron parts of the ship that were damaged in battle. Out of curiosity, I inquired about the number and use of buckets, and I was told they held cannonballs—heated in the blacksmith forge—to try to heat the somewhat open spaces where the injured and sick were. The crewmen of that ship endured such hard times. It gave me such a new appreciation for the sacrifices of the many. Let the critics criticize the wars, but never criticize the warriors. God bless the warriors. We all owe them a huge debt for their sacrifices. We are all the recipients of unmerited favor.

I owe my country. What a blessed privilege to be an American. We are absolutely the greatest country on the face of the earth because we were founded on Godly principles. I can never have an attitude of contempt because I cannot live as I please. It disgusts me that ungrateful people (who do not recognize the grace of God, which is so evident in our country) want to destroy America—and remake it—without God's presence.

Gratitude for grace overwhelms me, especially when I obey this wonderful directive: "Be still and know that I am God" (Psalm 46:10, KJV). It is in stillness and meditation that I sense how wonderful it is to be His forgiven son, a blessed child of God!

# CHAPTER 25

# What a Beginning!

My first day of employment with Southeastern Freight Lines as Senior Vice-President of Operations was Monday, August 20, 1984. I met Mr. Cassels, Jr. at the Columbia Service Center for introduction and my orientation. The corporate office occupied a small portion of the service center/terminal because there were only a few officers besides Mr. W. T. Cassels, Sr. as Chairman of the Board, and his son, W. T. Cassels, Jr., President. They certainly were not top-heavy and had only the few officers needed for the size of the company at that time.

I had not inquired as to where my office would be, because it was not of a real concern to me. My new office was modest in contrast with my former office at Carolina Freight. However, the size of the office was of no concern because I was a man on a mission, and I knew Who had called and sent me. It was indescribably good to approach this new challenge, not with self-confidence, but with God-confidence. What a liberating exchange!

I moved my few books, papers, and files into my office, and we then spent the rest of that day meeting more Southeastern associates and discussing priorities. Mr. Cassels, Jr. explained that Southeastern had a very excellent reputation as a motor carrier, and I was aware of that and agreed. We also discussed competitive advantages that larger carriers with greater geographical coverage had over Southeastern, something that needed immediate attention and improvement for service and cost reasons. From a customer's perspective, would you rather be served by one carrier that could connect all your shipment origin points with each needed destination or deal with several smaller carriers, each of which could fill only a part of your required origin-to-destination shipment needs? From our perspective, a smaller route system meant we had cost disadvantages. For example, it costs about the same to make a pick-up collecting ten shipments or thirty, but when a big carrier doing the latter spreads that single pick-up cost over thirty shipments, the unit cost is about one-third of the smaller carrier's. Also, it is more advantageous to customers when one carrier can reach all destination points rather than needing more carriers. Thus, it was very clear. Southeastern must begin to catch up with at least most of our larger competitors by expanding our service area. At the time, we served most of Georgia and South Carolina and a portion of North Carolina. We needed to expand into Florida, Alabama, and Tennessee and into the underserved parts of the Carolinas and Georgia.

Fortunately, there was an offsetting factor to the scope of geographic coverage with our customers. It was Southeastern's excellent on-time delivery performance and the next day (overnight) service from the greater Atlanta area to most of the Carolinas. Southeastern had really pioneered this overnight service, and it had tended to offset the lack of a greater scope of service coverage. As a previous competitor, I was well aware of how very reliable Southeastern's service was. The second offsetting factor was the quality of the Southeastern Freight drivers who clearly knew how to care for customers in an outstanding manner.

The states of Florida, Alabama, Tennessee, and the unserved portions of the Carolinas made up the preponderance of the Southeast region of the country that Southeastern Freight was not serving at the time. The great challenge that lay before us was to expand our outstanding transportation services presently being rendered. Specifically, that challenge would be to expand into those new areas without diminishing or losing the outstanding and exceptional culture that permeated the company and set it apart from all our competitors. One thing I knew before I came was that Southeastern was a much respected, very reliable company of the Carolinas. Again, they had led in pioneering next-day service between Atlanta and most of the Carolinas. However, we knew that with growth comes complexities. We understood that when we began to expand and increase our coverage, Southeastern Freight absolutely must deliver the same high degree of reliability as what the company had been providing and was still delivering at the present time.

In addition, it must be rendered by superlative associates who possessed that same commitment to excellence. All of this provided a challenging scenario, but this we knew—people can, and people are empowered to excel. We also knew that the *want* and *desire* to excel in willing associates could be brought about and perpetuated only by authentic, caring leadership.

There was another significant factor that had to be considered. That factor was capital with which to buy land, build service centers, buy tractors and trailers, and develop state of the art Information Technology systems. All of these were needs, along with all the while keeping the present fleet in the optimal, economic operating condition.

I did not know it at the time, but Mr. Cassels, Jr. was, and still is, the best steward of capital and resources of anyone I have ever known. For years he had been forward-looking in regard to resource planning. He told me on that day, "We just don't do short-term things." That consoled me substantially because I knew God had sent me there for the long term! Mr. Cassels also said, "We need to build a Raleigh, North Carolina, service center and a corporate office sometime next year." It was now late August, and that only left a sixteen-month time frame in which to accomplish those objectives.

One of the most significant things he said was, "Paul, I want you to help train my son." I had been given this responsibility before, and I knew the greatest factor in such an assignment was, *Does the son want to be trained?* I said a silent quickie prayer, "Please Lord, let him be willing to be trained." Even at that, I wasn't too sure I possessed nearly as much wisdom and knowledge as needed to meet that requirement. But, by divine providence, an event happened which led to optimum development in the son. That event prompted choices that matured and prospered his son. And the son has become a perceptive, outstanding, and wise Christian leader who has so well honored his family and his Creator.

By the end of that first day, I knew what I had thought initially: My Lord had called me to work for the most competent, clear-headed, unpretentious, qualified business leader that I had then, or even now, have ever known. What a blessing! Mr. Cassels genuinely loved, appreciated, and respected all the people who comprised that company...and they all seemed to know it. The mutual respect was a real blessing to behold, and now by the grace of God, I was allowed to be a part of.

Mr. Cassels also informed me of an established practice that was carried out every spring. He, along with his father and perhaps another of the company officers, visited every Southeastern Freight location. They knew the people who served diligently and with excellence deserved to know what the operation results were. They met face-to-face with all the associates for the following purposes to share:

» Southeastern's operating results for the year just ended.

» Recognition awards for safe driving and service awards given in five-year increments.

» Planned equipment purchases.

» Planned new facility openings (expansion).

» Comparison with competitors.

The associates would then be given the opportunity to ask any questions they may have of the presenter. There were no boundaries. It was open communications with no parameters. When you always deal in truth, there is nothing to hide. The beauty was that the meetings were held at various times in order that people would not have to make a special trip to attend a meeting if they were off duty.

I could conclude only one thing from these established practices: It was very important that communication lines stay open and that all team members be informed, listened to, and responded to. This would become more of a growing challenge to continue as the company opened additional facilities. Yet, it was such a uniquely essential part of showing people how important they were. We would find, for certain, a way to continue in the same vein.

As I began to think about all we had discussed, it caused me to become more and more certain about information I had been exposed to previously in St. Paul, Minnesota. I truly knew that information was the single best way to energize and prepare people to enthusiastically produce excellence and enjoy the benefits true differentiation brings. I am still thankful for the vision the Lord gave me concerning this wonderful approach in the workforce to produce excellence. I believe our Creator is pleased when any organization embraces this approach of inclusion, quality, and excellence as their way of creating a successful God-honoring business. Those words that had been so imprinted on my mind in St. Paul described much of what was already being practiced in this company. They were:

» Inclusion: who doesn't want inclusion?

» Alignment: everyone on the same page, serving customers better.

» Encouragement: constantly provided by leadership.

» Vision: to build something where everyone could truly win—customer, company, and associates.

And also to be the industry leader, to be the best. Why not?

Little did I know when God led me to Southeastern, Mr. Cassels would embrace Quality Improvement Process in such a completely unlimited and absolute way. Perhaps it was because Southeastern was already doing many of the things the QIP would later introduce, especially Valuing People Completely.

The loyalty these people had all throughout the company for their leaders was evident. That loyalty was no doubt earned by the respect and gratitude the owners had demonstrated for them.

As Mr. Cassels, Jr. described the communication meetings to me, it was clear the associates who made up this company were respected, valued, and informed. And they loved it. This effort to interconnect on the part of the ownership spoke volumes about their appreciation for all these hardworking, loyal associates. It was also evident these people truly enjoyed being part of something unique, different, special, and better. (DS & B= Different Special and Better).

It was also unmistakably apparent we had a solid foundation on which to build a world-class transportation company. There was also a right motive to do this... for the benefit and well-being of every single stakeholder. There was and still is a profound sense of togetherness and unity there.

When the company was founded in 1950, founder W. T. Cassels, Sr., said, "Take care of the people who take care of the customers, and that will take care of our future." Mr. Cassels, Jr., being the respected, disciplined person that he is, had made certain over that long period of years that the wisdom of his father's direction had not been neglected. He knew that taking care of the people included inclusion, respect, and individual attention. The result was now a company full of people working diligently to satisfy customers and helping to build something Different, Special, and Better (DS & B). They had already collectively begun to decisively differentiate the company. Trucking can be considered a "sameness" business, and it takes real accomplishment to be a company set apart. This company had left the pack, and the best was yet to come! On my first day, my Heavenly Father put an exclamation point on this place, His choice for me, by showing me he had put me in a unique place to represent Him. He also put a second exclamation point on this profound truth: we are empowered to excel, and this is a special place where we all surely could. He made this apparent to me, people are empowered to excel because there was evidence of excellence, and they were already in process of excelling at this very special place.

# CHAPTER 26

# Authentic Leadership

Given my limited formal education, I missed almost all the usual instruction and lessons most college students receive. But I found a complete guidebook of even higher learning in the Greatest Leadership and Human Relations Book ever written, the Bible. It is a book of truth that offers every leader a great source of wisdom and a pattern for leadership. At the same time, it encourages a genuine love and concern for those associates one is responsible for leading and encouraging. This is a simple, uncomplicated truth—encouraged people accomplish more.

The dictionary definition of "leadership" is "people who have authority or influence."[1] But experience has shown me we need to take this one step farther and affirm the following truth. Effective leadership is demonstrated by people who have authority or influence *and use it for the benefit of those for whom they have responsibility.*

Now, we agree man was created for success, so the question is what determines whether a person achieves success. It is clear, as stated earlier, that making up one's mind without wavering and simply *deciding* to be successful is a primary or foundational ingredient in achieving real success. There is a world of difference between *wanting* to and *deciding* to. An even more important ingredient is being in a right relationship with our Creator, the One who knows us best. When we are in that forgiven relationship, we can claim the amazing promises in the Owner's Manual, which is the best Leadership and Human Relations Book ever written. Also, a true believer will have the continuous prompting of God's Holy Spirit as a Counselor, Helper, Guide, and Advocate. Every practicing Christian has access to God's "Library of Leadership," and it is invaluable as an unmatched resource.

Before we go any farther, it is important to define the most important role of a true leader. It is almost too simple but so often misunderstood. It is

1    *Webster's Collegiate Dictionary*, 10th Edition

to help their people succeed, even when the follower may be difficult, hard to instruct, or halfhearted in effort.

People need to know you believe in them. It is a principle Jesus taught and lived: "It is more blessed to give than to receive" (Acts 20:35, NIV). Leaders do not have to actually believe this. All they have to do is try it, and this principle will prove itself. When true leadership is not embraced and carried out, there is a very negative result from that deficiency. Sure, all too often, taking the easy way out is to fire and rehire someone else, but to be totally honest, that requires no talent at all. The sink-or-swim approach will never produce acceptable results, let alone best discretionary efforts from the participants. Why? Because "best discretionary effort" is most often given by people who genuinely respect their leaders. Willing followers are most often created by respected effective leaders.

It is far, far more satisfying to work with an imperfect person, show them respect, be patient to a reasonable point, and know that when you put your head on your pillow at night, you have done "to others as you would have them do to you" (Luke 6:31, NIV). You are making an extra effort to help one of God's most important creations. There are no throw-aways with Him. Think about it this way. If the person was your son or daughter in a similar situation, how would you want their leader to deal with them?

Another very important role of a real leader is to help each person see the value and benefit of achieving the objective at hand. Yes, that involves taking time to sell or inform and educate each person on the value of accomplishing the goals. Helping one visualize a real image of a promising future for them is another powerful persuader. Your communications must be authentic, genuine, and from your heart, if you expect it to be taken seriously. The *why* of an instruction is so helpful in getting it accomplished. "Because I said so" will never be a motivational phrase that comes from a true and wise leader.

As each person begins to understand the value of alignment—everyone working toward common goals that create advantages for every person—then progress begins to be the daily objective as well as the very satisfying result.

A really effective leader will genuinely care about everyone in that workgroup. If you are a leader and don't feel a genuine concern for the success of everyone that you have responsibility for, ask our Lord to give you a heart for each and every one. There is a promise you can believe if you are a Christian: "The effective, fervent prayer of a righteous man availeth much" (James 5:16b, KJV). If you are His child, God will hear you, and God will help you on behalf of the people you are responsible to lead. People always know when someone is sincere.

Remember this, when God allows you to move into a leadership position, you can know He will equip you to represent Him well and to take good care of all your people. Besides, He loves it when we look to Him, in faith, for wisdom to know how to do well, whatever He has called us to do.

The workplace is an especially wonderful place to show the world that God's principles always work better than man's anywhere. Similarly, don't you love it when your children humbly and honestly seek your advice? So does God when we seek His.

The Bible is replete with specific and important examples of people God called out who were not trained and prepared for a task larger than themselves. Some of the better known are David as a very young man facing the giant Goliath and David killing the giant with only a sling and unwavering faith in God. David released it, but God then guided the stone that He had created deep into Goliath's forehead. Another is Moses, who was not eloquent in speech, yet God called him out to lead the children of Israel on a miserable journey through the wilderness for over forty years. Perhaps, one of the most compelling examples is Solomon, David's son, becoming king of Israel. As this very young man became king, he asked for wisdom to govern his people well rather than asking for great riches for himself. God not only gave him much wisdom but also made him the wealthiest king to ever live (2 Chronicles 1:11–12, NKJV). God gave Solomon riches because of his unselfish prayer for wisdom to benefit others, the people God had given him to lead.

There are many others who God called out for specific duty (myself included), who had to learn to trust and have faith in God because we were inadequate within ourselves.

Everyone deserves a leader they can respect. It is almost the equivalent of servitude if one has to work under the direction of a leader who doesn't act like a true leader. Followship becomes so much easier and natural when a leader leads in an enthusiastic, respectful, exemplary, and caring fashion. That is so much easier to do when we follow the Owner's Manual, a source so loaded with wise counsel, provided from the Source of all wisdom.

A real and effective leader is also to be a keeper of the vision, just like a keeper of a lighthouse. That real leader will always be providing a clear and certain direction to a safe and secure and worthy destination or objective.

Another of the most important qualities of an effective leader is to be a serious and intense listener *and* responder. I remember well an instance where an over-the-road driver at Carolina Freight was at the check-in window in the dispatch office, and he motioned for me to step up as he complained angrily about a dispatcher in one of our New England service centers. He said, "Henry has it in for me and my buddy, and he always pulls us out of the line-up and sends us down to Putnam, Connecticut, to load a whole trailer load of heavy cartons of yarn. Then we, sweaty and dirty, have to drive twelve to fifteen hours home, and we're d—n tired of it." An over-the-road driver is one who moves the trailers between service centers. In those days, some of the trips were twelve to twenty hours one way. Team drivers shared the driving and sleeping in four-hour shifts.

I assured him I would get to the bottom of their discriminatory allegation. Somehow the note I had made to follow-up disappeared, probably in my pants pocket in the washing machine, and in my busyness, I never gave it another thought. Several weeks later, that driver, Bob, was checking in again, and he motioned for me to step to the check-in window. I thought to myself, *What a hypocrite I am. You promised to speak up for these men, and you've done nothing.* The very first words he said to me were, "I don't know what you told that blankety-blank, but you sure got him straightened out." All I could say was, "I'm so glad things are better for you." But I, at that moment, realized how dependent others are on our leadership. That's just like we are dependent on God's Spirit for our leadership. That incident with Bob made a lasting impression on me as a leader. Others are dependent on leaders always being willing to listen attentively and then do what is promised. In this case, just listening was therapeutic. That driver became a lifelong friend of yours truly. That was not my objective, however. Helping someone feel like they were worth being listened to surely was.

The effective leader will always be honestly open to suggestions and ideas from those he or she is responsible for. Those closest to the work always know far more about the job they work at every day simply because they are closer to the work. Listen to them and then value them. It will shock you at how often, once they know you are open to their thoughts and ideas, they will bring meaningful suggestions for improvement. The associates will actually help you become a valued and encouraging leader as they become individual leaders in advancing quality improvements in the processes they work within. If you genuinely care for people, you will be so blessed to see the pride in their eyes as they see their contributions valued and at work.

Effective leaders inspire others to give their best discretionary effort and to become enthusiastic, satisfied, contributing team members. Never take those team members for granted. Their consistent inclusion in decisions is more than a paycheck. It is significant fulfillment and purpose for them.

While an effective leader is the strongest voice affirming the truth *people can* in such a positive way, it is important to know there will be, though infrequently, times where firm leadership and resolve are necessary also.

Shortly after I joined Southeastern Freight Lines and we had charted a course for growth to further differentiate and separate our company in the marketplace, an incident arose that required firmness. On a return trip from Charlotte, I decided to stop by our Florence, South Carolina, facility just to say "hello" and greet as many people as possible. It was a bit out of my way, but I always found it a good practice to visit other locations as often as possible.

I found it to be a simple way of saying to people, "What you are doing is important, and so are you." When I arrived and walked to the open door of the service center manager's office, he appeared to be surprised when he noticed me. He then asked, "What are you doing over here?" I answered, "I just came for you to tell me what's going on." To this day, I do not know why I answered his question the way I did. He then responded with, "I was planning to call you later this afternoon." This was really becoming interesting because he now seemed nervous. I knew, however, that Dick was an honorable and loyal person and the consummate team player. My response was, "Well, since I am here, you can tell me all about it now."

He proceeded to tell me there was a political "faction" developing within the corporate office. It consisted of a group of four to six people. Apparently, they did not like the approach we were taking to grow and secure our future, but they never came to sit down and discuss it. They chose another route—the route of division. Division is a costly and destructive hindrance to real progress. Jesus spoke to it emphatically in Matthew 12:25 (NIV), "Every kingdom divided against itself will be ruined, and every city or household divided against itself will not stand." It is recorded again in Luke 11:17 (KJV), "But He, knowing their thoughts, said unto them, Every Kingdom divided against itself is brought to desolation; and a house divided against a house falleth." This also applies to businesses, athletic teams, churches, and families.

One of my most admired friends speaks to this so profoundly. His name is Charlie Schram, and he is a devout follower of Jesus, up close. I have known him and his wife, Bobbi, for over forty years. Charlie and I served together for many years as board members under Dr. Clyde Dupin, one of America's most effective small-town Billy Grahams. I highly respect Charlie. His writings are profoundly truthful and consequently profoundly impactful. Recently, Charlie wrote this in an article he named *National Suicide*.

"It is hard to imagine a time when our nation has been more divided than it is now," Charlie wrote. "Only the Civil War could have been more divisive." Let me elaborate—there is open hostility toward Christianity and increasing disregard for the family, God's great institution and plan for mankind, just to name a few issues that divide us. There is not just a difference of opinions and not just a lack of respect for our leaders and for each other, but actual hatred with venomous words, lies spread, and uncontrolled violence.

"Our national leadership campaigns on a platform to look out for the people's best interest, but once elected, their interest turns to party politics and the preservation of their own position of power."

Forget love for our fellow man. There is not even enough civility to work together for the common good. (And I'll add this—Congress is a complete disaster.)

"While we are busy trying to destroy our political enemies within," Charlie writes, "the world is a powder keg ready to explode."

I agree completely. This is so true.

"Our Lord gave stern warning of where this will lead us if not corrected," Charlie states.

I am in absolute agreement with Charlie and banning God's truth from public places and places of higher learning does not keep it from still being absolute truth. It further shows the error of our ways as well as how far we have fallen away from the principles established by our founding fathers.

Charlie continues, "Wake up, America, we are destroying ourselves!"

Charlie speaks to division earlier in a profoundly perceptive way. It is destruction on steroids! I could have never described this destructive practice better.

Look at the political scene today. What was at one time simply disagreement on different points of view in our country is now clearly hatred. It is absolutely shameful. That division is utterly and always destructive, regardless of the side it originates on. Let our Creator unite us as we submit to His perfect will. Our land desperately needs revival and civility.

Why would I be so concerned about division and those who create it? It's like those who caused the "stand-up meeting" that I will soon tell you about. It is because those who cause division for personal gain, and often because of immaturity, jeopardize everyone else's future, both economically and emotionally. It is a dangerous and damaging practice.

Godly, commendable, moral, political leadership for the common good is so rare, almost non-existent today. Moreover, it is clearly dangerous what we are experiencing in our nation. It is the extreme opposite of what God expects and desires. The division has become so ugly that even our current President, Joe Biden, while campaigning for office at one of his CNN town hall events, said, "If you don't defect from your faith and embrace leftism, then you're going to be added to the government's terror watch list." That statement appears he would prefer an America where there are no Christians, or they should at least stop opposing the radical LGBTQ agenda. How deluded can he be?

Anyway, back to my impromptu visit to our Florence facility. I was shocked, to be completely honest, to hear what Dick disclosed to me. I think he probably thought I already knew, but I was just making conversation about why I had stopped by. I assured him he should not worry about any of this, and I would handle it from here on out. It is pure conjecture, but I believe because Dick was a long-term associate, they were trying to convince him to become part of the dissenting group. He was a loyal associate, however.

All the way back to Columbia, I was thinking, *What is the best way to handle this?* I knew there would always be small resistances in the way of changes that not everyone would agree with, but to overtly badly politicize needed corporate expansion and direction was just not acceptable. As I drove, it became clear what should be done. When I returned, I went immediately to Mr. Cassels, Jr.'s office and told him what was happening. He apparently was also unaware of this beginning resistance to what he and I both knew had to be done to strengthen and further prepare our company for the future.

The plan for correction with this small group was divinely inspired. I shared it with Mr. Cassels and invited him to attend if he would like. He expressed confidence in me to handle it and seemed to be pleased with my intended approach to dealing with it.

At my request, the custodian removed all the chairs from our conference room, as I invited all the disgruntled players to a four o'clock meeting. I made sure I arrived at the meeting first, as to be there as they began to arrive. When the first one came in and saw there were no chairs, he asked, "Where are all the chairs?" I replied, "It is going to be a very short meeting; just pick a spot at the table where you would like to stand." The second person came in and asked the same question and got the same answer. He chose to stand directly across from the first person, and they both had very questionable, puzzling looks on their faces. The other three arrived, and it was a very quiet place. I explained the meeting would be very brief and there would be no need for discussion. I don't believe in their minds there was any question why they were selected to be there.

My short address was also simple. "Gentlemen," I said, "you have been invited here because I know what you are doing behind the scenes, and it is divisive and destructive. I am not going to tell you that you must stop the negative politics because I cannot make you do that, but I am going to tell you that if you do not stop, you cannot stay in this organization. Because I will stop your paycheck, and I can do that!" I did not enjoy speaking this way, but it was essential in order to maintain the unity that is so important.

I continued, "Politics in business is an expensive waste, and it is always destructive, and we have not budgeted any monies for politics, and we never will. It is also unfair to the loyal associates. We must grow and grow fast, and alignment is the most powerful force to accomplish that. I hope you will each do the right thing. *Meeting over.*"

Not one of them ever came and asked me a single question about the whole matter. I knew why. They knew I knew what they were up to. It was the only stand-up meeting I ever needed to have. The reason for that kind of meeting is that it can never be forgotten. It's also important to know this—you never invite any of the first meeting attendees to a second stand-up meeting.

You may be wondering why the word *manage* has not been addressed here along with the word leadership. These words are not synonymous. In fact, they are not even close in reality.

In the broadest terms, *leadership is about the continuous development of others via motivation, encouragement, detailed instruction, and inclusion in decision-making.*

Management is more about supervising and controlling others. Man was not created to be controlled. Man was fashioned to be motivated, to be encouraged, and to be challenged and prepared to live up to our innate potential. That comes by way of the positive encouragement of true leaders.

*Leadership is about a way of guiding,* of going in advance, of mentoring. More notably, true leadership is being out front in essence as a role model, doing the work, leading the way. It is about motivation and respect. It is about every leader taking a sincere interest in each associate's progress and success. Listen up. It is about every leader owning the success of all those who make up their group, where "owning" means taking sincere responsibility for the success of every one of their people.

Please do not misunderstand me. There are excellent leaders who have the title *manager*. The title doesn't make the person—the actions of the person do. For the most part, true caring leadership will produce in others "best discretionary effort."

When someone tells you, "I am the boss," you are probably looking at a manager.

A leader will almost always show you he or she is a leader, and you will like and respect what you see.

Also, a leader's words *do matter*. When we, in the mid-1980s, originated a world-class Total Quality Improvement Leadership approach, we needed to make a number of decisions. Those decisions included how we would always keep our commitment to same in the forefront. We knew it had to be more than just another program. It was a key to our continued success, which would benefit every associate. It was not the latest fad. So we knew correct structure was so very important. In most organizations, there will be an executive committee and/or a management committee; these names, however, do not speak of functions or objectives at all.

At Southeastern, we desired to lead correctly and to embrace seriously our wholehearted commitment to Total Quality Improvement. We did not believe we should have the *words* "Executive Committee" at the very top of our organizational structure. As we sat and debated the matter thoroughly, this question came up. What is our most important objective? The answer was clear because we were excited about becoming the "best and biggest in the Sun Belt." Our objective was *the never-ending quest for the advancement of quality*. By definition, "quality" is defined as meeting the customer's requirements every time. Thus, we chose this descriptive title, "Quality Advancement Leadership Group." The leaders who made up this group led the company on a continuous journey of progress. Every associate helped to achieve our objective and was/is the beneficiary of that progress. The beauty of this approach is that it opens the minds and hearts of every associate to provide input consistently on how we could continue to out-perform our competitors and completely satisfy our customers in every transaction. Our people loved, and still do, this opportunity to really influence anything that allows continuous progress.

Since corporate quality is no more than the sum total of the results of all individuals, the concept of I.Q. (Individualized Quality) was very logically developed. This made alignment behind the corporate objective a natural company-wide focus. It also gave each associate a very personal, specific, and important role. That ownership of something so important gave our people a strong individual sense of pride. It also gave real value to the clearly defined superlative objective.

Never, *ever,* underestimate the power of alignment, with everyone enthusiastically pursuing the same objective. It is a great experience to be surrounded by people who are pursuing excellence with the same passion you, as a leader, are. It is the same principle that we see with all people who are filled with God's Holy Spirit. They are all pursuing the wonderful will of God for mankind.

Every person desperately needs and deserves a leader (role model) who can and will earn their respect as their leader.

Every wise leader knows he or she must plant—make an investment of time, patience, and encouragement— before he or she can ever expect to receive the harvest of willing "followship." That wise leader also knows that earned respect from their people is the greatest motivator they can ever create. People will do more out of respect than for any other reason. This investment creates an unbelievable result, but the onus is on authentic leadership.

People were created and empowered to excel at their roles. God's plan is to ultimately empower every person to excel in life. However, authentic, caring leadership plays a critical role in helping each and everyone live up to their God-given potential.

The very best leaders will go out of their way to work with everyone they are responsible for. They will genuinely care about the progress and success of each of their people. Nothing else produces loyalty more than people knowing their leader cares about them personally as well as their success. It is simple: treat your people the way you would want your own children treated. That's what the Owner's Manual teaches.

There has never been a greater need for ethical, effective, admirable leadership in our world than the need today. Integrity and honorable character are so essential today for these challenging times. The Word of God is the most complete resource anyone can follow to become a revered leader.

God's Word is a book of divine wisdom that has been proven over and over for thousands of years. It continuously reassures us that we are empowered to excel, and we have the Difference-Maker to help us. This wonderful book includes the wisdom we need in order to excel. Application of its wisdom by true leaders advances the high probability of success. One of the most profound truths I have ever learned is people can excel, they really can, but leadership determines whether they will or won't. Furthermore, authentic leadership helps people *desire* to willingly excel and then rely on God's empowerment to do so.

Leadership also carries a heavy responsibility—to lead followers correctly, as a mentor who always leads toward God's will for their benefit. Consequentially, it is so rewarding and fulfilling to see people begin to respond with appreciation and accomplishment.

One of the most enjoyable emotions I have ever experienced is seeing people exceed their limited belief in themselves and their potential progress. Time after time, because someone believed in them, encouraged them, and urged them on, they achieved far and away more than they ever thought possible.

Leadership is the urging voice, and God's Holy Spirit is the catalyst that completes human power and allows God's most beloved creations to excel. God's Spirit is the power that makes all the difference on our journey, and it is a wondrous thing to behold.

Speaking of wisdom, someone long ago defined wisdom as "being able to *see life from God's point of view.*" Wisdom also understands what to do with education and the information that you possess. Leaders need wisdom. In the book of James, God says, "If any of you lacks wisdom, you should ask God, who gives generously to all without finding fault, and it will be given to you" (James 1:5, NIV). It will always be an advantage to be able to call on the Lord for wisdom and advice if, in fact, I have a personal relationship with Him and have invited Him to be my personal Lord and Savior.

Over a career that spanned more than forty-five years, I was privileged to work with and interface with hundreds of people in leadership positions. Many of them were outstanding in carrying out their roles. However, as I have had retirement years to contemplate the people and events of those many years, there is clearly one individual who stands undoubtedly above all the rest. The other people were not inferior; he was just that much superior. That person is W. T. Cassels, Jr. It is a blessed privilege to have a leader whom you can respect without any reservations or "buts." And it was my unique privilege to have such a leader. Allowing me to work at the direction of someone I respected so unreservedly and completely was God's special and enormous blessing.

At his ninetieth birthday party, attended by more than five hundred people, it was a special blessing to be part of Mr. Cassels' introduction. He is the only son of the founder of the Southeastern Freight Company.

The following reflects what I said to that admiring audience. I believe every word of it, and I am convinced it is what our Lord wanted me to say because it is so very true.

"Southeastern is a unique company, and it was a special blessing for me to be a part of something so different, special, and better, and to work closely with Mr. Cassels, Jr. for almost seventeen years. I must confess, I lack the vocabulary to do justice to the man we celebrate and honor today, but he is described accurately in the Word of God, and he has met God's requirements for a lifetime. The prophet Micah wrote it down as the Spirit of God gave it to him (Micah 6:8, NKJV), and this describes Mr. Cassels:

'And what does the Lord require but *to do justly... to love mercy...* and *to walk humbly with your God.*'

We can all see God has blessed His servant, W. T. Cassels, Jr., for his lifetime of obedience."

When Mr. Cassels was inducted into the South Carolina Business Hall of Fame, I had the opportunity to express what a unique leader he was. This is what I wrote and shared: "The most important thing about Bill Cassels is not what he does; it is who he is. I am convinced that our doing comes from our being. Bill Cassels is not about self-confidence; he's about something far more important—God-confidence.

I have never known one so wise, patient, consistent, disciplined, competent, and concerned for others. He is a pillar of integrity. He has helped shape so many of our lives by his consistent example. Certainly, he was a mentor for me.

He is the consummate leader—easy to follow.

He taught me many things through his gracious conduct.

He taught me that it is what you do for people who can never repay you that brings personal fulfillment and so pleases our Lord.

When you sit behind closed doors with him and discuss people and money, people always come out on top. By that, you can be certain you are in exceptionally rare and wonderful company.

How much does this man we celebrate today really care about others?

Here's a great example. I received a phone call one Friday afternoon. The caller introduced himself and the well-respected, wealthy company he represented and said, 'We are putting a transportation network across America, and we want to start with the best. We want to buy Southeastern, and the price will not be a consideration.'

I thanked him for his compliment and told him I would return his call. I then went to Mr. Cassels' office and relayed the message since this offer had a unique caveat. 'Price will not be a consideration.'

He pondered and pondered for a good twenty seconds and then said, 'The people have built this company, and I want to be certain they have a place long term. It is not for sale at any price.'

How many others do you know who would have made that decision?

And now, Mr. Cassels, my most respected and admired role model, when your work on earth is complete, and we hope that will be many years from now, and you rejoin your beloved Charlotte, I say to you, I am sure, with the consensus of all who are here, you will hear from that One you have obeyed, loved, and followed so consistently, 'Well done thou good and faithful servant' (Matthew 25:21, KJV)."

In a world that so needs leaders filled with God's wisdom today, we can know we will never have a finer example than W. T. Cassels, Jr. We should all be challenged by the exemplary leadership he has provided. That example says to every leader, "Go and do likewise." Our Creator stands ready to help us do so.

This special leader and servant of God knew all along this great truth—people are capable, and they are empowered to excel. He also knew real leaders would understand their leadership role. It is simply to help people reach their fullest potential. Mr. Cassels inspired so many, including yours truly, to make my best effort to do just that, help others reach their fullest potential—out of respect for our exemplary leader. He lives in such an exemplary way he made it easy for each of us to follow. And it was his leadership that has built a sound company.

*Mr. Cassels, Jr. and Paul*

# CHAPTER 27

# To Be the Best

In 1985, though limited in geographical scope, Southeastern Freight Lines was a very reputable company. But it was also an established fact in that era that a smaller company must grow or slowly fade away.

Deregulation of trucking during the Reagan administration in the 1980s had created tremendous opportunities to enter into new markets. Growth, however, creates risks and can cause morale problems, as some associates may feel less important since more of the leadership focus must now essentially be on the expansion.

At Southeastern Freight, we in the leadership positions (Mr. Cassels, Jr. had named me President in 1988) were well aware of this possible downside of expansion. However, we knew our answer to avoid a morale issue during expansion was a simple, proven approach every leadership person should know. It is—work hard to change things that need to be changed, but work twice as hard to keep things from changing by neglect—those things which should never be changed. In simple terms, take care of essential morale issues no matter what. Keeping loyal, faithful associates pleased, informed, and believing in the organization will always be Job #1. We also knew we could not continue to take care of the people who take care of the customers unless we continued to grow and provide the best possible tools and methods for them to help distinguish and separate our company from all the competitors, setting us apart.

It had now become more and more apparent that what I had been exposed to at 3M Corp. in St. Paul was by divine appointment. Never before my redemption could I have imagined God could and would lead my life in such a profound way, step by step. The 3M conference revealed what authentic quality improvement could do as the optimum business approach and impacted my thinking about a service industry approach. I knew Dr. Deming had really influenced Japan's post-war recovery, but primarily in the manufacturing sector. Obviously, machines could be finely calibrated and recalibrated, and adjusted to produce consistently defect-free products. However, there was a major difference between a manufacturing industry and a service industry, like trucking. Our implementing a quality process would require all pick-up and delivery drivers, freight handlers, long haul drivers, mechanics, billing and accounting associates, in fact, all associates of Southeastern Freight, to be enlightened, trained, motivated, and consequently determined to produce quality in a real-time arena. All these associates could not be calibrated to provide quality without question. That would be our exciting challenge. Real quality improvement would require an unwavering commitment from *all* associates to error-free work. However, I still believed the presentation at 3M provided the perfect catalyst to be used to invigorate our expansion effort at Southeastern. An embraced Quality Improvement Process was evident not only as an exemplary motivational tool but also as the absolute best way to create completely satisfied ultra-loyal customers. QIP also provided confident, proud, excited providers of those services as well.

We had been thinking about a best-in-class Quality Improvement Plan for Southeastern Freight. I had not gotten over 3M's presentation, and Mr. Cassels was very supportive of the goal of our company becoming a leader in our industry by completely equipping our people with the tools and training needed. Yes, it was ambitious, but not risky, because of the outstanding associates who had worked diligently to cause Southeastern to already be somewhat set apart. We had the culture and the people to undertake this exciting new approach which would ultimately be so beneficial to all. After all, this approach would result in a win/win/win, and those opportunities are rare. We knew a proven, winning strategy embraced consistently by every associate and excitedly applied was the very best approach we could take to win in a deregulated environment.

More and more, it became clearly evident this business approach was divinely appointed, and we now had an even more optimal way to separate our company from our competitors. This vision for our future was now compelling.

And what was written earlier about vision is worth repeating here: "A grand vision will get you up early, keep you up late, and keep you excited most all day."

We were now in such an advantageous position to begin a more aggressive expansion without being overly concerned about the expansion being able to negatively affect the outstanding culture we enjoyed throughout the Southeastern Freight system.

As we planned, we knew our real responsibility was to create a company that was uniquely different and superior in customer satisfaction and efficiency. Trucking had always been somewhat of a *sameness* business. In marketing, we refer to this as a *"commodity* or *undifferentiated product"* business. Now, we were determined to help lead our people to further become a unique, one-of-a-kind company. The safest place in any industry is at the *top* of the customer's list of suppliers. What every customer, or at least most, desire is value. When any of us get what we pay for consistently, we know that is value, and its provision to customers is a sure way to stay at or near the top of the customer's selected list of providers.

At that point in time, Quality Improvement was not a well-known business approach in America. Consequently, there were limited providers of Quality Improvement training available. Phillip Crosby and Associates was the best-known provider of Quality Improvement training at that time. Most businesses, meanwhile, were unaware of the outstanding work Dr. Deming had been doing for a good while in postwar Japan. We began our adventurous journey with the Phillip Crosby choice.

It was a very exciting time for us. After all, who doesn't want to win and win big? Tobin Cassels, Mr. Cassels' son, became our first Director of Quality Improvement. His enthusiasm about what he taught, his sincerity, and his love for his fellow man gave him a very attentive audience of participants. Tobin painted an exciting picture of what can be for group after group of excited trainees. Every person in our organization, including our Chairman of the Board, received extensive training.

The picture revealed the real advantages of an existent Quality Improvement Process. As we began to implement enthusiastically our Quality Improvement Process, we found a number of substantial benefits.

» It allows a business to create a competitive edge and thereby differentiate itself. Otherwise, a business most likely will become one of many with no uniqueness, and that business will be filled with people who consequently work too cheaply.

» It reduces turnover of associates and reduces that consequent wasteful expense. Who wants to leave the best and take a step backward?

» It improves morale substantially. Every associate feels more and more important because they now have a more important role. That new role is to bring forth ideas and suggestions to improve a process. That is done in a formalized system, with accountability to make certain none of this valuable input falls through the cracks.

» It solidifies customer loyalty. Who would want another supplier when the one you presently have is obsessed with meeting your requirements every time?

» It substantially reduces the waste created from errors, accidents, and poor, inefficient processes. The cost of inefficient processes in many organizations often exceeds twenty percent of revenue at a minimum, and in most cases, even more.

» It binds and unifies a company together with a focus on an error-free, excellent result. There are many processes that create that positive result. The customer is generally, however, only concerned with the excellent positive end result.

» It creates a workplace of vision expansion, pride, and healthy confidence, which ultimately permeates the entire organization.

» In essence, it converts any top-down autocratic organization into a bottom-up organization. We all know synergy always works best and produces more. Synergy is ultra-valuable. Someone in the group will have the answer.

» It frees up time for planning and looking forward with uninterrupted focus. That's simply because mega hours spent in handling errors and problems will have been freed up for forward-thinking, planning, and recognition of the accomplishments of worthy associates.

» In essence, it creates a win/win/win. The customer wins, the company wins, and every individual associate wins. It is clearly a superlative strategy. It unifies an entire organization to collectively provide excellent services or products like no other approach can.

Simply put, as everyone worked to identify and improve processes, our costs would decrease. It was very encouraging to see this effort to eliminate waste was so completely embraced by all the associates. It was an exciting beginning as we all realized what great opportunities lay ahead for a trained, excited team. Life was good.

Southeastern Freight identified internally and externally our market offering as "Quality Without Question." Those three identifying words were abbreviated as QWQ™ and trademarked in 1985.

As mentioned earlier, all our people were taught that Quality Improvement has two parts.

The first was satisfying customers completely every time, and the second was becoming more and more efficient in the process. We also made certain everyone knew the statement, "The order is everything," was critically important: In essence, providing the customers the promised excellence will always be the number-one priority. We knew if we always did that, our revenue would increase, and our costs would not increase proportionally.

We believed our people also needed to know how we take care of our customers and how we provide the financial security to take care of our people and our future.

Our leaders' business approach had now become enhanced with an exciting additional approach to guarantee a successful future for every participant for many years to come.

The U.S. Department of Commerce, in an effort to focus more industry on Quality Improvement, soon began sponsoring the Malcolm Baldrige National Quality Award. It was a very prestigious award.

In 1991, we decided to enter the contest, not so much to win the award but to get their valuable feedback as to how we could continue to make improvements in the future. It was a major undertaking, but well worth the effort. We were one of only five companies in the U.S. to receive a site visit by the examiners. They spent days in some of our service centers. They also spent days in our corporate office. Their purpose was to make sure our described activities were accurate and actually being accomplished.

The selection process called for the examiners to make recommendations to others in the Department of Commerce. The others, however, had the final say in selecting the winners. Based on some anonymous feedback, we were told the examiners had recommended Southeastern Freight as a winner. In the end, we were not selected for the award, but we did receive a wealth of good recommendations to further improve our Quality Improvement efforts. Disappointed though we were, the examiners' feedback was a winning prize for us. We seriously began to make application of that most helpful feedback.

Anyway, when we initially started our quality process, we realized rather quickly that everyone must be a willing participant and embrace this wonderful new approach to being the best. It was and is a strategy too promising not to have the positive participation of everyone. We knew it could be a serious mistake to leave participation to whosoever will. Our role was to convince our people that, with everyone participating, we could set ourselves apart from the pack, but only with everyone participating. We were well aware corporate quality results were no greater than the sum total of individual quality efforts. Therefore, we gave this matter much attention and established "I.Q." as our solid inclusive approach to achieve excellence.

I.Q., or Individualized Quality, became our way of creating individual ownership of Quality Improvement. It worked wonderfully well, as our associates responded so favorably. In fact, it worked so well that this is what the Malcolm Baldrige report had to say about it: "The I.Q. process is an innovative and remarkably effective driver of the widespread development of quality at Southeastern. The I.Q. process constantly reinforces the focus of Southeastern associates on the customer, the requirements of their jobs, and the importance of quality. Southeastern's I.Q. process is a world-class approach for creating and maintaining a focus among all employees on both the customer and on the importance of quality. It would be difficult to exaggerate the excellence of Southeastern's I.Q. process."

When these skilled examiners verified at least some world-class practices were in place, we knew we were charting a course to become a uniquely superlative organization. It was exciting.

In the summer of 1994, Wachovia Corporation wrote in their corporate publication an article entitled "Taking Care at Southeastern Freight Lines." It included this observation: "Long before names like Deming and Crosby and Ishikawa began to ring in executive suites across America, Southeastern already had an admirable quality process in place. But the Baldrige Award process in 1991 was a defining moment for the company and its approach to the future."

I believe there is a clear analogy relative to the I.Q. Process. If we are in God's family as believers, He sees and interacts with each of us as if we are an only child, and each of us contributes to the good of God's great plan and His body of believers. Though there are many of us in Christ with different functions and different gifts, we form one body (Romans 12:4–6, NKJV). The I.Q. Process also focuses on the individual and gives each person that special and important identity in a workplace as a part of the Southeastern family.

Over a course of several years, knowledge of Dr. Deming's incredible success with a focus on Quality Process Improvement became more widespread. Consequently, an excellent company, Qual Pro, located in Knoxville, Tennessee, began to teach the Deming more-refined approach, and that interested us. The primary enhancement of the Qual Pro approach offered us the surprising use of data. We realized we needed to continue to learn all we could about anything as valuable as Quality Improvement enhancements and to continue to provide our people with the absolute best tools and methods available. The Qual Pro course was very comprehensive, eighteen months in length, beginning in 1992 and wrapping up in 1994. Before it commenced, they described the needed skills and background wanted for our representative whom we would enroll in that first group. A higher math background was the first essential. Fortunately, and much to our advantage, we did not really have that such person with higher math background, or we would have probably selected them to be trained.

More fortunately for us, we had a person in the company who had started their employment as a temp employee in 1986. She had been used to fill in for various clerical persons when absent, but clearly, from the beginning, she demonstrated she was capable of achieving and contributing at a much higher level. Quickly she became the secretary for three different corporate directors and department heads. She was promoted to that first corporate director's secretary position in less than five weeks after she worked her first day as a temp. That's a pretty enlightening accomplishment that attested to her potential.

She did not have an outstanding resume. She did, however, have a God-given gift of intelligence and ability to not only solve problems but to regularly offer suggestions to improve practically everything she touched. What she lacked in completed higher education, she was blessed with something even better, the innate ability and desire to work hard and excel. It was natural for her, always desiring to do her very best. She always loved to help and always improved anything she was involved with. Therefore, she was our clear choice to be trained, rather than someone with a higher math background. Her name is Carmen Smoak, and she became our Resident Quality Consultant (RQC). I am confident there was some concern at Qual Pro about our decision, but it did not take long for them to realize why she was our wise choice for the very specialized training.

There were approximately twenty-five people in the class, and she was one of the youngest but, as it turned out, one of the brightest. She excelled by acing some of the most difficult exams. Not only that, of the class of twenty-five, she finished the course that was apparently too difficult for the thirteen who did not complete the eighteen-month course. More importantly, she learned how to take Quality Process Improvement to a whole new level. As a result of her grasp of the knowledge, she taught us, in leadership positions, how to make continuous improvements using the newly acquired methods.

One of the most important things that Dr. Deming's approach taught was, "If you really want to know how to improve a process, you must ask the people who are doing the work for their ideas on how to improve it. You must listen to those ideas and then use the data to guide the decision-making."

Providing people with the best tools, systems, leaders, and helpful advisors like Carmen will always be a part of "taking care of people" at Southeastern. Educational development will never become too expensive. Providing what they need to excel, including special training, is a critical part of taking care of people. That was a part of Southeastern's business strategy from the beginning.

When my Heavenly Father first impressed me to write this book, I recognized I was not an author, and I put the idea out of my mind. However, my resident Reminder would not relent. I believe the reason is that we need to be continually reminded that God wonderfully fashioned us in His image to excel. I have worked closely, moreover, with hundreds of people but have never worked with anyone who more epitomizes "people can, and people are empowered to excel" than Carmen Smoak. In addition, her work is always done with such a positive willingness, excellence in quality, and humble spirit. Because she loves Christ and is grateful for her salvation, she loves people. God is the giver of abilities and of love. Because she loves people, she loves to serve people. Awareness of her and many, many others like her, would not let me abandon writing this book and sharing their story as well.

When I think of her and of others, I am amazed at the wonderful God-given capabilities they possess. That is exactly why I chose the book premise, *Obedient Journey: Guided by the Difference-Maker*. She applied her God-given abilities, sought to do her best following in His ways, and was empowered and guided by the Difference-Maker. It is also why, when I tried to avoid writing same, I could never have peace about abandoning the project.

Our Creator wants us to know profoundly that we are empowered to excel. Satan wants us to believe otherwise. He knows if he can keep our Lord from being loved, appreciated, and worshipped, then we will follow him, who is the enemy of both God and man.

Our Creator (who cannot lie, misrepresent, or exaggerate) spoke the truth to David, the psalmist to describe mankind:

"You formed my inward parts; You covered me in my mother's womb. I will praise you, for I am *fearfully and wonderfully made*" (Psalm 139:13–14, NKJV).

God created us to know for a certainty *we can* because we are empowered, and thereby, we are equipped to excel. We all need to be reminded often of His Holy Spirit's power within us. He is counting on you and me to represent Him well in a world that has lost its way.

The negativity in too many places in our world is making a concerted effort to drown out the bold truth that we can be obedient because we are empowered to excel, but God's Word renews our faith when we believe it and claim it. Ephesians 3:20 (NKJV) is so profoundly true: "Now to Him who is able to do exceeding abundantly above all we ask or think, according to the power that works in us."

I thank God the Father, Son, and Holy Spirit for this truth. People are empowered to achieve, to excel, to be faithful, and to bring glory to our Creator and Savior. We can never have greater purpose than to honor Him with our very best efforts to represent Him well.

The Quality Process endeavor attests that we are enabled to excel. The attraction of the QIP was that it focuses on the wonderful ability of mankind when we follow the Owner's Manual God put in place for us. To date, Southeastern Freight Lines has received the Logistics Management Quest for Quality Award in the South-Central Regional LTL category for thirty-seven consecutive years. This award is the most extensive market research study done in the transportation industry. Southeastern was rated number #1 in all of the five categories. Additionally, Southeastern's dedication to consistent, dependable service has resulted in more than four hundred eighty varying quality awards from some of the most respected companies in the United States. By the way, 3M is one of those companies.

The proceeding material shared how we came to put our quality processes in place and then how we further embraced same. Miami is an excellent example where those processes took root well and were implemented with enthusiasm.

As we began to expand into the entire Southeastern region, we had some concerns about the large Southern portion of Florida. It was new for us, and we did not know what to expect in the greater Miami area. Consequently, we worked diligently to select the very best people—drivers, freight handlers, sales reps, leadership, maintenance people, and so on. Simultaneously, we did our best to explain who we were, why we were decidedly different, and how we could clearly win in the Miami area in a big way, especially with a group of winners on the payroll.

One of the fondest memories of my entire career is of a meeting I attended with the entire group of new Miami associates. It was organized as an opportunity to express our gratitude for their belief in Southeastern Freight to people, who, in some cases, left their previous employers in order to sign on with us. And it was also an opportunity to paint a picture or create a vision of who we could become if we were willing to differentiate Southeastern Freight from all the rest. We emphasized that our associates were in a position to do just that—differentiate us—as they interfaced with customers. They listened very respectfully, and I spoke from my heart, with conviction about our future. My concluding sentence was, "We have come to Miami to be the very best."

Then I asked them if they believed we could do so to rattle the rafters. When I asked the question again, "Why have we come to Miami?" they indeed shouted back in unison, and with passion, "To be the best!" It made chill bumps in a very warm Miami and still warms my heart to this day.

Whenever I returned to Miami for company update meetings, I would ask that same question. Even after we had doubled, tripled, and then quadrupled the workforce above the original number, they always rattled the rafters with that same response, "To be the best!" They would shout it with passion because they had made that vision a reality! That experience in Miami over and over created one of my fondest workplace memories. I loved to be with those people when they rattled the rafters as winners. I will always be indebted for the great way they trusted us in leadership positions initially and made a vision a reality.

A real Quality Improvement Process always does that very same thing. It makes a vision a wonderful, winning reality. Today, Southeastern is among the top leaders, if not the leader, in LTL market share in the greater Miami area. Excellence always has and always will pay off. We prove once again what Truett Cathy so wisely said many years ago, "There will always be a market for the best." Each and every one of us at Southeastern Freight determined long ago we would always be the best. Excellence and unity will always be keys to winning. Authentic leadership is essential in leading that effort.

I can take little credit for the wonderful success of that great organization God allowed me to be part of. Why do I say that? It is simple; I was surrounded by leaders who knew God and consequently loved their fellow men. They applied the ethics of Jesus in the workplace. They did not preach to those for whom they had responsibility. They simply applied the teaching of Christ. There is no more ethical way than Christ's way to create a business that allows success for every associate and kept promises for the customers.

# CHAPTER 28

# God's Unique Provision

It is beyond my imagination to believe I could ever meet anyone besides my sister Ruth, who enjoyed accommodating and giving to others as much as W. T. Cassels, Jr.

When the new Southeastern Freight Lines corporate office complex in Columbia, South Carolina, was completed, it included a domed recess in the center of the reception area or entrance to the building. Unbeknown to me, Mr. Cassels had commissioned a well-known artist, Christian Thee, to do a special painting within the domed area. Christian Thee was a uniquely talented and much sought-after artist.

I had not been to see the progress of the building for several weeks as it neared completion. When I walked in and looked up, I was shocked to see a beautiful likeness painted of a majestic bald eagle soaring on broad wings. It had been painted on a background of blue sky with fleecy white clouds.

Mr. Cassels knew my strong affectionate thoughts about the eagle as the symbol of Southeastern Freight. He also knew I, as a hobby artist, really admired Christian Thee's creative and unique work.

Being the consummate giver he is, and always has been, Mr. Cassels secretly had this work done by Christian Thee. He knew how much I love God's creation and wanted me to always enjoy this special blessing. Even to this day, every time I walk into that building, I look up and am reminded of his great kindness!

*Painted Dome with Eagle at SEFL*

Less than a week after we moved into the new office, I was standing at my office window admiring the beautiful landscape below, which included the Saluda River, less than a quarter-mile away. The river's water is crystal clear and cold because it flows from the bottom of the Lake Murray Dam. And that cold, fresh water is so well suited for trout that they are stocked in the Saluda each spring.

To my amazement, as I stood there, suddenly a beautiful bald eagle with white stunning tail feathers and a pure white head came floating over our new facility. This was so totally unexpected and rare because eagles usually do not fly near urban areas. Never had I seen one in this area before. My guess was that the eagle was there in pursuit of the trout, one of its favorite foods. Regardless, I was impressed with its magnificence and could hardly wait to tell Mr. Cassels about it. When I did tell Mr. Cassels, he smiled and asked, "Do you think it could be an omen?" We don't hear that word often, but *Webster's Dictionary*[1] defines it as "an occurrence or phenomenon believed to portend a future event." It did not occur to me then, but later as I have thought both about that idea and a very distinctive behavior of eagles, it has become clear; it was an omen.

What is that distinctive behavior? What do eagles do when the strong storm clouds move in? They stretch their broad, powerful wings out and begin to fly in circles. Invariably they will locate an updraft which will begin to immediately lift the eagle. They do not even have to flap their wings and make an effort or expend energy once in the up-draft. All they must do is keep the wings extended and stay in the updraft. In short order, they are carried above the fury of even the most powerful storm! Similarly, *God always makes provision for all His creation, especially for you and me.*

I have pondered Mr. Cassels' question about the omen many times, and the answer is very clear in my mind and heart today. I believe that future event, or omen, was to see this great company, Southeastern Freight, soar above the industry which they have been a part of for now over seventy years.

God has continuously provided the updraft, and Christian principles permeate everything this company does. This has been the case since its very inception. They have not used Christianity in an effort to make money. They have, because of their faith, honored God by clearly demonstrating the guidance and wisdom they have received from God. The Word of God provides clearly the best guide to accomplish anything and especially a successful business. God's principles always work twenty-four-seven. Those principles work in homes, colleges and universities, the professional sports

---

1     *Webster's Collegiate Dictionary*, 10th Edition

world, government, and the entertainment professions. They also work wonderfully well in a business where trust, integrity, and respect at all levels are so very important.

Do you know why God's principles are not at work in so many of the other organizations listed above? It is simple. They are not applied. For some reason, there are people who are led to believe Christianity is just for church on Sunday, mealtime prayers, and in emergencies, and certainly not for business purposes. After all, haven't you heard that long-enduring statement "business is business," as if business is somehow exempted from the Godly teachings of our Savior?

Let me repeat. The Godly principles that are referred to above have never been given a chance to work in so many endeavors. But any endeavor where they are applied will work all the better for it.

I can state emphatically that I have never heard anyone say, "I am so sorry that I gave my life to Christ." On the other hand, I have heard more than a few say, "I wish that when I was convicted of the sin burden in my life, I had given that burden to Jesus and become free of the load of guilt."

Christianity doesn't have many dissatisfied users. They are rare. There are, however, many critics who have never yielded to God's great purpose in their life. They judge from afar. Those critics have not experienced His peace. Satan also has a multitude of those people hoodwinked into believing they will have to give up their most enjoyable habits if they become Christians. But God's Word has proven itself over and over, "Where the Spirit of the Lord is, there is liberty" (2 Corinthians 3:17, KJV). Satan does not want his captives to know that when we yield to the love of Christ, God's Spirit begins to change our *want-tos*. His presence will bring more real satisfaction to any life than any previous habit ever could. Then, our new *want-tos* are to do the things that will honor the One who has set us free from a judgment of death and separation from Jesus and God's people in eternity.

Too many people make judgments about Christianity, and they have never even "tasted the peace and freedom it provides." Satan loves it when God's plan is condemned, and Satan's enslaved ones continue in binding habits. It is really hard to understand why there is such absolute rejection of and hatred for Christianity. These very people rejecting it have no comprehension because they have never given Jesus an opportunity to speak peace to their troubled souls.

There is, however, a great truth that critics of Christianity need to know. God would never call us to follow Him in peace and fulfillment unless He provided the necessary strength and power to do so.

When life becomes really challenging, we must remember God always makes provision for all He has given life to and created. Just like the eagles avoid the fury of dangerous storms, God provides provision for you and me. All you and I need to do is to stay faithfully in the up-draft of His deliverance, love, and power.

# CHAPTER 29

# That Remarkable Enterprise

In 1950, W. T. Cassels, Sr. decided to start his own business. At that time, he was working as a banker, although he had grown up on a farm, but he decided farming was not what God had created him to do as a life's work. He had probably seen with the bank's customers some successes and some failures in their businesses. Without a doubt, familiar with the possibility of either of these outcomes if he began a business, he moved forward.

As a devout follower of Christ, he determined that Christian principles would be the bedrock foundation on which the business would be started and built. And to this day, these divine principles are still the fundamental truths at the core of Southeastern Freight Lines, just as they were in the beginning.

Mr. Cassels, Sr. knew God's plan for anything would always produce a better result. His faith gave him conviction that Christians are expected by our Creator to demonstrate to the world that Christian principles always produce a better result than secular principles ever will, in any business or other endeavor. As a Christian, he chose a strategy believing that if he did his part, God could be fully trusted and would bless. Since the first day a Southeastern truck was purchased, the business has been operated with applied Christian ethics. Time has proven there is no better way to conduct a successful business than by following Christ's teachings. In faith, Mr. Cassels, Sr. ventured out, believing that with God's help, he could create a successful business. Why would he have chosen a Christian strategy? The answer is that he had a vision. Someone said, "Vision is a picture of the future that causes passion in your heart." He also knew if you expect God's leadership and blessing of your life, you do not compartmentalize your life. He knew God saves us as full-timers, not part-timers. He, being a devoted Christian and humanitarian, never embraced that idea that "business is business," almost as if it can be set apart with a different set of values and ethics.

From inception, Mr. Cassels, Sr. determined the business strategy would be simple yet profoundly wise, and it would become the cornerstone of this great company. He said, "Take care of the people who take care of the customer, and that will take care of the future." He knew this was a strategy that would please his Creator. He had a genuine awareness of the value of treating every associate with respect and dignity. He knew just hiring and firing would never produce the culture that would excel. He also knew nurturing, encouraging, and developing on the part of leadership would produce an extraordinary culture. Christian-based leadership works because everyone is respected, equipped, and expected to honor God with *quality* work. And he also realized in order to shape a culture, you must be actively interacting with the people consistently.

The leadership torch was passed to the second and now third generation. Both Mr. Cassels, Jr. and son Tobin Cassels have seen and helped carry out that simple yet profoundly successful plan. They have now embraced same, with perhaps even greater commitment today. Truly, the apples did not fall far from the tree.

As the founder began to age, his only son became the primary leader. He, like his father, also brought these outstanding attributes of wisdom, vision, great faith in his Creator, and great faith in his fellow man. His role was to maintain the wonderful existent serving culture, and at the same time, greatly enlarge the area of service. The customers were anxious for Southeastern Freight to expand its geographic service area, and the company wanted to make its consistently excellent service available to more customers.

Fortunately for everyone involved, the Cassels had not taken substantial profits out of the business, which is often the case when a business is prosperous. Because of the wisdom of the founder and because of the family's discipline and kept promises, this company had the essential resources needed to fund the expansion necessary without penalizing the associates monetarily.

Unfortunately, history tells us that as a business becomes larger, all too often, the personal touch is diminished. Growth can and often does bring disproportional complexities in human relations and morale issues also.

We were certainly aware that the most important responsibility we had with the expansion was to take care of the people by not allowing anything to interfere with that sacred duty. How would we do so? Southeastern was growing and had now become a well-established and highly respected transportation company. Deregulation of trucking during Ronald Reagan's presidency had now provided unlimited opportunities for expansion. The answer for how to expand as needed and yet still take care of the people is rather simple, though not always easy to do. Duly noted, we would work hard to continuously change the things that needed to be changed and improved, but we would work twice as hard to keep the important things that did not need to be changed from changing for want of attention.

First and foremost, on that list of important things to preserve was, and forever will be, taking care of the people who had diligently and faithfully helped build a great company.

It is difficult to believe that any astute business persons would knowingly allow morale to decline without a response from leadership. However, sometimes simple, obviously unplanned neglect is all that is necessary for people to begin to feel unimportant. I expect at some time in our lifetime, we have heard people say, "The place I work at is not what it used to be." That is the beginning of the end if left unattended and uncorrected.

The leaders at Southeastern Freight were determined that our very essential growth and expansion would never lead to a seemingly less appreciated workforce. The old adage "an ounce of prevention is worth a pound of cure" is certainly true as it pertains to the encouragement and morale of loyal associates.

There had been four primary elements that had led to Southeastern Freight's success. The first was the vision by Mr. Cassels, Sr., and the faith to persevere in making that vision a reality. He saw a prosperous future as people felt truly appreciated and consistently encouraged.

The second was the absolute inclusion of every associate. They were not just regularly told how important they were; they were included in significant ways. One of those ways was the sharing consistently of important information relative to the company. The people genuinely felt they were an integral part of this company, and it has created a great sense of pride for all.

The third was the unity and alignment with every service center focusing on what was best for the customer even if it was inconvenient for that facility. Kept promises were more important than territorial statistics.

The fourth was encouragement, regularly given by leaders who knew a primary responsibility was to always be seeking opportunities to encourage their people.

There was a genuine respect and strong bond among the people who comprised this unity. They knew division was a destroyer and had clearly eliminated same. The objective embraced by every associate, of keeping every promise to the customers, had united them.

There were probably many others, but these were the primary elements that had contributed to the development heretofore.

## Vision

The vision had been a constant of ours at Southeastern Freight. The Bible teaches us this great truth, "Where there is no vision the people perish" (Proverbs 29:18, KJV). The teachings and applied principles from God's Word had been consistently prevalent and practiced in the company from inception. The associates knew they would always be treated with respect and dignity. That Christian vision brought a sense of genuine security.

Now to be sure, as a Christian business, Southeastern Freight did not have a prayer meeting every morning at the office. Neither did it have a Bible reading period. Our people just lived out and applied the principles in God's Word in a very practical, consistent way. It was at that time, and still is a matter of always, always doing the right things as they serve customers externally and associates internally.

Mr. Cassels, Jr. and his son Tobin have now faithfully embraced and consistently practiced what the founder had expressed and implemented. They are both devout practicing Christians, and they had both observed how well the founder's strategy had created a unique corporate culture. They also knew the strategy of respect and care for others and kept promises that had come from the Word of God. They knew those same principles work best everywhere—in families, even in government, and certainly in business. God's principles and taking care of your people had clearly been proven effective as they worked diligently and faithfully to make application of that simple strategy.

That strategy had created a company of contented associates who reflected their contentment as they interfaced with customers. The respect they received from the leadership was reflected to the customers consistently, and there is no question as to how well the strategy had worked. Kindness with consistency and reliability is still somewhat rare in the business world. It is hard to find other companies who so embrace the honorable and respectful treatment and care of their people as prescribed in the Bible.

*Paul, Mr. Cassels, Jr. and Tobin Cassels*

## Inclusion. Unity and Alignment

Within every person, there is the desire to be included. It is a very natural thing. Inclusion causes associates to genuinely feel and know they are a valuable part of an organization. It is part of a divine plan to treat others as you would want to be treated. It will always produce a better result.

One of the great strengths of this company is inclusion, a powerful persuader to cause associates to give their very best effort and receive the personal benefit from same. Because of that inclusion and constant recognition and encouragement, there is a remarkable commitment to unity and alignment in return.

I remember vividly a Sunday morning when the majority of our long-haul drivers were attending a Road Drivers Appreciation celebration. Sunday was the only day those who moved the loads between service centers could attend without interfering with the moving of the cargo. Mr. Cassels, Jr. gave a devotional message, and wouldn't you know he quoted Solomon, the second wisest man who ever lived. "Though one may be overpowered by another, two can withstand him. And a threefold cord is not quickly broken" (Ecclesiastes 4:12, NKJV). He focused us on unity without the destruction of division.

It was interesting to me that out of such a comprehensive book as the Bible, he chose this verse. In the New American Standard Version of the Bible, there are 31,303 verses. What are the odds of that one verse of 31,303 being selected? I cannot help but believe Our Lord Himself helped Mr. Cassels select that verse. Why do I say that? Because God hates division! He knows what a destroyer division is, wherever you find it, in the church, home, government, workplace, or wherever. Matthew 12:25, NIV is clear about division's destruction: "Every kingdom divided against itself will be ruined, and every city or household divided against itself will not stand."

Unity is critical to any group, family, church, and business that is trying to succeed. By this, I mean getting everyone on the same page. God is our helper, providing His Holy Spirit to indwell and unite His people. Holy Spirit, the Difference-Maker, provides the power which allows His people to overlook the minor things that so often separate and destroy others.

The wise founder of this great company and certainly his son knew how very important it is to be in unity and aligned against the things that divide and prevent the creation of excellence. Oh my, how we desperately need alignment and unity with a fresh commitment to morality and brotherhood in America today.

There is a unity within this great company, Southeastern Freight, which is so rare and so remarkable. Every person fully understands customers buy the promises made. Those promises are then backed up by performance, and the customers expect those promises to be kept. All employees are then unified in this effort. The process will always be done best only by a team of unified, aligned, and focused associates who are bonded together in the effort, and Southeastern Freight has that proven team.

From its humble beginning, Southeastern Freight has been about inclusion and unity. Constant positive reinforcement, as a result of the founding vision, has become a wonderful reality. This can happen only when the leadership teams genuinely respect and take care of the people who create those outstanding results.

The spirit of serving internal and external customers is in place because the second and third-generation heirs have so honored the founder with a very protective commitment to that beginning philosophy. By the way, God has honored it also because He is always pleased when man treats man with God-ordained respect and dignity.

## Encouragement

Encouragement, continuously carried out with sincerity, has also been an important factor in creating an outstanding culture at Southeastern Freight.

Jesus, Himself made a profound statement: "It is more blessed to give than to receive" (Acts 20:35, NIV). What He is saying is that it is more fulfilling and will make you happier to give or commend someone else. To be an encourager of others is a wonderful characteristic to have. Honest and sincere encouragement permeates this great company. Encouragement and recognition are essential tools in a real Quality Improvement Process. Southeastern has one of the most effective QIPs in any industry. Encouragement and recognition are two keys in making that process so very effective and encouragement is such an essential ingredient in creating excellence.

The entire Cassels family has lived out values that make their leadership easy to follow. People will do things out of respect that they will do for no other motivation. Those values lived are solid Christian morals found in God's Holy Bible, which is the best leadership and human relations book ever written. They are guaranteed to work and produce positively for every stakeholder. Alignment, with unity and added encouragement are so very powerful in any endeavor, but especially so in business.

The presidency of Southeastern Freight was given to me in 1988. It was the best job I could have ever imagined. God had put me in an organization that was solidly united in the effort to outperform all our competitors and always do the right thing. There was already an embedded culture of service providers who were absolutely committed to providing the promised service to our customers.

I lack the words to describe how graciously I have been blessed to be a part of one of America's finest companies. My work was never a dread because my workplace was a place of unbelievable unity and alignment, inclusion, and encouragement. It was not occasional; it was consistent. Why was it so vastly different than so many companies where people tolerate the corporate culture because they need a paycheck? It was and is different because it was based on the biblical ethic for a business lived out every day. The Bible is a profound book of truth. It is full of profound instructions and encouragement.

Our world, and our country, and our homes truly need alignment behind our Savior—following Jesus up close and fearlessly like Peter after Pentecost and after being filled with the Holy Spirit.

We have the "aligner," the Holy Spirit of God, to keep us in alignment and following Christ faithfully. He provides the only lasting answer for mankind today!

Perhaps the most likely question after hearing all of this is, what has all of this accomplished and created. It has created clearly superlative results. What is so interesting and outstanding to me is this family has simply applied God's principles within the business. They knew the great potential God has put within mankind, made in His image. In response to that faith in them, the associates have responded with superlative results. People *absolutely can* achieve any tasks before them when we follow God's most wonderful plan for our lives. There is such value in following God's instruction. These truths are available for all to follow and benefit from. Why would any continue to resist something so wonderful when people can excel so remarkably by obeying God's instructions?

# CHAPTER 30

# Missions Beginning

Many, many years ago, if you had asked me about doing missionary work in foreign countries and in the United States as well, I would have said, "No way." It is now interesting that the Lord has guided me and Lynette (some together and some between us) on twenty-three different mission endeavors. I lack the words to describe the joy in my heart for being allowed, though unworthy, to take the gospel to so many hopeless and desperate people. So many of those hopeless people readily accepted the truth of the gospel and became heaven-bound saints. It is interesting as I think back to how it started.

Approximately twenty years ago, we began a Thursday night prayer meeting in our home with a group of our dearest friends and fellow church members. We would come together and pray earnestly for an extended period of time and then enjoy a time of fellowship. Several in our group at that time would continually talk about missions and how important it was that we all support all the mission activities in our church. They had a real passion about it. We also had a young associate pastor who was passionate about missions. I really had not thought through the seriousness of making disciples, but as I did, realized it must be really more important than I had realized since that was the last commandment Jesus gave us before ascending back to the Father.

During that time, God's hand had been on my life. I was doing my best to follow the wise counsel which was given to me by my pastor that night I was born again. God had called me to teach Sunday school every Sunday, to participate in a Bible study every Sunday evening, and to be in prayer meeting every Wednesday when I was not traveling. Also, I had already chaired several pastor search committees and served as a deacon for many years. I would gladly share the gospel when I encountered someone who clearly exhibited a need. All of this I did willingly and happily. After all, I owed my Savior a debt I could never repay. However, when short-term missions in foreign countries were discussed, I let the enemy deceive me by whispering in my being, "Paul, you are already doing your part." Satan is so clearly deceptive and destructive with his half-truths. And half-truths are still lies.

Anyway, as we gathered to pray, it was evident everyone in the group was committed to the great commission. There was one lady, one of God's most faithful servants, who loved horses. Riding horses had been her favorite pastime passion for years. Yet in order to fund her mission trips, she sold her horse and saddles. She traded these things in order to go places she had never been and to tell people she had never met about the love and forgiveness of our Savior. Our learning of this sacrifice was a most inspiring and encouraging event to all the rest of us. In essence, while she said nothing about what she had done, her actions spoke loudly of her decision to obey Christ, no matter what the cost. That clearly describes the passion within our small group. I was again convicted (later to the point of obeying God's call on my life) to also do missions, even to the point of doing what I never thought I could or would do.

Finally, my opportunity came. It was on my knees that God so convicted me of my need and His call to go and to share the gospel by doing short-term mission work. I really wanted to do God's will, and He made it clear that this was His will for my life. What a blessing it was to follow my initial reluctance with obedience.

Once I realized it was clearly God's will for Lynette and me to do the mission work before us, He opened the doors and blessed the results of eight trips to Cuba, seven trips to India, two trips to Africa, one trip to Bangladesh, three trips to the Czech Republic, one trip to Panther, West Virginia, and also a trip to New Orleans, Louisiana. I will share more about some of these trips in future chapters. I have never been able to forget the great needs in so many places for people to be introduced to Jesus and true life. Nonetheless, it is impossible to describe the joy we received as we observed the power of the gospel delivering so many enslaved captives. Praise be to God!

Now, it had occurred to me, and I then realized, my part was to listen and obey God's Holy Spirit regardless of what I may have deemed my part was previously. I learned this: God will never call anyone unless He equips that one. After all, He is calling us to do the most important work in the world! What an honor to re-present Him and obey Him with God-confidence, not self-confidence. Yes, re-present is what we are doing. He once walked this earth, paid our sin debt on the cross, and went back to the right hand of the Father. We now have the privilege of representing Him to hurting, lost, and needy people.

By the grace and goodness of God, He allowed me to do mission work in Cuba on eight different occasions. Every one of those is memorable because of the kind and humble nature of the Cuban people. They, as a whole, are a gracious and unpretentious group. The great majority are downtrodden and with very little hope.

The overthrow of Juan Batista, the cruel dictator in the 1950s, was thought to be the beginning of a better life for the Cuban people. They had finally been delivered from the tyranny of Juan Batista. However, over time it became evident they had been delivered unto another dictator, Fidel Castro, a man they had idolized earlier as their liberator. The result, though, whether intended or not, was that Cuba has now become, for the great majority, a communist country. Those few at the top live a very affluent lavish lifestyle, and the majority of others live in abject poverty, with little hope for a better life on this earth. While in Cuba, I also saw what socialized medicine was about. It was simply to let those whose illnesses (if allowed to continue) would cost the state the most, to die without the withheld expensive treatment.

What a blessing it truly is to experience the joy when hopeless people become liberated from that hopelessness, such as those did whom we met in Cuba after they were introduced to the gospel of Jesus Christ. They really begin to realize this short life on earth is just a rehearsal for the real thing: eternal life in a place of peace, beauty, and rest. But eternal life in heaven is conditional, and we can have those blessings only if and when we choose to repent of our innate sin, ask for forgiveness, accept Jesus as Savior, and follow Him in Lordship.

My former pastor and great friend, Dr. Rob White, and his wife, Sandy, have been burdened for the lost people in Cuba for decades. They are the ones who invited me to go on eight mission trips. The ultimate goal of these trips was to:

» Always conduct street evangelism.

» Strengthen and encourage "house church" Christians.

» Provide special ministry for ladies and children.

» Provide medicines and other health care needs.

» Teach and encourage church leaders.

» Preach in "house churches" while we were there.

» Work diligently to help start new "house churches."

"House churches" may be a relatively new term for you, but it is the only acceptable way Christianity is allowed in Cuba. "Why," you may be asking, "is that the case?" The answer is very logical. The overthrow of Batista was by a large gathering, and those who participated in his demise realized the power of large gatherings. There is no political danger from small group gatherings, whereas larger groups are a threat and not allowed. Therefore, there are now a number of small house churches, where twenty to thirty Christians gather regularly to worship our Savior. The house churches are simply residences that are opened for congregants to worship in. Rarely do they have more than thirty persons in attendance.

If you have ever led a person (with the gospel, urged on by the Holy Spirit of God) to accept and follow Jesus Christ, you know there is no greater emotion of joy than to be the voice delivering God's truth and watching the captive be set free. "Where the Spirit of the Lord is, there is liberty" (2 Corinthians 3:17, KJV). This verse declares one of my most favorite biblical truths! The power of its truth is such a blessing... freed from the bondage of sin.

I lack the vocabulary to express the great fulfillment and joyfulness I experienced on mission trips as I saw hundreds and hundreds delivered from the clutches of Satan into the perfect watchcare of Christ. I am reminded of the demoniac described in Mark 5. The man was demon-possessed, he had been cast out by the town's people since they were afraid of him, and his people had already given up on him. However, when Jesus arrived by boat in the country of the Gadarenes, the deranged one "when he saw Jesus from afar off, ran and worshiped Him" (Mark 5:6, KJV). Don't forget, the demoniac was a deranged one, yet miraculously he was drawn to worship Jesus! Jesus then delivered the man from his torment. The demons were commanded by Jesus (Yes, He is Lord of all, even the demons) to go into the swine, and "after the unclean spirits entered the swine, the herd ran violently... into the sea" (Mark 5:13, KJV). "So those who fed the swine fled, and they told it in the city and country. And they went out to see what it was that had happened. Then they came to Jesus and saw the one who had been demon-possessed and had the legion sitting and clothed and in his right mind [transformed]. And they were afraid" (Mark 5:14–15, KJV). The people did what you and I would probably have done. They began to beg the delivered one to depart from their region. His behavior severely hurt the pig business!

When Jesus got in the boat, the delivered one "begged Him that he might be with Him." Jesus said to him, "Go home to your friends and tell them what great things the Lord has done for you and how He has had compassion on you." This is exactly what He tells every disciple—*Go!* "The delivered one departed obediently and began to proclaim in Decapolis all that Jesus had done for him and all men marveled" (Mark 5:18–20, NKJV). Right away, he began to go and share Christ, making disciples along the way). His "special needs" had been supernaturally met.

Wow! We go from a man deranged, who was literally under the control of Satan and cast out of the city, to a man delivered by our Savior and given special instructions: "Go and tell what great things the Lord has done for you, and how He has had compassion on you." And he obeyed, (Mark 5:19, NKJV).

In summary, we see three things: a hopeless case (demon-possessed), a heavenly cure (Jesus Himself), and a happy Christian (because he was obedient).

And what was the result? "All men did marvel."

Every true born-again believer now has the Holy Spirit within them. Peter made that clear when he preached the first sermon in the church at Pentecost. Peter spoke to the townspeople about it, for they did not know what was happening.

Peter said, "Repent and let everyone of you be baptized in the Name of Jesus Christ for the remission of sins; and you shall receive the gift of the Holy Spirit. For the promise is to *you* and *your children* and to *all* who are afar off, *as many as the Lord, Our God, will call*" (Acts 2:38–39, NKJV, emphasis mine).

Now every time I read Matthew 28:18–20 (NIV)...

*All authority in heaven and on earth has been given to Me. Therefore, go and make disciples, baptizing them in the name of the Father and of the Son and of the Holy Spirit and teaching them to obey everything I have commanded you. And surely I am with you, to the very end of the age.*

... I realize Jesus was and is speaking directly to me. I am His disciple, and so is everyone who has truly repented, asked for forgiveness, and professed Jesus as Savior and is growing spiritually. Jesus would never call us to go and tell unless He equipped us with divine power to do so. After all, each one of us has the opportunity for the most wonderful story of deliverance from worldly mayhem and unhealthy wicked desires to deliverance into His perfect peace. If our experience of salvation is real, we also have the power of the Holy Spirit resident. The same Holy Spirit power that raised a dead Christ is given to help us be obedient to take the gospel effectively to others, just like He commanded each of us to do in His last words on earth. There is a very important point to be made here. When we obey Christ and go to share the gospel, we never go alone. We are to spend time with God first in prayer. The resident power of God's Holy Spirit empowers us. Then John 16:14 (NIV) promises that the Holy Spirit in us will glorify Jesus when we obey Christ and share the gospel. What a Helper we have (John 14:16, NIV).

Just like Jesus delivered and set free the demon-possessed man, He expects us to obey and reach out so others can be set free. What if the original twelve disciples had not been obedient? What if they had decided it was too difficult or too dangerous or not their job to go tell others how wonderful it was to be transformed? Thank God they obeyed Jesus' command in His last words, which are also written for you and me in Matthew 28:18–20 (NIV). The disciples were faithful to the point of martyrdom because their lives had been so radically transformed when they were truly born again and filled with the promised Holy Spirit. They spent three years in His presence as He performed miraculous deeds and spoke, never heard before, profound truth. They knew that they had clearly been in the presence of the risen Lord. We owe those first disciples a debt we can never repay. Their faithfulness and obedience took the gospel around the world, having given their lives—spiritually and quite literally—in obedience to Him.

» Matthew, also called Levi, was a publican (or tax collector) who suffered martyrdom in Ethiopia, killed by a sword.

» Mark, the first to author a New Testament gospel, was the founder of the Church in Alexandria, Egypt. He died in Alexandria after being dragged by horses through the streets until he was dead.

» Luke was a physician and companion of the apostle Paul who wrote the books of Luke and the Acts of the Apostles. He was hanged in Greece as a result of his remarkable preaching to the lost.

» John, son of Zebedee, was a fisherman and one of the first disciples called by Jesus. John faced martyrdom when he was boiled in a huge basin of oil during a wave of persecution in Rome. He was, however, miraculously delivered from death. John was then sentenced to the mines on the prison island of Patmos, where he wrote his prophetic Book of Revelation. The apostle John was later freed and returned to serve as Bishop of Edessa, which is in modern-day Turkey. He died an old man, the only apostle to die peacefully and of natural causes.

» Peter was a fisherman known also as Simon Peter or sometimes Simeon, and brother of another of Jesus' original twelve, Andrew. Peter was crucified upside down on an X-shaped cross. According to church tradition, it was because he told his tormentors that he felt unworthy to die in the same way that Jesus Christ had died.

» James, also called James the Just, was the leader in the church in Jerusalem and the oldest brother of Jesus. James was thrown over a hundred feet down from the southeast pinnacle of the Temple in Jerusalem when he refused to deny his faith in Christ. When the Pharisees discovered that he survived the fall, James was beaten to death with a fuller's club. This was the same pinnacle where Satan had taken Jesus during the Temptation.

» James the Great was the brother of John and son of Zebedee. Like his brother, he was a fisherman by trade when Jesus called him to a lifetime of ministry. As a strong leader of the church, James was ultimately tried and sentenced to death by King Herod Agrippa. The Roman officer who guarded James watched, amazed, as James defended his faith at his trial. Later, the officer walked beside James to the place of execution. Overcome by conviction, he declared his new faith to the judge and knelt beside James to accept beheading as a Christian also.

» Bartholomew, also known as Nathaniel, was a missionary to Asia and witnessed about our Lord in what is now Turkey. He was martyred for his preaching in Armenia, where he was flayed to death by a whip.

» Andrew, the brother of Simon Peter, was crucified in a manner similar to his brother on an X-shaped cross in Patras, Greece. After being severely whipped by seven soldiers, they tied his body to the cross with cords to prolong the agony of his death. Andrew's followers reported that when he was led to the cross, he saluted it and said, "I have long desired and expected this happy hour. The cross has been consecrated by the body of Christ hanging on it." He continued to preach to his tormentors for two days until he finally expired.

» Thomas, who is known today as Doubting Thomas because he did not initially believe that Jesus was resurrected, was stabbed with a spear in India during one of his missionary trips to establish the church in the sub-continent.

» Jude the apostle, sometimes called Judas (not to be confused with Judas Iscariot, the betrayer of Jesus), was killed with arrows when he refused to deny his faith in Christ.

» Matthias was the apostle chosen to replace the traitor Judas Iscariot. He was stoned and then beheaded.

» Paul, whose Hebrew name was Saul of Tarsus, was tortured and then beheaded by order of the evil Emperor Nero at Rome in A.D. 67. Paul endured a lengthy imprisonment, which allowed him to write his many epistles to the Roman Empire. These letters, which taught many of the foundational doctrines of

Christianity, form a large portion of the New Testament. Paul's body may have been imprisoned, but his spirit was still beautifully free.

Perhaps this is a reminder to us that our sufferings here are indeed minor compared to the intense persecution and cold cruelty faced by apostles during their times for the sake of the faith. "And ye shall be hated of all men for my name's sake: but he that endureth to the end shall be saved" (Matthew 10:22, KJV).

Jesus' Last words are Lasting Words, Matthew 28:18–20 (NKJV), the Great Commission. "All authority has been given to Me in heaven and on earth. Go therefore and make disciples of all nations, baptizing them in the name of the Father and of the Son and of the Holy Spirit, teaching them to obey all that I have commanded you; and lo, I am with you always, even to the end of the ages."

What if the disciples had not, by Holy Spirit power received at Pentecost, stayed faithful to this command of Jesus? You and I would still be lost. Who, out there somewhere in your world and mine, might miss out on Jesus' forgiveness? If I do not persevere and do as these first disciples and make the world's most important truth known, who will never hear? Jesus said, "I am the way, the truth, and the life; no man cometh unto the Father, but by Me" (John 14:6, KJV). Who has the Lord saved that He wants to share the gospel? It is every one of us. We are to share the gospel and make converts who will ultimately become disciples.

The Lord has equipped His people, by Holy Spirit power, to go and make truth known. We have the most important calling, opportunity, and duty in the world. Think about this, really let it soak in: No church would be in decline today if all God's people were sharing that truth and if God's people were sharing a testimony to God's wonderful, fulfilling presence in their lives. Think about this question: What am I willing to do in response to God's precious gift of grace and peace through Jesus Christ? Also, know this: you will never be alone and without God's Holy Spirit "(the Difference-Maker)" as you share Christ and obey our Savior.

God will always bless obedience and faithfulness! Success in missions is simply going forward without reservation. The results are in the hands of our gracious God. He is always more than trustworthy.

# CHAPTER 31

# The Decision (Submission)

While my time at Southeastern could never have been more fulfilling and rewarding, I had begun to realize God's call on my life to short-term mission work, and it was not going away.

With seriously mixed emotions, I decided to retire at sixty-three, a couple of years earlier than later at the age of 65, to pursue God's call to missions. It was a final step in Lordship for me. In my spirit, I knew God wanted me to be a faithful, obedient disciple, sharing Christ at every opportunity. That was what I had done with regularity within the company and anywhere else as God prompted.

It was evident through all those years after becoming a true follower of Christ that God was leading me to allow Him, and desire Him, to be more than just Savior, but more importantly, to be my Lord. I loved being under His new and wonderful leadership. When we limit what we will do in response to God's indescribable grace in our lives, we miss many blessings and the joy that comes from grateful obedience.

Because Southeastern Freight had been so very good to me, I was seriously conflicted by God's urgings to do the mission work that lay ahead or whether to stay and continue to help build a better future for this great company. But the fact that the owner's son, Tobin, was to become my successor made it somewhat easier to retire and answer God's call. Tobin had become a faithful, obedient, born-again child of God who had matured greatly; additionally, he had a wonderful personality, always the same. He was very intelligent and had grown spiritually by leaps and bounds. He loved people and continuously demonstrated his God-given servant/leader skills. I became convinced Tobin had the family heritage of wisdom, and he could now easily more than fill the position I held.

I so wanted to please Mr. Cassels, Jr., the most respected man I have ever known, by staying several more years. He had been more than gracious to me, but I knew the company was in equally as good, or in better hands, with Tobin. He was a natural-born and now reborn servant-leader, ever-increasing in wisdom. He had already proven clearly as much. As time progressed, my confidence grew that God was leading me to do the mission's work. The year was 2001. I had enjoyed seventeen wonderful years with the finest people you would ever want to know. God had been so gracious to allow me to be part of something so uniquely different, special, and better. But knowing I could trust God's calling because He had blessed me so much, I listened to His call to move forward in discipleship and missions. I tendered my resignation to do same.

## On Mission, Finally

One of my first trips was to the Czech Republic to a beautiful small town, Mikulov, which is in the eastern section of the Czech Republic and near the Austrian border.

*Paul and Lynette in Czech Republic, Holy Hill, 2002*

Our purpose for going there was to help evangelize for the purpose of strengthening the church. We did various things to create opportunities to evangelize. More so then than now, we (being Americans) were somewhat admired in most of the world. That may have been more so because of the prosperity of our country than anything else. Whatever it was, simply being Americans opened some doors, especially in the schools. It was evident they wanted to know more about America than they did about religion. After all, they had been exposed to much religious activity over a long period of time. There was a bit of coolness with the people toward religion, and understandably so. Truth is, they were, in fact, hardened, or so it appeared, to any form of religion even though they received us graciously and treated us well. I believe this was because they had been through extremely difficult times in World War II, and religion had not helped them. That made them stoic and skeptical about same. We were, however, attractive to them because we were Americans.

Our approach was to work as much as we could with the younger ones, the middle schoolers and early high schoolers, because they were the most receptive. On a very warm Saturday, we organized an activities day, and we had a large crowd of about two hundred children. It became my lot to do face painting, which because most had never seen it before, was a huge attraction. That had taken almost 4 hours to paint all the children, and it was a very hot sunny day. Then, the worst thing that could have occurred did. One of the children saw a painting on the face of another child that he liked better than the one he had gotten painted on his face. He quickly came back, turned his bare cheek to me, and asked me to do the one he liked best on the other bare cheek. You guessed it—it started a revolution. Before the day was over, almost all two hundred of them had a face painting on each cheek. And I had a weary body and a sunburn. Nevertheless, the children were elated with their face paintings...or perhaps, more so, loved the attention they received from us Americans.

There was another thing we did to attract people. Since I've always enjoyed drawing and painting, I found a busy street location and began to sketch a portrait of Christ in pastel medium. Even though I am only a hobby artist, it is something I had always liked to do when there was time to do it. One young man was captivated by the image, and as someone shared the gospel with him, he accepted Jesus as Lord and Savior.

Overall, our trips to Mikulov were eye-opening to us. This had been one of the most religious places in Europe previously. It had been the home of some of the Anabaptists who had originated with the reformation. For clarity, Anabaptists were more devout and differed with the Catholics to the point some were martyred and burned at the stake. But such devotion was clearly not the case anymore.

There may be a great lesson for all of us here—a place where once people were willing to die for their strong beliefs in their faith was now practically devoid of spiritual life. Their *religion* had turned into mere form and rituals.

Mikulov was a nice place to visit and a historically interesting place. However, it is a place that desperately needs to know about the wonderful plan God has for each of us. That plan is not religion but a relationship, for the *forgiven*, through acceptance of His gracious provision, by the Lord Jesus Christ (the gospel).

Prague, the capital of the Czech Republic, is one of the most beautiful cities in the world. Unfortunately, spiritually, it is also still somewhat dark, and the people are not that open to the gospel. Some of the most beautiful and ornate structures ever built are now decorated with ugly graffiti. I could not help but be somewhat saddened that graffiti was a more important American influence than the liberating gospel of Christ. Also, could it be that the yoke of rituals, fads, and rites without a clear focus on the gospel had created a serious lack of awareness about how important the simple gospel is?

In the next chapter, I will contrast Prague with Cuba, where the Cuban people warmly welcome the hope that the gospel brings. The following chapter will cover teaching lessons learned about missions from my eight Cuban trips. Then it will conclude with two stories, one about Somalian refugees in Kenya and the last about Americans devastated by Hurricane Katrina. I share these varying stories because each has an important mission or discipleship lesson, and I want many others to know the blessings that obedience always brings forth.

I must not fail to say with each mission trip we were diligent to request prayer from other faithful Christians and to be prayed up ourselves, praying much like Paul in Colossians 4:2–3a (NKJV), "Continue earnestly in prayer, being vigilant in it with thanksgiving; meanwhile praying also for us that God would open to us a door for the word, to speak the mystery of Christ." We were well aware anything could happen, and we knew Satan would always try to interfere in any way he could. Hence, we continually claimed 1 John 4:4b (KJV), "Greater is He that is in you, than he that is in the world," as we moved forth.

# CHAPTER 32

# On Mission

## Yes, It Really Matters

After He was resurrected, Jesus gave his disciples the great commission, as recorded in Matthew 28. As a Spirit-filled child of God, I came to a point where sharing the gospel with those around me, those I came in contact with, was challenged. God wanted me to up my game. Jesus did tell his disciples to go into all nations, and I, too, was so informed.

Taking a missions trip is, for me and everyone I know who has done so, a life-altering experience. It gives one a new lens into witnessing the power of God. It takes us out of our familiar comfort zone and reminds us of the diversity of God's creation and of the masses of humanity who need the saving knowledge of Jesus Christ.

Have you ever thought about the fact we can be really nice people—perhaps we are disciplined and determined to be nice—yet we can still be lost spiritually? On one of our mission trips to Cuba, we were going door to door and sharing our faith. We had just left a home where both the husband and wife were joyously saved. While there, we had inquired about their next-door neighbors. They told us about the three people who lived there, a husband, wife, and mother of the wife.

When we went next door, graciously they welcomed us in. They were warm and friendly to us. Then they shared that they had recently returned from America where they had been visiting their son and the brother of the mother. It was evident they were very proud of their son because he was a pastor of a Protestant Church in New Jersey.

We complimented them on having a relative called out to lead a Christian congregation and began assuming they were all Christians as well. We can only credit the Holy Spirit for leading us to ask the mother about her own "reborn" experience. She appeared really surprised and began to ask us to explain that term. When we asked again if they had ever asked Christ to save them, they all three indicated they had not. It was quite unusual since they had just returned from visiting their pastor son.

Next, we shared the gospel carefully and fully. Then we asked if they would like to invite Christ to be their Lord and Savior. It was evident God's Holy Spirit convicted them of the truth of the gospel. All three of them answered affirmatively and were gloriously saved. They were so grateful to know the liberating truth of the gospel and to be certain of their eternal home in heaven with God's people. It was a wondrously happy time for all of us.

*Cuba Mission Team*

The lesson I learned that day was to never take anyone's Christianity for granted. These dear people had religion, and they obviously felt religion was a good thing because that was all they knew. They were good, moral people trying to live honorably by doing good works. But they did not have a relationship with Jesus.

Does discipleship really matter? Yes. There are people that God—the only One who knows the future—expects every one of us to share Christ with. If we do not, who will?

It may seem intimidating to become a faithful witness for Jesus, but here is what we must never forget. We will never face a lost person alone. God's Holy Spirit is in us. His Word tells us, "He shall be in you" (John 14:15–17, KJV). Personally, I am of the persuasion that a person who has been the recipient of the shared gospel, presented by a faithful witness, never forgets that experience. Even if that person does not accept Christ at that time, they are much more likely to do so the next time or at some time in the future. The truth of the gospel is powerful and really challenging to dismiss, especially since man is created in the image of God.

Too often, the clever, deceiving enemy of God may whisper this lie in our ear, "But that's the preacher's job. He knows so much more about the Word of God." If that happens, we must then ask ourselves this penetrating question: Why did Jesus then, as His very last words on earth, say to His disciples there, and to *you* and *me* as his disciples today, "All authority in heaven and on earth, has been given to me. Go therefore and make disciples, of all the nations, baptizing them in the name of the Father, and of the Son, and of the Holy Spirit, teaching them to observe all things I have commanded you, and lo, I am with you always even to the end of the age?" (Matthew 28:18–20, NKJV).

Experience has convinced me "regret" is the most difficult thing anyone must live with. I cannot help but think about the twenty-one wasted years from the time I was baptized until I asked Jesus to save me and fill my heart with the Holy Spirit. As a lost church member, I never shared Christ with anyone. *I had nothing to share*! I cannot help but think about how many people I could have shared Christ with, but I did not do so. I was an observer, a bystander. By God's grace, however, He has forgiven me. Hopefully, someone else was faithful to share and did what I should have been doing: helping those people with an eternal death sentence to be set free to live abundantly.

Does it really matter that I share Christ? You bet it matters! And it matters for all eternity to those God has planned for you and me to be exemplary witnesses to, just like Joe Alexander was to me.

We may not be aware of just how much it really does matter because we most certainly live in an era of individualism, all too often focused on ourselves rather than our fellow man.

God saved us to be concerned for others and to share so they might enjoy His blessed peace and presence as we do so. It really, really matters how we respond. It matters for all eternity if we go and tell.

He said, "Follow Me," and He forgave our grievous sins. At that point, He sent the powerful Holy Spirit, the Difference-Maker, to empower us to live in grateful *obedience*, and share. Share the most important thing that could ever happen in anyone's life with people who need hope and forgiveness.

What a saviour!

## Radical Transformation

On every mission trip to Cuba, our primary purpose would be evangelism. The sharing of the gospel was something we were always prepared to do and something we always sought opportunities to do. We also made a special effort to listen to Christian leaders who lived there and helped us with priorities they identified. On this particular trip, one of those priorities was to go door to door in a rather remote area with the intention of identifying enough interested people to plant a new house church where there was no church there at all.

This remote location was about an hour's drive from where our team was staying in Alomar. When we approached this remote area, we turned off the main highway onto a narrower road, a paved road that was in need of much repair. It shortly led to an unpaved and very rough road. The farther we traveled on it, the narrower and rougher it became. In short order, our driver decided this was as far as we could safely take the bus. It was clearly remote.

The vegetation was lush and beautiful, and there were scattered homes, but it was not a village, and our work was clearly cut out for us. Our mission for this day was to find enough people to share the gospel with, who would then become the nucleus of a house church, which is simply someone's home that opened same for prayer and worship.

We were there for the purpose of sharing the gospel and then explaining the benefit of a local house church. We trusted the Lord to help us enlist twenty or more people to do just that. Our driver had stopped the bus at a place overlooking a valley bursting with lush, green vegetation. We prayed earnestly for God's presence and guidance and then departed the bus.

As we were preparing to separate and go in different directions, a very pleasant-faced, middle-aged man approached us and nicely asked us what we were doing so far off the main road. I am doubtful he had ever seen a bus venture so far into such an isolated area.

He was very friendly to us, and when we told him our purpose was to seek out enough people to begin a church, he smiled. I believe most of us were surprised by his reply when he said, "Oh, a church will be nice here." He told us he was responsible for the large farm here and seemed sincerely pleased we had come to this place to start a church. We were all impressed by how well he spoke, and he clearly displayed an air of confident leadership. It was almost as if we had encountered an old friend.

After we prayed earnestly for God's Holy Spirit to go before us, we all left the area walking in teams of two and three. We were excited about the challenge of reaching enough people with the wonderful, liberating truth of the gospel.

There were five or six teams that day, and we traveled a mile or so along the rough, unpaved and rocky road. We stopped at every dwelling, and the acceptance of the truth of the gospel occurred at practically every one of them. It began to be evident we were on a mission ordained of God as attested to by the enthusiasm about having a church in this, up until now, somewhat neglected area.

As I think back to what happened that day in such a profound way, I cannot remember a time that was more gratifying. It was exciting as these people listened intently and responded to the great good news of God's forgiveness.

Farther down the rough, rocky road, we saw one of our teams sharing Christ with three people, so we knelt and prayed for God's Spirit to lead them. As we were praying there on the road, a husband and wife riding bicycles approached us. We asked them if they were Christians, and they indicated they were not. We took our time and shared the wonderful truth of God's grace, so demonstrated by sending His sinless Son, Jesus, who willingly came to die cruelly and thereby save us from our sins.

They had never heard the powerful description of what God has done to restore whoever chooses to be in a right relationship with God. That person can then enjoy a peaceful, fulfilling, and rewarding life.

They got off their bicycles and bowed humbly but gladly, and on that rutted road, gave their lives to Jesus. They happily accepted the gift of salvation. The three people down the road whom we had been praying for also accepted Christ. There were five people joyously saved, delivered from an eternity in hell, in that one spot in a matter of about ten minutes.

We were in the middle of nowhere, and we experienced this truth: "Now unto Him who is able to do exceedingly abundantly above all we can think or ask, according to His power that works in us" (Ephesians 3:20, KJV). His power works in anyone who will repent and accept Jesus as Savior, and this promise from God is to everyone who accepts Jesus as Savior.

As we walked on, we could not help but rejoice that so many people were being set free from the bondage of sin. The Lord was even so gracious to send them on their bicycles while we were praying for God's will with the other three. Our God is an awesome God, and nothing is remote to our omniscient God.

Why do we ever doubt God's blessing when we (with pure motives) are doing His perfect will and honoring the last command He gave on earth to go and make disciples?

As we gathered back at the bus and started to board, a colleague named Sandy White asked, "Why don't we walk over to the farm and say goodbye to that nice man who greeted us when we arrived?" We all agreed we should do just that and headed that way. We had no idea there would be four or five farmworkers there with him.

He greeted us warmly and told us about the farm he was responsible for. It was an excellent opportunity to honor God by letting him know that God had so obviously blessed the hard work of him and his farm hands, which is exactly what we did. Sandy White then asked him, "Who are your heroes?" He proudly responded, "Marx and Lenin. I study in Russia." He told us he was a Lt. Colonel in the Cuban Army. Since military needs had diminished, the army had assigned him this responsibility to develop the farm. God had blessed his efforts to do so in an abundant way. Sometimes I forget that God is the only One that knows the future, but he knew this man would someday accept Jesus and become a true follower and worshipper of God.

Sandy turned and looked at the man and said, "Would you like to hear about our hero?" He answered very heartily a positive "Yes," and Sandy turned to me and said, "Paul, why don't you tell him about our hero?" At that point, I was glad we had already seen God's Spirit work so powerfully, and I approached this opportunity not with self-confidence but with God-confidence.

This man, by the way, reminded us of a young Paul Newman. He was very nice looking and so very hospitable. If you know anything about Castro's army, you know, however, they were brutal to people, keeping them subservient somewhat in order to avoid any hint of another rebellion. Castro's Army also continued to control the people even though this man was very kind to us.

*Cuban Lt. Colonel and Paul*

I placed my hands on his shoulders, looked into his eyes, and shared the glorious gospel of Jesus Christ. I asked him if he would like to become a Christian. He enthusiastically said, "I want to know this Jesus." He prayed the sinner's prayer and became a child of God. What a glorious occasion we celebrated as he chose eternal life over death! The other farmworkers there accepted Christ as well. We embraced these new members of God's family and started to walk back up the hill to the bus. As we did so, the Paul Newman look-alike asked if he might ride back to the city with us. We were pleased to give him a lift, and after we boarded the bus, someone in our group gave him a small blue Gideon Bible. He took that Bible, raised it heavenward, and said very firmly, "I will memorize this Word of God."

Six months later, I just happened to be back in Cuba when my new Christian brother was, after attending church that Sunday, baptized in the Gulf of Mexico. God was so gracious to let me be there without even knowing it was going to happen. When he came up out of the water, he raised his hands to heaven in victory. What a blessed sight to see—a man changed from being a Lt. Colonel in the cruel enforcing Cuban army to being a forgiven saint in the army of the Lord. It was beyond description.

It's important to know that by his initial comment welcoming a house church, we thought he was already a Christian. We had almost left the scene before God's Holy Spirit prompted Sandy to suggest we go over and thank the nice man for his greeting. Clearly, it was the Lord prompting us through her. People can be obedient, for God so equipped us, and our Father is so honored and pleased when we "go and make disciples." This was a unique experience that only our gracious God could orchestrate.

## The Shirtless One

My experiences in discipleship have taught me that Christ has not given up hope on any person on earth. The world is filled with people eager for salvation if Christ's believers would just take the initiative to explain His message and invite them. Like the previously discussed Cuban Army Lt. Colonel, here is another story of a least-likely person, someone many people would have just passed by when they saw him, who discovered the glories of Christ. We should keep in mind that during his earthy mission, Christ Jesus had particular interest in the downtrodden.

Once again, our effort for the day was to share Christ with enough people to begin a new house church in a rural area of Cuba. As we were driving off the paved road with sparsely scattered palm trees, now onto a dirt road to the location selected by the church leadership, we passed a shirtless man who was playing a guitar. He made for a very unusual sight— shirtless and shoeless, and he was perhaps about forty-five years old, sitting on a gnarled tree stump very near the road. We actually debated a bit about whether we should stop and witness to this person. After all, his dress—or lack thereof—was uncommon and made us more than a bit uneasy. But we stopped the van nonetheless and backed up the short distance to where he was sitting.

We introduced ourselves and found out his name, José, I think, and asked him if he was a Christian, and we soon learned he was not. We began to share the good news with José, and when he heard the gospel (possibly for the first time), he enthusiastically accepted Jesus as his Savior. We then explained there would be a new house church in the neighborhood he could attend. He joyously replied, "I will play the music for the church." We loved his enthusiasm, but we wondered if he would follow through on his promise.

As I have thought about this over the years, it was as if God—by divine providence—had led José to be there on that stump, that day, beside the road as we passed by. And perhaps it was all to teach me a lesson. It was not by chance he was there. I shudder to think we almost passed him by because José did not appear as one who would be receptive to the message we had to share. What a tragic mistake we would have made if we had continued driving, passing him by. Don't we often prematurely conclude things and prejudge others so incorrectly? God's word further verifies that truth in Acts 10:34 (NIV): "Then Peter began to speak: I now realize how true it is that God does not show favoritism." God sees everyone the very same way—each and every one of us is precious to Him. He expects us to see others in the very same way!

During the course of the day, as we met others, we shared Christ with them. Many were eager to be part of establishing a new place of worship. As we proceeded with our witnessing, we shared with each man and woman that the first worship service would be held the following evening. It was a very productive day, but we had not kept count of the number of people who promised to attend the first service. We did, however, know there would be enough for a good, solid nucleus of a new church. We were excited with the positive responses of the people and clearly realized they needed the wonderful news of the gospel.

When we arrived for the first service the following evening, there were twenty to twenty-five people assembled. We were awed and blessed when we found our shirtless friend, José—now very nicely dressed—in the midst of the group playing music for the church. He was playing as a born-again child of

God, surrounded by the people of God.

The Lord taught me a great lesson about this entire experience. Christ came as Savior for *all* mankind. God's Book of Truth states this in several places, but I'll just refer to one at this point. Profoundly and without question, Romans 5:6 (NIV) says, "You see, at just the right time, when we were still powerless, Christ died for the ungodly."

There are only two groups of people in our world. One group is the Godly, who have accepted Jesus as Savior; their sins are washed away by the Blood of Christ. The other group, all lumped into this category I'll call the "ungodly," are the ones who love the world and its allurements more than they love Christ and the cleansing forgiveness He alone can give.

No man will ever love the downtrodden, the outcasts, and the rejected ones more than Jesus Christ. In Matthew 11:28 (KJV), Jesus says, "Come to me, all ye that labour and are heavy-laden, and I will give you rest."

It brought us great joy to find so many new believers in this baby church surrounding the now well-dressed one playing music in honor of Christ. That whole experience acutely reminded us of why we were in Cuba—to share what was, by far, the most important thing that had ever happened in our own lives—our relationship with Jesus Christ.

## Once Blind and Angry, Now at Peace

One of the challenging things on many mission trips to countries where the English language is not the primary language is having enough competent translators.

On our trips to Cuba, when doing street evangelism, which was most of the time, we would usually divide into groups of two. Sometimes if we had a large group of a dozen or more, we divided into groups of three. That meant we would always need five or more translators. God always provided ample translators, though sometimes we scrambled trying to locate enough bilingual people. Perhaps God was saying, "Trust me."

On one of my last mission trips to Cuba, my partner and I were assigned a twenty-one-year-old man as our translator. He spoke five languages fluently, and we found it remarkable for someone to be that gifted at such an early age. We had never seen him on any of our previous seven trips in this same area, and it was really a blessing to get to know him and do God's work with his help. He had a wonderful personality, and, in some ways, he was unusually mature. I have wondered many times since then as I have remembered him, could he have been an angel? Let me tell you why.

We had just finished witnessing to a husband and wife who lived in a house on the corner of a downtown intersection. As we exited the house, our translator took me by the arm and said, "See that man in the white shirt on the corner? He needs us!" I was taken aback since the man he pointed to was at least forty yards away and on the other side of the street. Our young translator repeated, "He really needs us. Let's go!"

The man in the white shirt was sitting on a large concrete base of some kind that was perhaps three feet high. At that time, neither my partner nor I knew that he was blind. Perhaps our translator did know because he was eager for us to quickly meet this man's needs.

Our translator began to talk in Spanish with him, and immediately, he began to wave his arms and loudly said, "I hate God, He will not help me. I cannot see, and God does not care." That was a bit unsettling for us because we had never encountered anything like this, let alone the urgency with which our interpreter convinced us that we were sorely needed. People began to gather around.

We would usually take turns sharing the gospel, and the others with us would simultaneously pray earnestly for the Holy Spirit to bring conviction into the life of the one being witnessed to. It was my turn to share with this man who was continually proclaiming, "I hate God, He will not help me," in a real angry fashion. I remember silently asking the Lord for wisdom as to how to even begin to share Christ with such an angry person.

Not surprisingly, God began to provide. I inquired how long he had been blind. "For many years," he said, and with that reply, I realized at some point in his earlier life he could see. That told me he had seen at least some of God's beautiful creation, sunrises, and sunsets. The next question I am convinced God gave me to ask him was, "Do you believe there is a heaven and a hell?" He was honest and told me he did. I then asked if he knew hell was a place where people rejected the gospel and rejected God's love and would be tormented forever.

He was now calming down, at least somewhat, and acknowledged that this is what he had been told about hell.

The next question was, "Do you believe heaven is a special place of love and peace and beauty like none of us have ever seen before? And do you believe the light of heaven will be special and pure because of God's glory?" I went on to say, "the colors in heaven will be more beautiful than any of us can even imagine. Have you never heard these things about heaven and how wonderful it is and that it will be that way forever?" By now, he had begun to listen attentively.

I continued, "Then, are you really sure you hate God who has sent His only Son to pay our sin debt in order that we can spend eternity with Him in such a wonderful place?" I concluded with, "When we go to heaven, we will be glorified, created anew, with no desire to sin. And we will have perfect vision to see indescribable beauty like we cannot even imagine. Jesus has paid your way to that wonderful place as a gift, but the only way any of us are going there is by accepting that gift!" It was a sobering moment that God orchestrated because we certainly weren't able to.

This blind man was now very calm, and he thought for a moment. "I want to accept Jesus and go to heaven and see again and see Jesus," he said finally.

He confessed his sins, then prayed the sinner's prayer, and had a completely different look on his face.

We asked him to tell us about himself. He then proceeded. He said he had a thirteen-year-old daughter he was responsible for. His wife had left him because he was blind, and he could not work. He admitted he had felt abandoned. But not anymore. He was now smiling and pleasant, intently listening as the interpreter told him about a house church where he would have spiritual brothers and sisters who would become his spiritual family.

*Paul with the Blind Man and Interpreter*

I have written these details to say that, without question, I am not capable of being a part of something this special apart from the leading of God's Holy Spirit, the Difference-Maker. John the Baptist said in John 3:30 (KJV), "I must decrease, but He must increase." We saw that demonstrated. A blind man, both literally and spiritually, was given a sure hope of eternity in heaven as the Spirit of God led him on a new and wonderful journey to that place of eternal rest, peace, and beauty.

He was a changed man when we walked away. I still think about the real possibility that God directed that young translator to us. And I still cannot help but wonder if that translator was an angel on a mission that none of the rest of us could have accomplished.

We serve an Amazing God!

## Trust and Obey

My missions team was in Cuba in late October of 2012, and the effects of Hurricane Sandy were now beginning to reach this small island country.

Rains were torrential, and winds were steadily increasing in what would be the deadliest and most destructive hurricane of the season.

These conditions brought our mission team to a place of decision. Should we call off the evening's planned evangelistic service in one of the house churches? Should we stay inside, out of the severe weather, or should we place our trust in God to protect us as we in faith carried out our work?

We unanimously agreed to proceed as planned even though we had no idea if there would even be anyone attending the planned service because of the extreme weather. As we drove to the house where the service was to be held, the rain was steadily increasing in intensity.

When we arrived, we were more than pleasantly surprised to find the largest room in the house completely filled with people. We did not realize at the time that God had led these people to attend just as He had led us not to cancel the planned service.

In order not to over-crowd that larger room, my colleague Maxie Roberts and I stood in an adjoining hallway and listened to the message being shared. Despite the leaky ceiling above the hallway, neither Maxie nor I missed a word Dr. Rob White preached that blustery night. It might have been stormy outside, but God was clearly at work within the hearts of the listeners inside.

Dr. White preached from John Chapter 1. As he preached through verses 1–13 (NIV), he explained that Jesus, the Creator, had come into the world to restore sinful man to a right relationship with God. In verse 12, the Bible tells us, "Yet to all who did receive Him, to those who believed in His name, He gave the right to become the children of God." Verse 13 continues, "Children born not of natural descent, nor of human decision or a husband's will, but *born of God*" (emphasis mine).

Dr. White made the truth of God come alive, and it was convicting. Afterward, he gave an invitation to anyone who would like their sins forgiven and to begin a wonderful new life with Jesus as their Savior for all eternity. Three people were saved, and, amazingly, one of these ladies saved was the wife of the house church leader.

We all knew from experience that mission trips often require discomfort, inconvenience, and unpredictable obstacles. That knowledge helped us make a right decision not to abandon any part of our mission because of weather, rejecting the notion to pause or cancel and instead moving forward. After all, every Spirit-filled Christian knows the Creator God can control all that He has created.

Many of us will remember the story recounted in Matthew 28. Jesus and His disciples were crossing the Sea of Galilee. They were weary from a long day of ministry, and Jesus was asleep in the stern of the boat when a fierce storm arose. The disciples woke Jesus because they were terrified and fearful they were going to perish. "Jesus then arose, rebuked the winds and the sea; and there was a great calm" (Matthew 28:26b, KJV).

That evening in the midst of a great storm, this is exactly what we had witnessed in the three lives that were changed through faith in salvation. Jesus had brought about a great calm in their hearts. That is exactly what He stands ready to do for anyone who desires "the peace of God which passeth all understanding" (Philippians 4:7, KJV).

God's Holy Spirit was always present with us in Cuba. He was doing what God the Father sent Him to do, and that was to glorify Jesus. The Holy Spirit brings conviction of sin and repentance of sin and reminds us of the great price Jesus paid to set us free. With just three full days on the street, two-hundred thirty-seven precious souls were born into God's family. It was a blessed time and reassured us that the most important thing we can do is worship and give glory to God first, and then be faithful. Despite the dangers presented by Hurricane Sandy, God provided an umbrella of protection over us so that we could follow the Spirit's leading in witnessing to these lost souls.

We upheld the importance of the great commission—to go and make disciples in obedience to Jesus' command—knowing that His mighty power goes before us and within us.

## Expecting Death but Finding Eternal Life

On Tuesday, October 24, our team of six rode for an hour or so to a small, rather remote village. As we were exiting the van and deciding where three teams of two could go to begin to share the gospel, we were approached by a frantic middle-aged lady. When she neared the van, she was panting from running, and she was laboring to recover her breathing. With concern all over her face, her desperate plea was for us to come quickly to her father's home. She was seriously anxious about him. She revealed why she was when she said: "Please come quickly, my father is old and dying, and he is not a Christian, and I need you to talk with him."

As mission volunteers, you really never know what to expect, but the urgency demonstrated by this lady was highly unusual. It was evident by the fear in her eyes that she was convinced her father might even be dead before we arrived at their home, even though we were trotting at a very good pace to get there. The home was approximately a quarter to a half-mile from the place our van had stopped. To say the least, it was a very unusual start to our mission work that day.

As we ran along the dirt path, it took us a few minutes to get to the home, which was a typical Cuban house similar to most modest concrete block homes in the rural areas of Cuba. The home was clean but somewhat Spartan with rather plain furnishings.

When we arrived, she told us more about her father, Carlos, who was 84 years old. He appeared to be slightly overweight, and he was short in stature. It was obvious there was something wrong with his eyes as they appeared to be very irritated. He was not completely blind but could barely see. He was seated on a small couch with his head resting on a pillow as we entered the home, and the daughter introduced us to her father.

"I am going to die tomorrow," he had told his daughter the day before, instructing her to "give my clothes to my sons."

My partner for the day was Maxie Roberts, a true friend, lover of Jesus, lover of people, and consequently lover of mission work.

333

*Maxie Roberts with Paul headed to Cuba*

Our total focus was on getting to this home before this lady's father died. We were so preoccupied with getting there so quickly, we never even gave a thought to how this well-spoken daughter could have known we were coming or why we had come at all to this remote settlement. There was no signage or identification on our van to indicate anything about its use for Christian causes.

Anyway, once the daughter had introduced us to her father, we began our conversation with him. We asked him, "Do you believe in God?" Even though it was evident he was very physically uncomfortable, he indicated he did believe in God. That led us to the most important question, "Do you believe in Jesus Christ?" He did not pause or hesitate when he answered, "I do not believe in Jesus."

In Cuba, we always use the EvangiCube to share the gospel. It is a 4 x 4-inch cube made up of six smaller hinged sides. As the cube sides are opened and turned, they pictorially tell the gospel story. We have found it to be a very effective way to introduce Jesus to people who have never heard the gospel.

The first picture is of a man in a sinful state. Others are pictures of Jesus on the cross, the sealed tomb, and the next-to-last scene is the radiant risen Christ. The very last one we share with people we witness to is the changed heart. It is a large red heart surrounded by a kneeling person in prayer, a Bible, a hand of fellowship (church). There is also a cross that reminds us that we have been saved, belong to the body of Christ (church), and we are to consistently share the gospel with others who do not yet have a personal relationship with Jesus as their Savior.

When we started sharing the cube, Carlos was attentive, but not overwhelmed. We explained there are many gods that people worship, but that the Creator God had sent His sinless Son, Jesus, to restore us sinful people to the one true holy God. He listened patiently and more and more intently. However, when we came to the last panel with the large red heart in the center of the EvangiCube, he became very excited. As he leaned forward when we explained Jesus changed our hearts, he raised his voice and said, "I see! I see! I will now live with Jesus as my Savior." Before we left the home, we made certain that he fully understood that Jesus had forgiven his sins and died in his place that Carlos might live eternally. When we had asked if Carlos wanted Jesus to be his Savior, he said yes. In that moment of weakness and dying, he was gloriously saved.

It was exciting and dramatic. Only the *Difference-Maker* can orchestrate such an instant transformation. Carlos was almost blind, but when we turned the cube to the picture with a large red heart, he said, "I see it," and became very excited. We had explained that Jesus changes our hearts, and he became very excited about his salvation. He was now thinking about truly living and not dying.

How did this dear daughter know of our coming and arrived just as we did? Could it be a coincidence? Not at all! If we pay attention, God will take that word, coincidence, out of our vocabulary. There is a verse in the Bible that helps us understand events such as this. It tells us that God is always at work carrying out His plan for mankind. Second Peter 3:9 (NIV) assures us: "The Lord is not slack concerning His promise, as some count slackness, but is long suffering toward us not willing that any should perish but that all should come to repentance."

God loves mankind, and He made us for fellowship with Him eternally. We can know He is continually orchestrating events that will lead to the repentance and salvation of persons just like the aged hopeless man. Our omnipotent God orchestrated that day what man cannot!

After we prayed for his health and his sight, he said to us, "I am so glad you came, and I feel so much better." We explained, "Now, you will never die. One day you will go to sleep and wake up in heaven, in the arms of Jesus." We then told his daughter, "Carlos helped to give you life as your father, and today you have helped give him eternal life through his heavenly father. Please take your father to your house church if he is able in order that he can worship his Savior and grow spiritually strong."

It was a divine experience. God is seldom early, but God is *never late*.

This man literally was snatched from eternal damnation by his new faith in Christ. Just in time.

When Carlos arrives in heaven, if he has not already, his vision will be 20/20 in both eyes because everything there will be perfect. The perfect Savior guarantees that!

## What? Riot!

As you may know, Somalia, Africa, has been for many years a very unstable country, with various factions fighting, crippling, and killing rival factions to stay in or gain power. It had become so unlivable in the early 2000s, and its people had become so desperate, they were fleeing as refugees to any country they could get to in order to escape persecution and death.

Because of the close proximity of neighboring Kenya, a large number of the Somalians had become refugees there. Most had left practically everything behind in an effort to save their lives. An estimated 110,000 settled into a large slum called Eastleigh, just south of Nairobi. Most refugees had no jobs and little hope of one in the future. Because most did not work, the streets were busy and crowded with these refugees almost all the time. About 99 percent were Muslim.

One of the first things we were told by the International Mission Board missionaries who did our orientation was, "You need to be out of there before 1 p.m. on Friday when the call to prayer for the Islamists is called. These people really get cranked up, worked into frenzy." There are five large mosques in Eastleigh. Without any doubt, we made certain we would not be there past noon on Friday.

Our residence was in a gated compound located on the western side of Nairobi, a place owned, we were told, by another Protestant denomination. We were thankful to have a relatively secure place to stay and recoup each evening after a challenging day working in Eastleigh.

What we did not know until we arrived was that men and women are not allowed to even walk together in public. As you probably know, Islam places enormous restrictions on women, how they behave, and what they can and cannot do. We adapted pretty quickly as soon as we were made aware of this expectation. We men began to walk in front, with the three ladies, one lady being Lynette, walking respectfully behind us.

Our objective for the seven days we were there was to make some friends and then to give them the gifts of scripture that the local International Baptist Missions had wrapped completely in brown paper. The purpose of the trip was to get the Word of God into Eastleigh and leave it there. The gifts of scripture consisted of separate biblical books such as the gospels and a number of whole Bibles. None of these were identifiable because of brown paper covering. This was done because the Muslims would not accept the Bible or any of its parts if it was recognizable, especially in public.

Our instructions were to seek out restaurants, food stands, or tea houses—which appeared to be no more than tea shacks—and spend time in these places until we could establish some relationships. Due to all of us being Caucasian, our skin color was a dead giveaway; we were not very successful over the first several days.

We later found out that Eastleigh citizens were often watched—spied upon—by Islamic leaders. Obviously, this raised fears that their acceptance of our friendship would somehow indicate they were in agreement with American or Christian ideals.

After several days, the ladies found a place of refuge, a Mennonite School, which made them welcome to stay. They ministered there. Meanwhile, Troy, the only other man in our group, and I continued our effort to carry out the mission and give out the scriptures.

The strain and tension were mounting among us because, by midweek, we were not making much progress kindling friendships, and we had been robbed twice. Two other robbery attempts failed. These thieves had developed a technique that worked really well in the crowded streets. Pedestrians packed the streets as well as the sidewalks, getting in close proximity to our vehicle. Since it was terribly hot, we rode with all our windows left completely down in our van. The open windows made it easy for a group of six or eight or more to ease out of the crowd and begin to scream loudly and beat on one side of our vehicle, which caused all of us to look to that side in astonishment. Several thieves on the other side would then reach in the open windows and snatch any valuables they could get their hands on, like our cameras, the ladies' handbags, whatever. Once they grabbed something, they would run and quickly disappear into the crowd.

On one occasion, Troy jumped out of our van and literally chased the thief down, and brought a camera back. It was a brave act, and none of us knew how dangerous it could have become if the crowd had turned on the American interloper. But we knew that God had sent us there, and God would see us through.

As I mentioned, for about three days Troy and I had made little progress in establishing friendships. When we would enter a restaurant or place of assembly, we could never quite engage any of the Somalis in conversation. On the fourth day, we met a well-spoken young man who befriended us and invited us to a tea house he regularly patronized. This tea house was like all the rest—a structure with a small shack in the rear, a rusty tin roof overhead, with open walls, rough wooden tables and benches, and banged-up drinking cups probably unwashed for days after previous use. Suffice it to say, if there was a local health department, its standards pale in comparison to those we enjoy here in America.

We learned our new friend worked for the UN, and we were so thankful to have someone now to help us carry out the mission. After all, our backpacks were still mighty heavy, and carting them around was tiring since they were still full of the printed Bible material.

His friendship opened a door for us, and, every day thereafter, we would meet at this tea house for "tea" or whatever else was resident in those battered cups. One thing we knew for certain—God was at work, and He would reward our persistence. However, what we did not know, after the first day of our being noticed, was that someone would be sent from one of the mosques to sit next to Troy and me every day in order to try to learn more about what we were doing in such a place as this. They were not hostile, but it was rather clear they wanted to know more about our reason for being there. Each day these men from the mosque became a little friendlier, yet we had not yet offered any scripture to anyone. Neither of us felt led to do so up to this point.

On the last morning, our friend from the UN did tell us they were sending the highest leader from a mosque to be with us that morning. When he arrived, we introduced ourselves and began a dialogue. He was very personable and, likewise, I endeavored to be also. We laughed, talked about grandchildren, and after an hour or so, I asked, "Could I give you a gift?" His answer was, "Yes, I would like your gift very much." With that, I sat my backpack up on the table and took out one of the books of John, which was wrapped in brown paper. When I did this, some twenty-five-or-so people saw what was occurring, and two of them stepped forward with outstretched hands, indicating they would like one also. With that, my friend Troy opened his backpack and began to do the same. By now, all of the people were out of their seats, excited about a gift and creating a loud disturbance as they competed for our gifts.

When the man who ran the place and brewed the tea heard the uproar, he came out, saw what was happening, and he went ballistic. He screamed, waving his arms in agitation. At that, the customers all turned on him, and it was a donnybrook. What we did not understand at the time was the man that was responsible for that tea house was accountable to the Islamic officials who controlled Eastleigh. An uproar or uprising of any kind was surely a large concern for him and the other Islamic officials.

With that, our friend who worked at the UN said, "I believe we should go now." Troy and I were both in a three-point stance and ready for what might happen. We had not been within a mob, perhaps ever, and we knew this was getting serious.

Our U.N. friend said, "We will go to the U.N. Building," so we started in that direction. When we were three blocks away, we could still hear the uproar from the people screaming at each other. It had become a riot. The great news is our backpacks had all of a sudden, in God's timing, become much lighter because they were both empty.

As I think back, I saw on the face of the man I gave the first book to, a gentle smile of gratitude. I am convinced that when he opened it and pulled off the brown paper, he knew what it was. That made the whole trip worthwhile for me.

As we were walking to the U.N. Building, our friend met an older man, and they greeted one another warmly. Apparently, the older man we met had been out of Nairobi for a while and indicated he had been in Washington, D.C.

At that point, we all decided to have lunch, which was a great challenge in this place. Nevertheless, when you are "in Rome, do as the Romans do," or you lose all hope of establishing a meaningful relationship with anyone. One of the true facts about being on mission is to always remember that we are on someone else's turf, and we show respect by honoring their customs and suggestions.

While we were eating lunch, our discussion turned to world affairs, and Al Qaeda was mentioned. Specifically, I do not remember how the subject came up, but this was not too awfully long after the World Trade Center Towers were taken down by a plot masterminded by these terrorists. I remember making a statement to the effect that "all the Al Qaeda participants should have by now been brought to justice." Yet, obviously, there was still the wicked extremist element out there plotting more evil in the world. I was not ready for the next words I heard. The man we had met on the street looked at me with menacing eyes and said, "I will have you know I represent Al Qaeda." With that said, our lunch was quickly over, and our U.N. friend suggested that the three of us go on to the U.N. building and spend the afternoon there. We hurried there at a brisk pace.

I learned then to be careful in a place like Eastleigh, with such a divergent and dissimilar culture to my own, because you never know whom you are interacting with. We had been told by our International Mission Board host group that there was an active terrorist cell within Nairobi, but we never expected to have to deal with any of them or their related parties, especially over lunch.

We did learn that radical Islam is more than a religion. Islam in countries like this has its tentacles inside the government. Everything that goes on in a place like Eastleigh is being observed. No one ever knows who is for or against them, or who is friend or foe. Unfortunately, there is no liberty or freedom because there is no Christ, but "Where the Spirit of the Lord is there is liberty" (2 Corinthians 3:17, KJV).

I am convinced to this day that if people were allowed to hear the powerful truth of the gospel and realize what a precious gift that forgiveness and restoration through our sinless Savior is, many, many would choose "the Way, the Truth and the Life" (John 14:6, KJV). I left that day, after all those events, filled with gratitude for the grace of God and thankful for the liberty we all enjoy as His children. That liberty is only made possible by the sacrifice of Jesus.

Our job in Kenya was to distribute scripture wrapped in brown paper, and God chose a very unorthodox way of getting it done—with a riot!

We learned later that our friend from the U.N. was running for the presidency of Somalia. At that time, there were forty-five other candidates. It was—and still is—a chaotic, godless nation.

Without a doubt, this was the most challenging mission trip I was ever a part of. Every evening our team would share the events of the day. We would discuss whether we should go back out the next day into such a strange, unfriendly, and really dangerous place. As we would drive in each morning, we passed by garbage heaps of unimaginable size. The stench was horrendous. There were always barefoot children walking through this filth in search of something to eat. That is still unforgettable to us as we think about God's grace in all our lives. Each evening we would arrive at this conclusion: How could we not continue the mission God had prepared and led us to carry out? Then as we went forth each day, He always strengthened us. God reminded us this was exactly what we were supposed to be seeing—His world the way it is. And He reminded us this is exactly what He wanted us to do; in fact, had saved us to do (Matthew 28:18–20, NIV).

Troy and I saw the hand of God when He sent our U.N. friend to help us gain access to the people who needed what we had brought—truth. It is then ultimately from that truth, hope, and assurance that there is a God who cares and saves. We saw that God would use even the most unorthodox method to accomplish His work.

We did not realize it so much then as we do now, but on that trip, God allowed us to see a microcosm of our great but needy world. He also allowed us to hear, as we listened to career missionaries whose very lives are on the line every day, talk about not their problems and fears but about the joy they receive as they see people liberated and set free to be the people God gave them life to be.

God reminded us that it is in our busyness that it's so easy to allow "out of sight, out of mind" to salve our consciences and keep us from sharing the most important thing that ever happened to us. It was one of the most challenging and humbling events of our lives.

On the next morning, Alfred, our driver and Christian brother, picked us up, and we started a three-day safari at Masai Mara. God knew we needed a rest and we were so renewed just to see one of the most beautiful game reserves in all of Africa. Masai Mara was breathtaking beyond description. If I tried to describe it, I would say it is an undisturbed part of creation. In the first chapter of Genesis, after God had created everything, verse 25b (NIV) tells us, "And God saw that it was good," to which all of us who saw this great undisturbed portion of His creation, would say *Amen*!

When we returned to Nairobi that evening, we ate at a world-famous restaurant called The Carnivore. This restaurant serves almost every kind of exotic meat on the African continent. Helpful tip: Don't try the alligator.

Our return flight to America was from Nairobi. Unfortunately, one woman with us, Kaye, became ill. She was very nauseous and dehydrated for the entire trip home. She had to be taken off the plane in a wheelchair. Kaye was the person who helped us see our responsibility in mission's work many years before. She was also the one who sold her horse and saddles to raise money for this trip. She was admitted to the hospital and stayed several days to recover. However, she was not a victim; she was a victor. She did not withdraw from her mission's calling. She and my wife, Lynette, traveled to difficult and dangerous Bangladesh twice since then. That is also a dangerous and challenging place to do ministry. Nonetheless, missions becomes much easier when we realize our God will do whatever it calls for in order that His will to be done—even a riot. I am so glad I could be a part of and witness it in real time.

When it comes to missions, don't be afraid. That fear is not from our Father. God's Word promises, "For God has not given us a spirit of fear, but of power and of love and of a sound mind" (2 Timothy1:7, NKJV). God accomplishes His purposes, especially when we obey Him.

We did other mission trips to Africa where we saw great needs, but we always saw God's hand move in remarkable ways. Especially endearing but heart-gripping were the children we encountered at orphanages.

*Paul at Orphanage in Africa*

## Clarence

In 2005, Hurricane Katrina inflicted tremendous damage on the gulf coast and especially on New Orleans, Louisiana. As a result of that damage, Trinity Baptist Church, located in Cayce, South Carolina, organized a team to go there and provide food distribution for a week. The Holy Spirit led me to go and participate as a member of that team.

When we arrived, the weather was extremely hot, the air stiflingly humid. Celebration Church, which had only sustained minor damage, was our place of residence for the week. It was also the site from which we distributed the food. We worked under a large, dark army surplus tent on the church parking lot. For us older individuals, it was very tiring. By the last day, we were drained and weary.

Our mission was to be completed on Friday at 5 p.m. Friday had come, and with only five minutes left in our day, an elderly man and his wife shuffled into our tent. The events of the past few weeks were clearly evident by their labored walk. The wife registered and began to push a cart toward the food lines. Then the husband walked over and sat near where I stood. Registration was essential to keep people from coming too often, or every day, or gathering too much food for the purpose of reselling. Essentially, registration was a process to deter dishonesty and fraud. Immediately, my heart was burdened for him because it was evident he was completely exhausted and defeated by Katrina and her aftermath.

In my spirit, I knew the Lord was saying, "Go see if he knows Me." I looked at my watch again and tried to ignore that directive. My own fatigue and weariness caused me to hesitate. Yet, God's Spirit convicted me that I should determine if he was a Christian. While all too often I have disobeyed my Savior, I knew God meant business here. Further, I knew I would never have peace about this if I did not obey. So, I walked over and asked him, "How are you today, sir?" He replied in a weak and defeated voice, "Oh, I'm all right." I then asked him, "Are you a Christian?" He said, "I goes to church, and I tries to live right."

Every truly born-again believer knows we are Christians because we have repented of our sins, humbled ourselves before Jesus, and asked for His forgiveness. We welcome Him to become our Savior and Lord. It is that personal relationship with Jesus that assures us of salvation, not the rituals of religion. Or just going to church and trying to live right. When we are truly born again, we want to be in church to worship with God's people. We will desire to read His Word daily for direction and encouragement. We will need to and want to pray daily, and pray earnestly when we do pray. We will also seek opportunities to share with lost people what a wonderful peace and liberation true salvation brings. It was evident this precious older man needed encouragement. He needed Jesus, and there is no greater consolation than Him.

Following his response, I gently explained to him by way of analogy. I said, "going into my garage doesn't make me a car, just like going into a church

345

regularly doesn't make anyone a Christian." As the Lord led me, I asked this dear humbled man, "Wouldn't you like for Jesus to forgive your sins and give you the peace of God in your heart today?" I will never forget the tired voice that responded, "I sho' would." The Lord has since reminded me of His promise given to everyone, but especially to the weary, "Come to me, all you who labor and are heavy laden and I will give you rest" (Matthew 11:28, NKJV).

I then presented the gospel, and he prayed in such an exquisite, tender voice the sinner's prayer. "Now tell me about yourself," I asked him afterwards. "My name is Clarence," he began, "and me and my wife ain't got nothin' left but that old car." He then pointed out to the parking lot and said, "Katrina got everything else. We are living with my son. I'm 87 years old, and I found out last week I've got multiple myeloma."

*Clarence and Paul*

As I watched my new brother in Christ leave, I thought about how close I had come to letting Satan claim another one of God's creations just because I was tired. I was ashamed beyond words. I thought about my Savior and Lord while He was on the cross. My Savior was weary and bearing the enormous weight of mankind's sin, yet His mission compelled Him to be faithful to the end, as He forgave a repentant sinner beside him who was also being crucified.

We can never fully repay Him for becoming sin for you and me. We can, however, express our gratitude by obedience to the mission. He has saved us to share the gospel truth even when it isn't easy or convenient. After all, what a privilege it is, by the power of God's Holy Spirit, to take the liberating message to lost and often hopeless and dying people. We should live for and love to share the gospel. We know from Acts 2:4 (NKJV) that every person who accepts Christ receives the powerful gift of the Holy Spirit. It is the *Difference-Maker* who enables us to live *obediently* and victoriously and to share the beautiful gospel powerfully at every opportunity. God set His people free by the precious offering of His Son as a sinless sacrifice for sinful people, who are all descendants of Adam from the Garden of Eden. One of the most reassuring verses to me in God's Word is 2 Corinthians 3:17 (KJV), "Where the Spirit of the Lord is there is liberty." A true Christian has God's power to obey, to persevere, and do what God saved us to do as defined in His Word and empowered by His Spirit.

Clarence lived a few more months on earth. He now resides eternally in that beautiful place of peace and rest which Jesus made possible for those who choose to accept Him as their Savior and Lord. John 3:15–16 (NIV) declares that every human being, regardless of their past, has an invitation to that wonderful place in the presence of our precious Savior and Lord. God's Holy Word is absolutely clear. When anyone repents and invites Jesus to be their Savior and Lord, sins are separated from that person "as far as the East is from the West."

Second Peter 3:9b (NKJV) is crystal clear, "The Lord is not willing that any should perish." The choice is left to each person. To be certain of our own salvation, we must repent of our sins, be genuinely sorrowful, and trust Jesus as our Lord and Savior. Then as God's Spirit prepares and strengthens us to go and tell others, He brings an unspeakable peace to anyone who will allow Him to be both Savior and Lord.

Clarence was a humble, gentle man, but he was a lost man. He was too good for hell, but not good enough for heaven, that perfect place. Jesus made his eternal home there possible. Here was a man who came with *nothing* because he had lost everything, who found everything instead, and he left with *everything that matters*! He came for needed food and left with the bread of life (John 6:48, KJV).

I almost prevented his regeneration through flagrant disobedience, but God had a better plan. He always does. We just need to be obedient and make certain we are following His plan and not our own.

# CHAPTER 33

# America's Greatness?

As we have observed other countries where we ventured on mission trips it has brought to surface some concerning issues in those countries. Here's another thought. Could it be since God has so blessed America, that America has in return shared His blessing by taking the good news of the gospel to those countries and actually all around the world? I've mentioned there is an attraction of peoples all over the world wanting to flood to America to experience her freedoms and blessings. But what is it about America that makes her great? We will take a look at an unbiased historian's thoughts and cover some other considerations.

America in 2022 is clearly divided, with distinct and very rigid opinions about our history and many other issues. We need to ask, are these opinions about our country justifiable, or are they just diverting tools for dissenters to use for moving our country toward a socialistic form of government? Many people do not want to even say the word "socialism," but I have seen it at work firsthand. So I will raise the issue.

As some unhappy Americans today complain about our country, it is surprising that even a former President, Barack Obama, has marginalized and suggested that "America was never great." At this point, we would do well to realize the definition of "great" needs to be more clearly agreed upon. If I am a malcontent, I will probably never consider my environment great. Our role as God's empowered people, however, is not to condemn but to lead the return to those better days with God's sovereignty over our nation. There is only one way back—His way—repentance and then restoration by our gracious Creator God. It is clear it was by God's grace, unmerited favor, that America became great in the beginning.

On the other hand, if I am a patriot and grateful for the blessings we do enjoy in America, I will probably consider my country to be greater than any other country I am familiar with. I will say, however, that I believe God still has a far better plan to continue to make America a very desirable place to live. Unfortunately, there are now a growing number of politicians who are working feverishly and deceitfully to change our democracy into a socialistic form of government. I believe that former President Obama also believed a different form of government would be a better answer for America in order to make America great. Career politicians know with a socialistic government, they are in control; elections can be redesigned and or manipulated to keep those who are in power forever in power! This is the historical truth in all socialist and communistic countries. Invariably, socialistic governments then are ultimately taken over by dictators. Ultimately the people have no voice. Socialistic heads of government love this because successors can never rise from the populous. Those heads of state do not have to be concerned with pleasing the people since they do not stay in office by the vote of the people. I believe history will prove no country has ever been able to go back to being a truly democratic republic once the socialist leaders are fully entrenched. History has proven those countries consistently evolve into enslaving dictatorships.

It would be interesting to see how much of the populous in Cuba, if they were in our place considering a socialistic government, would support that change. Experience tells me their first emotion would be utter shock because there, even today, so many decades after Castro's takeover, they are rarely, if ever, given choices to decide anything under a socialistic/communistic government. They have simply become decreed cheerleaders on cue, and most are now severely impoverished.

My own personal observations have led me to a much greater awareness of the dangers of socialism. Its deceptions are many. Apparently, the idea exists that with socialism, everything will be equal. And supposedly, there will be no more inadequacies among people, and every need will be met by the government. Then there will be no need for God, since government officials will replace our need for God. Alas, all will live happily ever after, except that has never happened before. That idealistic portrayal never becomes reality, and the people are helpless to change it.

Wow! So why has this utopian idea never worked long term before? It is simple. In such a mediocre society, too many people gradually stop contributing and become takers and wait for the spoils of others to sustain them. Why would that be the case? It is simple. No matter how hard you work, you will all have the same reward. Also, many then give up on reaching their God-given potential. Strife is then reborn because Our Creator never intended for mankind to be an unmotivated taker but instead a productive grateful giver. Another point is that God never insists that anyone or any nation must allow His divine guidance.

The Cubans became disenchanted with their president or dictator, Juan Batista, because of the corruption and tyranny. However, the people saw hope in a gallant young man named Fidel Castro who claimed he was going to rescue and deliver the people from this cruel tyrant, Batista. But after the victory celebration ended, then reality set in. Over the months and then years after the overthrow of Batista, the populous realized they had only been delivered from one known tyrant to another unknown tyrant—Fidel Castro. All the promises of freedom and prosperity applied only to the new regime and to only a few at the top. The truth about socialism is it invariably leads to totalitarianism. Socialism reduces God's most cherished creations to achieving in very limited ways. We were created in the image of God to excel. Not just to exist, but to *excel*.

I spent enough time in Cuba to see how severely impoverished the people have become, even though they were promised a wonderfully better life with the ouster of Juan Batista during the revolution. Sadly, it doesn't matter how much they try to improve their lots in life; each person is just an unimportant number.

Many years ago, in 1835, Alexis de Tocqueville, a French political scientist and historian, came to America to study our prisons. After a stay of six months, he left with a wealth of more extensive observations encompassing more than our prisons and wrote *Democracy in America*. Apparently, the French people, and probably the rest of the world, had recognized the amazing progress and success of this remarkable young republic called The United States of America. How utterly in contrast this is to anyone saying America "has never been a great country." De Tocqueville was an astute, objective observer in our country. He did not come with an agenda but came here to learn and to know the truth. He spoke openly and plainly about socialism, which he had actually observed and studied in other places prior to coming to America. Here is what he said:

"It [Socialism] is not an endlessly expanding list of rights, the right to education, the right to healthcare, the right to food and housing. That is not freedom; that's dependency. Those aren't rights. They are the rations of slavery, hay, and a barn to human cattle." That dependency is exactly what socialistic leaders want. They become exalted in this way. They decide everything for everyone else by and large; it appears they do not believe in man's innate capability to excel. However, our creator God does know mankind has been created empowered to excel when we follow His direction.

Alexis de Tocqueville went on to write, "Democracy extends the power sphere of individual freedom; socialism restricts it. Democracy attaches all possible value to each man. Socialism makes each man a mere agent... a mere number."

"Democracy and socialism have nothing in common, but one word, equality. But notice the difference: while democracy seeks equality in liberty, socialism seeks equality in restraint and servitude" (serving the state). With socialism, "All are serving the few at the top who invariably live in lavish lifestyles." In most cases, it is apparent they believe they are the only ones intelligent and learned enough to govern the masses. Yet they, being privileged, often live in gated compounds and support notions such as defunding the police for others.

De Tocqueville wrote this further statement: "Liberty cannot be established without *morality*, nor morality without *faith*." No wonder the peddlers of socialism want the Bible banned because it declares this encouraging truth: "Where the spirit of the Lord is, there is liberty" (2

Corinthians 3:17, KJV). God created man to be free and to achieve great things. Those ideas are disruptive in a socialistic country. An important question for Americans to answer is, *Do I have faith in God's plan and God's morality? Or do I have faith in man's plan without God's morality?* God wants mankind to look to Him for a much different reason. He created man and loves man! God has promised, "I will never leave nor forsake you" (Hebrews 13:5, NKJV). He also says, "Call unto me and I will answer you and show you great and mighty things which you do not know" (Jeremiah 33:3, NKJV).

De Tocqueville's thoughts and observations as a political scientist and historian are revealing. Finally, he went on to write a summary of what he had observed in America during his six months stay. Remember, he had come to make observations and to see how America had risen so fast as a world power. He reached a not surprising conclusion: "Not until I went into the churches of America and heard the pulpits *aflame with righteousness* did I understand the secret of her glorious power." I love that statement... the secret of her glorious power.

He continued, "America is great because America is good, and if America ever ceases to be good, America will cease to be great." Why in the world would he say these things? It is simple. Because they are true. He came to America seeking truth, and he simply recorded the truth he discovered.

Even a former President Obama does not have to believe America is great for that statement to be true. America is still the greatest country in the world. In fact, based on his comments, I am of the impression this former occupant of the White House saw America as somewhat of a bully nation. His vision as a globalist apparently influenced him to begin laying a foundation for a one-world (global) government. Of course, it would have been his gain as he would have been in a strategic position near the top and in control if such a disastrous thing could have been brought about. By the way, that deceptive effort is still underway today by our politicians and others around the world. That globalist world would not be a democracy but socialistic in form. Could it have that great-sounding name, "The Great American Reset"? We could know for sure the true God of all creation would be left out. Why do I say that? Because if God was a priority, He would overshadow the world leaders, and their egos would not allow such. With socialism, there would be no valid elections for leadership, as in a democratic country today. We all understand the larger any government becomes, the more bureaucratic it becomes. Ultimately it becomes a do-nothing debate entity for the entrenched figurehead elites. It is difficult to understand how a person without any extraordinary leadership skills could be elected president in a country that was never great. Yet, it was great enough to allow him to be leader of the greatest country in the world, whether he acknowledges it or not. Someone's belief in something is not the measure of whether it is true. Truth, by definition, will always be the absence of deceit.

Also, when we think of America as a bully nation because of our superior military strength, let us never forget the price we have paid to protect freedom around the world. It is all a matter of perspective as to how we view anything. Thank God that America liberated Europe from the murderous tyrant Adolf Hitler in World War II and saved many other parts of the world as well.

If you remember, there is a biblical account of when this same one-world government idea was attempted. It is described in Genesis 11:1–4 (NKJV). The stated purpose of such an undertaking is in verse 4: "Let us build ourselves a city and a tower whose top is in the heavens...let us make a name for ourselves." We can read clearly how God dispersed and destroyed that venture. The collective effort to leave God out of the plan resulted in His utter destruction and absolute confusion of the language.

I am convinced our French historian, de Tocqueville, was exactly correct in both his assessment of socialism and his evaluation of America's greatness. America was great because the people of America had honored God and God released His blessing in return! God always has and always will keep His promises.

Without question, our founding Fathers placed great emphasis on freedom, morality, and faith in God. They trusted God to help them build the greatest country ever known to man. I have often wondered how dissenters believe America was not founded as a Christian nation and how they could deny all the evidence of God's influence, much of it in our capital carved in stone. America became the envy of every other country and still is to a majority today. How many would love to have what we have today, and all the while we have some elected officials—politicians, so-called—who constantly express their dislike of America. Oddly enough, they enjoy all the perks, benefits, and advantages of high office. Why, if socialism is such a wonderful form of government, do our borders stay flooded with people fleeing their socialistic poverty-ridden countries? Why do these people just pass on through other socialistic countries on their way to enter America?

Thank God, we still have some statesmen who are determined to do what is right, even if they are not re-elected. As an electorate, we desperately need the wisdom of God to elect those who will do what is morally right and good for America rather than what is good for their reelection.

Without a doubt, the majority of Americans who have lived a while, clearly know America is and has been a wonderful place to live. Probably, many of these same people, however, have sadly watched the moral decline, the hatred and division created largely by too many of our elected ones and the biased media, as well as the brainwashing of our students. Is there any sanity when Critical Race Theory (often referred to as CRT) has replaced civics? It is the most divisive subject ever dreamed up. It was evidently created purely for political purposes. The teaching of American history has become so distorted and willfully misrepresented that many of our younger generations have no awareness of our true wonderful Judeo Christian history. Is there anything more worrisome than an uninformed voting constituency? That brainwashing includes removing the vital inspiration and influence of our Godly Christian heritage. Unfortunately, brainwashing begins in the early grades now and is reinforced all the way through most of our institutions of higher learning. We are clearly at a place for great concern, a time when we need to return to our roots and restore absolute faith in God! We are at the place where students need to always be taught *truth*! There is no greater resource of truth than the Holy Bible.

History tells us of the rise and fall of various nations. Rome is a classic case since it at one time was the greatest country known to mankind. What caused that great nation to fall in such a profound and complete manner, and what can we learn from it?

The English historian Edward Gibbon wrote a book entitled *The Decline and Fall of the Roman Empire*. In it, he delineated a number of reasons for Rome's fall. Among them was *"the undermining and destruction of the sanctity of the home."* Also, he listed the *"higher and higher taxes which were spent for bread and circuses."* This practice kept the people entertained and diverted from the purpose of maintaining and further developing the nation. Another reason was the *"building of great armaments...when the real enemy was within."* In other words, that meant the decline of individual responsibility and complete dependency on the government. Gibbon went on to say there was *"the decay of religion, which had turned into mere form, rituals, and rites."* There is a verse in God's Word that describes their condition as "Having a form of Godliness, but denying its power" (2 Timothy 3:5b, NKJV). Another reason for the fall, he cites, is that the Romans *"developed a consuming desire for pleasure, sports, and entertainment."* Does that sound familiar? Apparently, they had little desire for, nor interest in, the things of God. They were too busy with pleasure. The more they were entertained, the more exciting they expected the entertainment to be. "Nothing is wonderful when you get used to it," the old saying goes, describing the conditions they were experiencing. The more the crowds sought and expected entertainment, the more exciting it became. It also became more and more immoral and brutal. It included gladiators and man-eating lions in the arena. How far they had fallen! We can clearly see how great nations can begin to decline and lose their greatness as they lose sight of their founding purpose and their founding source of wisdom and power, Almighty God.

The people who have been citizens of America for decades know America has been a great country, regardless of what malcontents say. We are aware there are, unfortunately, significant changes that are taking place today. We are seeing more and more people concerned about the decline of America, and there are clearly diverse opinions about why we are experiencing that decline.

Despite all the criticisms to the contrary, our forefathers were extremely wise in establishing America as a Christian nation. They knew the Christian ethics practiced would produce a wonderful environment. That did not mean other religions could not be practiced. They assured freedom of speech and religion to every person. These rights were guaranteed under our Constitution, clearly a divinely inspired document. But we have now violated our own laws with political correctness and measures to prevent the mention of Christianity, God, or Christ Jesus in public places and especially government affairs. It is ironic that it's perfectly acceptable to mention and discuss other religions publicly. Worse yet, Christianity is not taught in many educational institutions, while other religions are taught in practically all colleges and universities. Sadly, even our current president in a CNN town hall advocated for a registry of all religious organizations that won't toe the line of the LGBT agenda. He continued to elaborate about how he believed the federal government should be able to keep watch on these Christian groups who are similar to terrorist groups. That is comparing the practiced ethics of Jesus Christ to the brutal behavior of terrorist groups.

With our constitution, our founders intended for this country to rely on our Creator for divine guidance and protection. They intended we would live together in peace and harmony as we allowed the principles in the Bible to guide our moral behavior. It also meant we would rely upon/trust the wisdom of God and the Spirit of God to guide us as we grew into a unique nation. Our wise founders decided we would become a united people, "indivisible with liberty and justice for all." But division is a destroyer, no matter where you find it. It is impossible to describe the destruction of division. The increasing odious division is most disheartening, as observed among our alleged public servants in Washington today; it is now more like abject hatred than mere division. Whatever happened to unity and brotherhood? The true Creator God is a uniter! Why can we not understand that the ethics so clearly taught by Jesus Christ are unmistakably the way to meaningful brotherhood? Somehow, too many elected officials do not know true brotherhood and that it cannot ever be legislated. Only changed hearts will result in real acceptance of all God's created beings. It is not surprising that the unifying truths taught by Jesus are clearly rejected by socialists/communists. The truth is that all blood is red.

When Alexis de Tocqueville came to America, he found churches full of people who were profoundly grateful for the grace and provision of God, Our Creator. He found preachers who preached the Bible in the power of the Holy Spirit. Conviction of sin was a consistent occurrence, and repentance and return to faithfulness were its results. He found a people who worshipped consistently a Creator who was worthy of our complete worship. He found a people who were not ashamed to bow before God in repentance and ask for forgiveness, and he was impressed! He knew America's greatness was a result of America's goodness. He witnessed freedom, morality, and faith in God... and witnessed it in awe over his six-month stay.

He had every reason to reach that conclusion about America's goodness because he saw God's church "pulpits aflame with the gospel." He saw the people truly worshiping God faithfully because of gratitude for God's grace. He also saw the gracious blessings of God being poured out on our country! God greatly desires to continue to do that today! The answer for America is not a different form of government but to return to our sovereign Source of help. We desperately need His wisdom, His uniting presence, His influence, and His peace once more. There is only one way back, and that is His way of repentance and then restoration by our gracious Creator God. Remember, it was by God's grace that America became great in the beginning.

Many today may well take for granted our great country. But the true children of God, enlightened and empowered by His Holy Spirit, will always be grateful for His provision of the Land of the Free and the Home of the Brave, watched over by the Creator of the entire universe because it truly is great. God has been so gracious to America, a nation founded on individual freedom, morality, and faith in God. But God's people need to turn back to Him if we expect continued blessings. God promises in 2 Chronicles 7:14 (NKJV), "If my people, who are called by my name, will humble themselves and pray and seek my face and turn from their wicked ways, then I will hear from heaven, and I will forgive their sin and will heal their land." That is a wonderful promise from a faithful, good God!

Is that really possible? Of course, it is, but it must begin with God's people returning to our heritage. That means God's people becoming obedient people, replenishing God's churches, led by inspired teachers and anointed fearless "John the Baptist" preachers. In the simplest of terms, for the sake of those who will follow us, we must renew our love for God and serve Him faithfully. We must make Him our first love. It is not complicated. It is a simple choice to let God's Holy Spirit guide us as we humble ourselves in repentance before our gracious God. We simply need to make time for Him and allow God to revive His people and restore our wonderful country.

No country could have a better plan than the plan outlined in the Bible. It clearly delineates how each of us should interact with others. And God has given us a moral law that will renew American morality. As followers of Christ, we would also have the powerful influence of the Holy Spirit within us to help us live faithfully the ethics of Jesus. Reminder, it was God's truths that were used as the core of America's foundation.

It makes it difficult for me to understand how it is today that so many fortunate young Americans, who have never paid the price to defend, grow, and strengthen America... are so angry about what they do not have. They do not have it because they have not earned it. People can—but you have to try, not just cry.

The truths of God's Word also tell us what an awful enemy of man division is and what its end result always is. These words came from the lips of Jesus,

"Every kingdom divided against itself is brought to desolation, and every city or house divided against itself will not stand" (Matthew 12:25, NKJV). This is an absolute declaration from the lips of Jesus. And does "house" here also represent a nation? Absolutely. And yet, many of our elected politicians clearly pay no attention to this sobering warning. Rather, they continually purposely sow divisiveness and hatred toward others who have a different view. There is a decided lack of wisdom in that behavior since the result is chaos and failure.

In our present government, there is a pronounced decline in civility, with the resultant unwillingness to debate issues without condemnation and name-calling. The hatred and dislike have led to the closing of minds and hearts and unwillingness to do the fact-checking and/or research to find evidence and truth to support one's beliefs. There is an unquestionable defied unwillingness to even try to reconcile differences with accurate facts and supporting information. As we know, there is usually more than one way to approach an issue or problem. One of the worst effects of this situation is there is no synergy, for the most part, at work among our government officials. Our country is deprived of best solutions and potential progress because the petty hatred and dislike of the parties prevent them from working together to find those best solutions and answers. Logic and righteousness should always be the providers of the solution regardless of who provides it, and civility by our leaders should be demanded.

I wonder how many of these elected *alleged* leaders have any vision whatsoever of how much they could accomplish working together. I speak from personal experience about how fulfilling it is to begin in an effort to find the best solution with a room of people with differing opinions and end up with the very best solution. Working together in a civil and respectful manner and putting into practice Christian ethics in dealing with those who have different ideas enables all to strive toward the best solution, and then every person leaves the room as a winner. Then all will own the better result and its rewards.

What you are about to read may sound boastful or prideful, but I assure you it is not, for that is not my intent. It is just an example of what real unity, with a clearly defined positive objective, can accomplish. God allowed me to be a part of a trucking company that was scattered over many states. We were all dependent on each other, and we knew it. Although our associates were disseminated, there was a superlative effort of cooperation and serving of customers. Whatever effort it took to keep promises to customers was always clearly given because it was a matter of honor and integrity. This approach had been in place since the founding of the company in 1950. I tell you, it was most gratifying to be part of something where the commitments to the customers were foremost in every associate's mind. Southeastern Freight is a shining example of what a company can be. Those who are a part of Southeastern family simply decided petty differences would never interfere with the worthy objectives of the whole. If a trucking company scattered over a large geographic area can cooperate together to accomplish great things, why can't our alleged government leaders? Are they not supposed and expected to be exemplary leaders?

There is really no excuse for the pettiness and littleness of too many elected officials. Someone told me long ago, "You cannot be big and little at the same time." Gigantic egos always destroy progress and cooperation. It's time for those who claim to be big to act big.

I cannot help but wonder if too many of our alleged elected leaders can even grasp what it means to really *serve* and always *tell the truth*. Unfortunately, it appears their personal interests all too often supersede the needs and best interests of the citizens. Perhaps we need to establish a U.S. Leadership Institute and teach good governance and civility with virtue-based curriculum in a democratic republic and be certain all of the future leaders are graduates and, more importantly, strong advocates of its content.

God has blessed our nation from its very beginning for many reasons, not the least of which was our faith and trust in Him to help us create a special nation, one nation, under God. We would be wise to acknowledge what our French visitor discovered much over a century and a half ago: "America is great because America is good. If America ever ceases to be good, she will no longer be great."

President Ronald Reagan was one of America's most favored and respected presidents, and to me, he was a true statesman. He was a man who loved God and who loved his fellow man, and he also loved his country. Why do I say he was a true statesman? The answer is simple. He did what was good and right for America, whether his critics liked it or not. He was a man of honorable convictions, and for him, truth and principle were more important than political points. He was exemplary as a leader, and he was humble as he bowed before Almighty God.

Perhaps one of the main reasons for his success and the success of his administration was reflected in what he said and believed about the Bible, "Within the covers of the Holy Bible are the answers for all the problems men face." He, unlike some, believed America was a great country, and he knew God's guidance would be the only way to keep it great. The applied wisdom and truth of that book is the only hope for avoiding the destruction of our God-ordained country.

We will never, by way of legislation, create brotherhood because it is a heart issue, and it is God's book that gives us all the answers. Besides, if we were applying His instructions, we would already be enjoying brotherhood. There is no question God has been so gracious to America. Since we are now at a critical juncture, how do we respond? Because America is absolutely worth fighting for, we need the wisdom of Almighty God to preserve her and restore our values. We also desperately need the same great faith of our founding fathers to do so. They really understood the great power and value of unity.

# CHAPTER 34

# The Mystery of Mysteries

The rejection of God's authority over the world and the people He created began in the Garden of Eden and has been increasing to this day. As we should all remember, God had given Adam only one clear instruction, and Adam decided he was his own person and he would not obey that warning. Possibly Adam wanted to do it just because he was told he should not, or perhaps he believed no one would ever know. Isn't that how, even today, people view the matter of sin?

The Bible had not been written then, and Numbers 32:23 (ESV) had not been written before Adam's fall: "Be sure your sin will find you out." That truth, however, is correct, and we never cover any sin or focus attention away from sin by pretending it doesn't exist. God is aware of all sin, and He knows our great need for forgiveness no matter how much we pretend the sin doesn't exist or pretend that He has no right or no public place in our society.

Every true believer empowered by the indwelling Holy Spirit of God knows when Jesus came and was crucified, He died for my sins and yours. He took the enormous weight of sin upon Himself. He came to restore us back to a right relationship with a Holy God, who awaits our arrival in our eternal home with Him.

But why is there such public opposition to any mention of God the Father or God the Son, Jesus? If we go back to John, Chapter 15, and read the entire chapter, it explains that question. In verse 18, we read, "If the world hates you, you know that it hated me before it hated you" (ESV). In the latter part of verse 25, it reads, "They hated me without a cause" (ESV). Both of these sad but interesting truths were spoken by Jesus, our sinless Savior.

Why did the world hate and disobey the teachings of Jesus? After all, Jesus had done nothing but obey God the Father since He came to earth. Jesus never spoke any words but truth. However, one major reason many people do not love and honor God is because human beings have a sinful nature. When Adam, our earthly ancestor, sinned in the Garden of Eden, all of mankind thereafter was born with a sinful nature. But God is perfectly holy, and He cannot even look upon sin. Because of sin, humanity was separated from God. But our loving Creator did not give up on us and leave us with no remedy for our flawed condition.

God loved mankind so much that He provided a way to forgiveness and sent a Redeemer, Jesus. Jesus, the perfect, sinless Son of God, came to earth and clearly said, "I am the Way, the Truth, and the Life. No one comes to the Father, except through me" (John 14:6, NKJV). Jesus, being the truth and *the only way*, then and today, makes the world uncomfortable.

Do we get the picture now? Jesus exposes truth, and the Word exposes truth. John 1:1–2 (ESV) states, "In the beginning was the Word, and the Word was with God, and the Word was God. He was in the beginning with God." The Word was in existence before the creation of the world. John 1:14 (NIV) states, "The Word became flesh and made His dwelling among us. We have seen His glory, the glory of the one and only Son from the Father, full of grace and truth." Another way of saying this is Jesus came to us, and He was full of unfailing love, faithfulness, and truth, and we have seen His glory. Also, the Word, God's Holy Word, is the wisdom of God and reveals truth. And again, the Word is Jesus. The presence of the Son of God brings truth—as God's word brings truth—and truth always exposes sin. Therefore, sinful man does not want to be reminded of his secret sin and hear the convicting truths or be made aware of them. No wonder there is such an effort being made to eliminate any mention of Jesus.

Reflect again to where we see Adam in the garden after eating the forbidden fruit. "Then the Lord God called to Adam and said to him, Where are you?" (Genesis 3:9, NKJV) Adam replied, "I heard your voice in the garden, and I was afraid because I was naked; and I hid myself" (Genesis 3:9–10, NKJV). Sin caused Adam to be afraid and to try to hide from his Creator.

Sinful man has been running from God from the beginning and ever since. Sinful man also rejected Jesus, the very One who came to earth to redeem mankind and give us a fresh start. Recall again, when He came to earth to rescue and redeem mankind, Jesus said, "They hated me without a cause" (John 15:25, ESV). Man continues running from our only hope for spiritual salvation. Why is that? Because deep down, God's truth convicts us all of sin in our lives. Many don't accept Jesus is the only One who can ever change that sinful, guilty condition, and He very much wants to do just that. He, the Perfect One, paid for our sin debt on that cruel cross. He bled our sins away, a free gift to whosoever will accept the gift. This is the historic message every person in our world needs to hear. It is the history of the fall of man in disobedience to God and His statutes, rejecting His ways to do "what was right in his own eyes" (Judges 21:25, ESV). Man chooses to run from God because of sin guilt. But God loves man too much to have left us without remedy, so He sent the only One, His only Son, who willingly came to rescue mankind with His own perfect life and death. God planned this salvation and redemption from the beginning of the world for any person who wants this better life God made possible.

There is now a worrisome and malevolent effort to do away with Christianity in the public forum. We have never lived in an era where there is such a pervasive effort to quiet or "cancel" Christians. It also appears to be true that many people who do not have a personal relationship with Jesus Christ do not want to hear that truth. It is now politically incorrect for religion to be mentioned in a public place.

Dear friend, please understand that what I speak of is far more than mere religion. It is more accurately recognized as a love relationship with a resurrected Savior, who was the only One who could pay a debt that we could not pay. And He did it because He loves each of us like an only child.

I must ask this question at this point. What exactly is wrong with the ethics of Jesus Christ? Why are His principles hated and rejected? What is it about God that causes fear in people in the public forum? Think clearly about this.

The ethics of Jesus Christ are beyond our small vocabulary to describe.

His principles are actually brilliant. The mystery of mysteries is—now that He has provided them, why won't man follow them? What better way for man to live than by the ethics of Jesus? Why can man not grasp God gave us the law and His commands to benefit us because He loves us. Then Jesus came to earth and taught us in order to help us not scar our lives. *Obedience* to God's teachings promotes peace and essentially equals not scarring our lives. There is no better way for man to live than by the ethics of Jesus, which is part of an *obedient journey* with the *Difference-Maker*.

## The Ten Commandments

Read the commandments in Exodus 20:1–17. God gave us these wonderful instructions that we might live a most fulfilling life unscarred by ravages of sin. But man cannot obey if we do not read and know His word. Then we must trust Him enough to obey. Hopefully, you agree our world would be wonderfully better than it is today if we seriously obeyed these simple commandments.

## The Fruit of the Spirit

When we accept Jesus as our Savior and follow Him, He sends God's powerful Holy Spirit into each of us to help us represent Jesus so very well. When the Holy Spirit fills our lives, we will bear His fruit when we allow Him to guide us: "love, joy, peace, patience, kindness, goodness, faithfulness, gentleness and self-control" (Galations5:22–23, ESV). What society would not want these wonderful characteristics demonstrated by its people?

I am mystified as to why lives bearing these wonderful attributes are not welcomed in our society. The Holy Spirit, the Difference-Maker, has given us these wonderful gifts to show others who our Lord really is and how He changes lives. These attributes, or fruits, do not come from within us; they come from He who is within us.

## The Sermon on the Mount

We should also read the words of Jesus as recounted in the Sermon on the Mount, which comprises all of Matthew chapters 5, 6, and 7. Speaking to a great crowd, Jesus ended his sermon with words that are as poignant today as they were to the crowds on that Galilean hill so many years ago.

*Therefore, whoever hears these sayings of Mine, and does them, I will liken him to a wise man who built his house on the rock: and the rain descended, the floods came, and the winds blew and beat at the house; and it did not fall, for it was founded on the rock. But everyone who hears these sayings of Mine, and does not do them, will be like a foolish man who built his house on the sand: and the rain descended, the floods came, and the winds blew and beat on that house; and it fell. And great was its fall. And so it was, when Jesus had ended these sayings, that the people were astonished at His teaching, for He taught them as one having authority, and not as the scribes.*

*Matthew 7:24–29 (NKJV)*

This was a great parable founded on truth: The life that is truly founded on Jesus Christ will always stand, even in the worst of storms, and eternally.

I highly recommend to anyone that you read Matthew Chapters 5, 6, and 7 slowly, carefully, and prayerfully. You are guaranteed to have a much greater appreciation of our wonderful Savior when you do so.

It remains so puzzling. We ask again why does man try to question the message and ethics of Jesus? It continues to be a mystery of mysteries. Can one not see its wisdom? Can one not see His message was clearly brought from heaven to rescue us all, descendants of a sinful Adam?

*Paul's Jesus drawing inspired from a charcoal sketch by unknown artist*

# CHAPTER 35

# The Perfect Plan

God had a perfect plan for mankind from the beginning. Too often, man does not want to believe that plan and follow that plan because it requires humility, obedience, and dependence on our Creator. However, God's book of truth declares it, and the plan guarantees the optimal results for anyone's life. We're all on the journey of life. But the *obedient journey* is the one that makes a difference.

God created the entire universe, and then He created man for fellowship with Himself.

There was something special about God's creation of man. "And the Lord God formed man of the dust of the ground and breathed into his nostrils the breath of life; and man became a living being" (Genesis 2:7, NKJV). This wonderful act of our Creator differentiated man from all the other created animals. Mankind was the only living being that God marked for Him in such a unique way.

Genesis 1:26 (NKJV) further describes that wonderful creation event. Then God said: "Let Us make man in Our image, according to Our likeness." It could not be clearer that man's first breath came from our Creator. It was divine breath, unlike the breath of all other creatures.

Since God made us for fellowship with Himself, we can be assured He also gave us clear direction to be able to live victoriously and honor Him.

What guidance does He provide us to follow that will bring honor to Him and peace with our fellow man? Very specifically, He gave us the Ten Commandments (Exodus 20:2–17, NKJV):

1. You shall have no other gods before Me.

2. You shall not make for yourself a carved image.

3. You shall not take the name of the Lord your God in vain, for the Lord will not hold him guiltless who takes His name in vain.

4.  Remember the Sabbath day to keep it holy.

5.  Honor your father and mother that your days may be long upon the land which the Lord your God is giving you.

6.  You shall not murder.

7.  You shall not commit adultery.

8.  You shall not steal.

9.  You shall not bear false witness against your neighbor.

10. You shall not covet your neighbor's house, your neighbor's wife, nor his male servant, nor his female servant, nor his ox, nor his donkey, nor anything that is your neighbor's.

God desired for them and for you and me today only the best, thus, He gives us great direction and expectation here. Just like we do for our own children because we love them, we tell them what is beneficial and what is not.

Later on, Jesus, Our Savior, was born. He constantly gave us wise guidance in order for us to live faithful lives for our Creator.

He gave us that profound Sermon on the Mount in Matthew, Chapters 5, 6, and 7. It closes with these words in Matthew 7:28–29 (NKJV), "And so it was, when Jesus had ended these sayings, that the people were astonished at His teachings, for He taught them as One having authority, and not as the scribes." These passages include the Beatitudes, and every Christian would do well to read and reinforce these teachings very regularly.

As we read in God's Word after Jesus was crucified, entombed, and arose to go back to the right hand of the Father, He sent as promised the precious gift of the Holy Spirit. Every born-again believer then possessed the awesome resident power of God to be strengthened for faithfulness. The purpose of the Holy Spirit and of being faithful is simple; that we might represent our Savior so well, others are also attracted to Him. The fruits of the Holy Spirit born by God's power are love, joy, peace, patience, kindness, goodness, faithfulness, gentleness, and self-control. As we allow those fruits to ripen in our lives, people will clearly know we are children of the Living God: Father, Son, and Holy Spirit.

God has now given us the entire Bible as a guidebook for our lives. I have come to know it as the absolute best human relations and leadership book ever written.

It is so very helpful because it clearly gives us guidance on what we are to do or be, as well as what we are not to do or be. Proverbs 6:16–19 (NKJV) is also very definitive, "There are six things God hates: yes, seven are an abomination to Him: a proud look, a lying tongue, hands that shed innocent blood, a heart that devises wicked schemes, feet that are swift in running to evil, a false witness who speaks lies and one who sows discord among the brethren."

Here is an important list to make application of and live by. Can you grasp how much God despises and will seriously judge people who constantly create division and hatred? God loves synergy, such as when people pool their individual contributions to a challenge, and then the whole is greater than the sum of the individual parts. In other words, people working together can achieve far greater results than can be achieved solo.

Clearly, the study and application of God's Word every day will decidedly help us individually, help us keep America Great, unify us again, and help us live out the remainder of our days on earth obediently by living above the fray and staying in His heavenly updraft... which I plan to illustrate next.

CHAPTER 36

# Staying in His Updraft

We have read of the high expectations God has for us, His people. These are all for our good and His glory. The better news is our gracious and generous God affords everything we need to meet those expectations, provided in His Word, and enables us with the Difference-Maker. God wants so much for us to excel at life and to enjoy "life more abundantly" (John 10:10, NKJV). Why does He desire this so? He loves us, and He knows we are the ones who will enjoy the benefits of obedience as we honor Him with our willful obedience.

We have previously read how the magnificent eagles avoid furious storms when they occur. The eagles innately know they are no match for the violent storms of wind, rain, hail, and lightning. However, God has made unique provision for their protection. They simply soar peacefully, almost effortlessly, lifted by an updraft above the fury occurring beneath them until the storm subsides. They were uniquely created by Creator God, and they instinctively know to do this.

*Eagle soaring above the storm in God's updraft*

I find this fact about the eagles interesting, though not at all surprising, and reassuring about the care of God for all His creation. His provision, especially for you and me, can always be depended upon, even more so. How blessed we are to have His constant watchcare in our lives, and it is so easy in our busyness to take it for granted.

How much more does God love and value mankind compared to other members of His creation? Surely, it is much because Genesis 1:27–28 (NKJV) tells us, "God created man in His own image, in the image of God He created Him, male and female He created them. Then God blessed them, and God said to them, be fruitful and multiply, fill the earth and subdue it: have dominion over the fish of the sea, and over the birds of the air, and over every living thing that moves on earth." God graciously favored mankind from the beginning. Since God knows the future, He even made available the Holy Spirit to empower and help man represent God on the earth with excellence. It takes God's power, the Difference-Maker, to do that well since Satan is the acknowledged "ruler of this world" (John 12:31, NKJV).

It is absolutely factual that God made man far superior to any other creature for a certain purpose, that purpose being fellowship for eternity with Himself. We need to hear this well: If we miss out on fellowship with God, we have missed out on everything. But what a great honor and continuous blessing it is to be in fellowship with Almighty God. Think about this! No wonder man has been able to do such profound things as travel to the moon, split the atom, discover and harness electricity, and explore the great depths of the sea. Man was created to achieve greatly and to have an intimate relationship with his Creator, Almighty God. However, something disastrous happened. The enemy of God and man tricked and deceived mankind with empty promises that were not true. Satan is still doing that today, and it's what Satan does best. Satan is a master deceiver. He has had mega centuries of experience doing so, ever since the Garden of Eden. No wonder he is so crafty, deceiving, and masterful at evil. However, thanks be to God, He gave us a Savior. Not only that, but He has also given His children a powerful indwelling Helper

(John 14:26, NIV) to enable His people to stay faithful, even in the midst of the worst of earthly troubles. All we have to do is to decide to stay faithful and then rely on His divine powerful Holy Spirit to help us do so. We must, however, decide with determination and then rely in faith upon the power of the Helper to keep our commitments to our Lord.

Before you read any further, may I suggest you go back and prayerfully reread chapter 18, "The Difference-Maker." It is unimaginable that a cowardly Peter could instantly become so emboldened and so empowered. But once clearly empowered by the Holy Spirit, he was immediately completely competent to do exactly what Jesus had selected, prepared, and called him to do, regardless of the strife, turmoil, opposition, and difficulties that lay ahead. Peter knew he was divinely prepared for the most severe tests and storms. He realized God had already made provision for what he had been called and saved to do: "Go and make disciples" without wavering. Peter, now filled with the Holy Spirit, had God-confidence rather than inconsistent self-confidence. I must add here that I have never gotten over how that same power, the Holy Spirit of God, also transformed my own fallen life. I did nothing but submit. It was all a gift of God's wonderful grace.

If we read the Bible from cover to cover, we will never find an instance when God called out anyone or any group to carry out a specific mission that He did not always make provision for their success. They could then go forth with God-confidence! That is still absolutely true for you and me and anyone that desires His peace today.

In the Old Testament, specific power or Godly assistance would be given to the person or group as needed for carrying out God's will at that particular time. Whatever it took, He provided. He made provision. He will always be our faithful provider to enable us to be obedient.

But it was not until Jesus had come to earth, had been crucified, was resurrected, and returned to heaven that Holy Spirit (our special provision and Helper) was given to every born-again believer. God's gracious gift of divine power (covered in depth in previous chapters) is the absolute eternal reminder that God has already provided and equipped us with what we need in order to stay in His updraft. Just as God makes provision to protect and save the eagles, He provides you and me His Holy Spirit to keep us safely above the destructive power of Satan. Satan always wants to tear us down and make us stumble, but God does just the opposite and always lifts us up, ever nearer our eternal home. His heavenly updraft is always lifting us, growing us, maturing us, and empowering us. On the other hand, Satan is always endeavoring to pull us down, discourage, deceive, and destroy us. However, we must be careful here. Our salvation experience must be real, including repentance for our sin and life-altering, if we are to have God's power in our lives.

We are divinely inspired and divinely led as we humble ourselves before our gracious God. But man, just like Satan, has often rejected God's way, carnally choosing our own ways, and in doing so, we gamble with a slippery slope that will always become disastrous. We, as a society and a nation, are close to that calamity today with darkened minds. As I write this, there is wholesale rioting, as well as burning and looting and shootings in more than a few American cities, because man's heart is darkened with hatred and division. The light of positive greatness has dimmed, and we are reminded of Judges 21:25 (KJV), "there was no king in Israel; Every man did that which was right in his own eyes." Man did what was right for himself in his own eyes, without regard for his Creator or his fellow man. It was then—and always will be—a disaster when we refuse God's way and choose our own, worldly way.

Man was not created to do as he pleases and live in selfishness. We were created to walk in fellowship with our Creator and to obediently follow His perfect plan for our development, peace, and fulfillment. That is the real plan for brotherhood that will last. As we walk with Him in fellowship, He will more than satisfy our wants and needs and clearly enable us to carry out His plan. God always has a far better plan for man than man has.

Dr. Charles Carter, my wise pastor and friend, said more than once, "You may not be the president of your company, but you are the president of your life." That statement is so profoundly true. He was saying no one else decides how you live and where you spend your eternity. We decide, personally. However, I have since discovered it is wise to invite our Lord to be Chairman of the Board and take His rightful, guiding position in our life.

Ever so certainly, wickedness propagates. That is why we must avoid stagnating as God's people, and we must keep growing in truth and grace. You might be thinking, but why is it so important that I stay in God's updraft? I am saved and going to heaven, and that is enough, is it not? No, God has saved us for far more than that. We have a wonderful gift to share with others.

We need to understand this profound truth. God saved us to *grow* us into faithful, powerful disciples who can effectively carry on the most important work in the world. What a high calling! In fact, Peter reminds us to yearn for and be spiritually fed on God's Word, so we may grow up in grace and knowledge of our Lord Jesus Christ and taste the kindness of the Lord. First Peter 2:2 (NKJV) states, "as newborn babes desire the pure milk of the Word, that you may grow, thereby, if indeed you have tasted that the Lord is gracious." Peter is saying God's Word is perfect wisdom to guide our lives, and by studying it, we will realize the sweetness of Jesus. A little farther in chapter 2:9–10 (NKJV), Peter reminds us of who we are: "But you are a chosen generation, a royal priesthood, a Holy Nation, His own special people, that you may proclaim the praises of Him who called you out of darkness into His marvelous light." What a wonderful heritage, God's special people, and we too have the privilege of proclaiming God's praises! Peter had clearly defined why God expects us to grow as we stay in the updraft of His provision, so we are prepared to go and make disciples. We must stay obedient if God is going to use us to represent Him. We certainly are not all called to go and make disciples on foreign soil, but we are *all* called to Christian growth and making disciples where we are. As we obey, we will always be in the updraft of His provision. The passage "Go and make disciples" does not necessarily mean we must go elsewhere and do so. It simply means, "As you are going, make disciples" wherever you are, full time. God's church would never be in decline if His people simply obeyed this simple commandment. The commandment has not changed. It is equally or more important for you and me today than when it was originally given. It is not just the preacher's job; it is every born-again Christian's job to be equipped and to share the gospel.

Christianity is a *developmental process,* and staying in the updraft of God's Holy Spirit direction, power, and care is essential. We will never be completely satisfied until we yield to God's plan to grow us into complete faithfulness. Divine tension in our lives focused on faithfully pleasing God is a good thing. We are saved by the God that we can always trust. Always, because He is a good God and His nature is good. We will never give up anything in order to serve and obey God that He does not replace it with something better.

I can't think of anything more unfulfilling than being a non-involved Christian. A non-involved or disobedient, or indifferent Christian is a witness in reverse. Our disobedience confuses lost people with the question, *What does being a disciple of Jesus Christ really mean?* It gives the impression being a disciple is not really important or, in plain language, like it's no big deal. But we, as God's forgiven people, know this is the biggest deal of all. It is the biggest deal because its consequences are eternal for the people our Lord expects us, you and me, to share Christ with.

As we obey the prompting of God's gracious Power, we are being "transformed by the renewing of your minds" (Romans 12:2, NKJV). This is an expectation from our Savior. He guides us and empowers as we obey.

As we, the guilty but forgiven children of God, rely on God's resident Holy Spirit to prompt and guide us, we can expect the following promise to become a reality in our life. "You will keep him in perfect peace whose mind is stayed on You, because he trusts in You" (Isaiah 26:3, NKJV). When we truly trust God, we obey God, and we then are the recipients of God's peace. Obedience always brings blessings and ultimately profound peace.

As we are blessed with His peace, we obey more and more. We then, expectantly and hungrily, read our Bibles. We also look forward to spending time on our knees with bowed heads and yielded wills. We begin to share the gospel and the liberating difference He has made in our lives with others as well. Disciplined Christians' lives impress, and those disciplined lives open doors to share the gospel. We share from the overflow of blessings that continually come into our lives when we, out of gratitude, gratefully obey our Lord. This is what happens when we allow God's promptings to keep us in the updraft, constantly under the influence of God's Holy Spirit. We then, and only then, have God's indescribable peace "that passeth all understanding" (Philippians 4:7, KJV).

Updrafts are always predictable. They always move upward, and they always lift. It is wonderful to know the provision God makes for us is to move us continually upward. That upward motion is toward Lordship while here on earth and finally upward to our celestial home, where everyone is glorified. We don't hear that word *glorified* often, but it's a wonderful word. It basically means, as "glorified disciples," we will have no desire at all to sin. Imagine such a place as heaven where every heart is pure, and every motive is inspired by God. How refreshing! How uplifting! How absolutely wonderful! Can you imagine a place where no one ever has a sinful thought and absolutely no desire to sin? It will be our eternal home.

Romans 8:29 (NKJV) tells us we are all predestined to be conformed, *molded*, into the image of His Son, Jesus, "the firstborn among many brethren." That tells us God expects us to continually grow as His followers. As we seek Him and grow, we will always stay in the updraft of His perfect care, love, and empowerment. He is continually lifting us toward our eternal home. We just have to make certain we are being led by the powerful indwelling Holy Spirit, the Difference-Maker, while on earth.

The Word of God is clear. God had a plan from the inception of the world. He also made provision in order that His plan would become reality. His plan included giving mankind everything needed to withstand Satan's efforts to destroy our relationship between God and man.

God is for you and me. Romans 8:31–32 (NIV) should reassure us greatly: "If God is for us, who can be against us? If He did not spare His own Son, but gave Him up for us all, how will He not graciously give us all things" that we need? Think about that. Anything that can separate us from God must be greater than God. Absolutely impossible! Case closed. Don't we know, without a doubt, God will give us all things we need since He has already given His most precious gift, Jesus? What more assurance do we need?

Think about what you just read. God will, by His divine power, give us everything we need to stay in His updraft far above Satan's destructive reach. As we make a determined effort to obey, our lives will bear the fruit of the Holy Spirit—love, joy, peace, patience, kindness, goodness, faithfulness, gentleness, and self-control. That is a guaranteed promise from our Lord.

Think about how attractive such a life is (one bearing the fruits of the Spirit) in today's world. Those fruits are inviting to others, and think about how many people will come to know our Savior because we willfully decided to stay in God's updraft, and we relied on the Holy Spirit to empower us to do so.

God has saved us all to help spread the gospel and to share the most important thing that could happen to anyone. Every child of God has been saved to represent Him well on this earth and to lead others to His security in the updraft. God has made provision, the Difference-Maker, so that we can all be effective in sharing the gospel. We, without question, seriously need a spiritual check-up if we do not have a convicting awareness of our Lord's expectations and a convicting desire within to share Christ. If we really know Him and have the peace of God, we will want others to have that same wonderful experience.

As we have been talking about Jesus' clear commandment of going and making disciples in this chapter, it has taken me back some fifty years to an occurrence when I received the clear expectations God has of His children. They seemed almost impossible for me, a broken sinner who was just welcomed *home* into the kingdom of God. However, when I was first told of God's expectations, I did not know I would have a more than able Helper. What occurred that evening is worth repeating.

Dr. Charles Carter, my wonderful preacher and pastor, had asked me to stay after the service ended in order that he could discuss my future as a truly forgiven, born-again believer. He said, "Paul, you are a baby Christian. This is what God expects of you, and what I expect of you also." I knew he was exactly right. We come into the kingdom as baby Christians. God then has a super developmental process to grow us into what He identifies as saints. I must admit, I have never personally felt worthy of that identity. But I do know God sees the difference.

He continued, "You be in Sunday school (Bible study) and in worship service every Sunday morning. You be in Bible study and Worship service on Sunday evening. When you are not traveling, you be in midweek prayer service on Wednesday evening and learn how to pray. Start reading your Bible every day to know God's will for your life and what He expects. Start telling people right away what a difference Jesus has made and continues to make in your life." This was my first instruction to share the gospel. I knew God expected me to obey. Then he told me to "bring a tithe next Sunday."

It was, by far, the wisest and most important advice I have ever received in my eighty-plus years. In fact, it was so helpful, I am convinced every new believer should be hearing the very same thing today when anyone accepts Jesus as Lord and Savior. Why would we not tell a new convert that God has a great plan for your life, and He has certain expectations of you to make that abundant life possible? We can also tell the new convert God will provide the power (everything you need) for you to do so. Discipleship is a partnership, and we are the junior partners. There should be no fear of political correctness. We owe obedience to the One who died to set us free and affords us eternal life.

At the time I gave my life to Christ, I knew nothing about God's provision, that I would now be empowered by the Holy Spirit who had become resident in me. I just knew I had been profoundly changed. I was so glad to be free of the old me and my guilt from sin that I wanted to please my Deliverer. I knew in my heart that I should do all Dr. Carter had instructed me to do. I welcomed his forthright guidance, and I will be forever grateful that he did not mince words. He spoke important truth that I desperately needed to hear.

Dr. Carter made it plain to me that night, and I was ready to hear it. I was under new leadership, and I had a divine Helper. He said, "It will cost you something to be a Christian, but you will never regret it." He was so on point.

At that point, out of gratitude, I had to make a decision with a firm and determined resolve. Because I was full of gratefulness, I wanted Jesus to be my Lord and Master. I never wanted to feel less secure and loved than the way I felt that evening. *God's Spirit wonderfully helped me know obedience would be the key to having God's continued peace in my life.* That is a powerfully important truth for every Christian! Not only that, God said, "If you love me, you will obey my commandments" (John 14:15, KJV).

Ultimately, we each have to make firm decisions. The real question is, am I willing to accept God's will for me in discipleship? If I wholeheartedly commit, then I will enjoy His wonderful peace, as I do my best to allow His powerful Holy Spirit to lead me in my Christian growth and development. In reality, this development is in preparation for heaven and that wonderful final state of glorification.

As children of God, we must decide and not waver. Decide whether we will be resolute and obey. He gives us all the power we need to do so. Jesus said in Revelation 3:16 (KJV) to the church people in Laodicea, "So then because you are lukewarm, neither hot nor cold, I will spew thee out of my mouth." We must confidently resolve not to be "lukewarm" or part-time Christians, but resolve to allow Jesus to be Lord. In James Chapter 1:8 (KJV), we are told a "double-minded man is unstable in all his ways." Double-minded—a mind constantly wavering, uncommitted, undecided, inconsistent, and unstable—is an identity that brings shame to anyone, let alone one who bears the identity of a Christian.

It is really a simple matter. Inspired by God in Ecclesiastes 12:13 (NKJV), the divinely endowed wise King Solomon said this eternal truth thousands of years ago, and he still says this truth to each of us today in reference to our duty: "Let us hear the conclusion of the whole matter" of life, and he continues further to elaborate that the whole matter of life is to "Fear God and keep His commandments, for this is man's all." We are whole and complete only when we fear God (live in awe) and keep His commandments.[1] Just give this some thought. The second wisest man to ever live is worth listening to. By the way, Jesus was the wisest man who ever lived.

This truth for us, in the simplest of terms, is "fearing God is to respond to Him in awe, reverence, and wonder, to serve Him in purity of action (right motives), to shun evil and any worship of anything else (including entertainment, pleasure, and money) in His universe."[2]

It is no secret the church in America, made up of people just like you and me, is now in major decline and has been for many years. Never before, at least in my lifetime, has this condition existed. There is open hostility by the speech police and politically correct groups in an effort to totally eliminate the gospel, to remove the name of Jesus, and to exclude any other offensive Christian terms in public. There is a clear rejection and avoidance of same in the majority of our institutions of learning from early elementary to grad schools, but thankfully not in all of them.

It is sobering to think about how far from God and our Christian principles we have fallen, and it has occurred so very fast. The world and worldly ways have become more and more attractive, apparently more than ever before. Big Tech, which was so innocent looking at its inception, has now become a censoring force in our society with an apparent hatred, or perhaps fear, of Christianity.

There is no question today there are multitudes of people whose names are on the church rolls who have never allowed Jesus to be Lord. They have never committed themselves to a faithful life of worshipping, studying God's Word, giving God's tithe, and sharing the gospel with the lost. In essence, they have not matured at all as obedient Christians. I do not judge them, but God's truth in His Word does. I am so thankful someone cared enough about my

1      From commentary *NKJ Study Bible*, 3rd Edition, page 958, Thomas Nelson Publishers

2      From commentary *NKJ Study Bible*, 3rd Edition, page 958, Thomas Nelson Publishers

eternity that they did not give up on me and another one had the courage to declare God's expectations of obedience. People who loved God enough to pray continuously and earnestly literally prayed me into the kingdom of God.

Unfortunately, too many have never decided their relationship with Jesus Christ is important enough to honor Him with obedience. Thus, we can undoubtedly expect and know that's the real reason for such a decline in God's church. Avoidance of hell is not the most important thing about Christianity. Pleasing our gracious Savior is... by allowing Him to be Lord.

Yes, as I mentioned earlier, it is called making Jesus Lord. When we do just that, God's resident Holy Spirit begins to keep us focused on Jesus (John 16:14, NKJV). Without God's Holy Spirit, a person cannot fully understand God's Word and His will, let alone be empowered to do His will. First Corinthians 2:14 (NKJV) makes this very clear, "But the natural man does not receive the things of the Spirit of God, for they are foolishness to him; nor can he know them for they are spiritually discerned" only. The Holy Spirit makes understanding possible. The Holy Spirit is then constantly reminding us of whom we belong to and at what a great price we were redeemed (bought back) from the ugly dominance of Satan in our lives and an eternal hell that had awaited us. The Holy Spirit always keeps us focused on Jesus and what a wonderful Savior He is. Remember what Jesus said and says today about the Holy Spirit: "He will glorify me" (John 16:14a, NKJV).

There is an important truth God wants us to recognize. "Where the Spirit of the Lord is, there is liberty" (2 Corinthians 3:17, NKJV). The Holy Spirit is available to set all born-again Christians free from habitual sin and its consequent guilt. What a profound blessing to experience!

We have not only been set free but we have also been empowered to crown Jesus Lord by our choices. Think honestly about this. God's churches would be flourishing and prospering spiritually, as they once did if the people who are enrolled would just allow Him to set them free. Free would mean free from competing for worldly attractions that are so interesting and desirable, yet so non-essential and worthless in the end. One of the things that the Holy Spirit does best is to change our "want to-s" from earthly things to heavenly things. Why do I say such a thing? He has changed my desires and now empowers me when the world begins to attract me.

There is a truth that every church member needs to hear: If you and I are living our faith empowered by God's Holy Spirit, people will listen when we share the gospel. The Holy Spirit empowers us and guides and leads us.

Every day we must all make a certain number of decisions simply because life is always a continual series of choices. However, we all know some choices are far more important than others. They are also more consequential. When God made us, He made us free agents to be able to decide our own destiny. But, being a gracious Creator, He made a Helper available to us, as well as an Owner's Manual, to help us make the very best choices. Being perfect and gracious, God innately wants the very best for us, and therefore, He gave us everything we need to choose correctly about those things that matter most.

There is absolutely no question that choosing to stay in His updraft is the most important choice we could ever make. That means we, in the power of God's Holy Spirit, choose to honor and follow Christ obediently and consistently. We are "fearfully and wonderfully made" (Psalm 139:14, KJV) and made in the "image of God" (Genesis 1:27, KJV).

As we allow the Helper that God sent to us to lead and guide us (when we are truly saved), we will always remain in the updraft. That is truly a wonderful place of peace, fulfillment, and obedience. Without a doubt, when the Holy Spirit guides our lives, we will clearly demonstrate that powerful truth which so fulfills us and pleases God—people can obey and excel when we rely on the Difference-Maker to "do exceeding abundantly above all we can think or ask according to the Power that works in us" (Ephesians 3:20, NKJV). That is an absolutely awesome promise from our Creator. And it is undeniably too wonderful to reject or ignore—we were created to excel.

God has given us His absolute best. It is now our turn to show our gratitude by giving Him our best for His creating us in His wonderful image and for Him giving us a means to salvation. We will hereby clearly prove this powerful truth: *People can* because we are made in His image for precious incomparable fellowship with Him—eternally. If anyone of us misses that fellowship, regardless of anything else we accomplished, we have missed everything.

Purposely I repeat. God has given us His absolute best because He loves us so much.

» He created us in His image for eternal fellowship.

» He gave us His sinless Son to pay our sin debt.

» He gave us His Book of Truth and Wisdom, our Owner's Manual, to guide us.

» He gave us His powerful, enabling Holy Spirit to indwell, strengthen and empower us to live in victory and to obediently represent Him well in this world.

» He gave us opportunity to live in the greatest country in the entire world.

» He continues to give us a "peace that passes all understanding" as we enjoy His precious presence.

» He now gives us opportunity to re-present Him gladly in our desperate, chaotic world. What a blessed privilege to share the peace and joy He has brought into our life.

» He will protect, reassure and speak peace to our hearts no matter what worldly things we face.

» He will comfort us securely for eternity like no one else can.

» All we need to do now is to respond to His mercy and grace and allow Him with holy hands to lift us above Satan's destructive tactics and ever toward our eternal heavenly home, as we obey Him and stay in His marvelous heaven-bound updraft.

» He then gives us great excitement and anticipation as we so
look forward to our final. refinement—Glorification.

# My Prayer for You

I am not a theologian and would never pretend to be. I am, however, desirous to know as much as I can of God's plan for mankind and by His plan make application of same in my life.

Before I became a Christian and God's Holy Spirit became the resident power in me, the Bible was simply a very difficult book to understand. I really had no interest in it. It seemed outdated, restrictive, and of no real value to me. In my mind, it was for religious people, and I was not one of those. However, when I was truly born again, and God's Holy Spirit became resident, the Bible became important and relevant since I now had a Helper "to lead (guide) me into all truth" (John 16:13b, NKJV).

I have found the book of Romans to be especially informative and encouraging. It has become one of my favorites, and chapter 8 is a favored chapter. I love the powerful promise of the very first verse: "There is therefore now no condemnation to those who are in Christ Jesus, who do not walk according to the flesh, but according to the Spirit" (Romans 8:1, NKJV). That beautiful verse guarantees me Jesus has paid my sin debt and the Holy Spirit now indwells me, the forgiven sinner, in order that I might represent Jesus well! My part is to will to continuously *obey* by following the *Holy Spirit's leading.*

Second Corinthians 3:17 (KJV) further encourages me every time I read it. It promises, "Now the Lord is the Spirit and where the Spirit of the Lord is, *there* is liberty." That promise is about being liberated from the bondage of sin. When we are saved, we were set free from the punishment of sin through justification. Now, through sanctification, we are being progressively provided the power to resist sin. But only when we are glorified will we be free from the presence of sin forever, by our glorification.

As we continue to read Romans, in Chapter 8, we find verses that are powerfully encouraging truths for every believer. Romans 8:28 (NKJV) reads as followers: "And we know that all things work together for good to those who love God, to those who are called according to His purpose." Did you notice the small word *all*? The word is neither *some* nor *many*. The word is *all*, and *all* is *absolute*. What a promise from One who cannot exaggerate! And what a special purpose we were created for (fellowship with God), and then called to represent the Lord and do His will here. As we seek to love Him, fellowship with Him, and serve Him, He guides and empowers all our efforts for good. All we must do is to *will for Him to lead as we obediently follow*.

In this eighth chapter of Romans, God continues to give Paul the words of truth to write in verses 29 and 30 (NKJV) as follows, "For whom He foreknew, He also predestined to be conformed to the image of His Son, that He might be the firstborn among many brethren. Moreover, whom He predestined, these He also called; whom He called, these He also justified; and whom He justified, these He also glorified."

Glorification is one of the most exciting spiritual experiences we can ever imagine. It happens when God calls us *home*, one by one, or when the Rapture occurs. Here on earth, even though we are saved, we still have a sinful nature. We are still tempted because we are still in the flesh. However, when we arrive in heaven as glorified saints, we will have no desire to sin. Is that not exciting? How can this be?

First John 3:2 (NKJV) blesses us with the words, "Beloved, now we are children of God, and it has not yet been revealed what we shall be, but we know when He is revealed, we shall be like Him."

"Believers will put on immortality and become free from the sin nature that presently plagues us."[1]

Philippians 3:20–21 (NKJV)[2] promises the same. "For our citizenship is in heaven, from which we also eagerly wait for the Savior, the Lord Jesus Christ, who will transform our lowly body that it may be conformed to His glorious body according to the working by which He is able even to subdue all things to

1      *NKJV Study Bible*. Commentary, Page 1,921

2      *NLJV Study Bible*. Commentary, page 1,787

Himself." The commentary continues, "Our body now is weak and susceptible to sin, disease, and death. But God will change our bodies to resemble Christ's glorious resurrection body." We will be like Him sinless, gloriously, and indescribably satisfied completely, just by being in His presence.

God's Word tells us heaven will be a place where no one will be tempted or have any desire to sin. Can you imagine a place where there is not even a thought given to sin on the part of anyone there? The glorious presence of our Savior will more than satisfy everyone who is there!

We hear and read very little about glorification. Why? Apparently, it is almost too wonderful to be comprehended. Let me assure you it is a very comforting truth, especially when a loved one dies.

Our middle daughter, Sandra, was a truly loving, very thoughtful, really friendly, and gregarious person. She gave her life to Jesus as a young teenager more than forty years ago. She loved our Lord, and consequently, she had a genuine love for people. I cannot exaggerate how caring she was, sincerely concerned about and always checking on others. In May of 2020, she was diagnosed with cancer. The medical efforts to heal her were not successful, and cancer cruelly ravaged her body. But she faced each stage of her difficult journey with enormous grace and courage. She trusted Jesus with her life, her illness, and her future.

*Our dear daughter, Sandra, 2008*

At the time of her diagnosis, we began to pray and believe two very specific prayers on her behalf. They were that the perfect will of God would be to extend her life much beyond the short time period of the medical prognosis. The second was that she would not suffer extensively. Our glorious God answered both in a wonderful way. What Christian is surprised at God's grace? We are extremely grateful for His kindness to us.

Several months ago, she closed her eyes here and awoke in an instant in glory, with Jesus and with other Christian loved ones, glorified saints. She also awoke with absolutely no desire to sin, and she is now among all those who accepted God's gracious gift of grace through Jesus. Praise God she is now at *home* in that indescribable place as is recorded in God's Word.

Our Sandra awoke to glorification, that perfect state made possible only by our Savior. Heaven is inhabited only with glorified saints and a place where no one has a desire for or is ever tempted to sin. Just think about a place where no one ever has a sinful thought, let alone a sinful action. No wonder it is called heaven! No wonder Jesus called it Paradise when He forgave the dying thief on the cross. Once glorified and in heaven, our wonderful, most satisfying focus will be on our precious Savior, the One who makes it all possible.

Paula Lynn is our second oldest child. About a year after Sandra's homecoming to glory, Paula was also diagnosed with a terminal illness.

Not only was Paula outgoing and friendly, quick-witted and funny, happy and full of life, she was also strong-willed, energetic, and a very hard worker. Often amusing, she spoke with candor, saying out loud what others might think but kept to themselves. She was "her own person."

Paula had a remarkable certainty about her faith and a Christian confidence. Therefore, she was fearless as she faced death, (passing a mere fifteen months after Sandra.) She consequently wrote out her entire funeral service. As her health declined in her last days she was praying for Jesus to take her so she not linger, and asked other loved ones to also pray that prayer.

Choosing to be cremated prompted questions she confidently replied to. She emphatically stated "I do not want people standing over my casket speaking to me or coming to my grave talking to me, for I will not be there." Her absolute faith in God's promises was so evident. She knew she would be in that wonderful glorified state, at HOME, in heaven.

Paula completely trusted God's promise for a "born again" Christian: to be absent from the body is to be present with the Lord (2 Corinthians 5:8). Paula is now glorified and at HOME with Jesus and Sandra.

*Our dear daughter, Paula, 2019*

Giving one's life wholeheartedly to Jesus Christ is the way to peace and fulfillment here on earth and for all eternity. To that point concerning peace and fulfillment, God passionately desires we excel in life and live life "more abundantly." As His children, we can confidently depend on His care and provision. Thus, *obeying*... being, and staying in God's updraft by the *power of God's Holy Spirit's direction, power,* and *care* will be the single most important thing any born-again Christian can do. We have His profound Helper to assist us to be divinely inspired and divinely led as His disciples, as we study His word, make application of His instruction, seek Him in fellowship, pray, and humble ourselves before our loving and gracious Difference-Maker.

Respond to Him as He leads you on your *obedient journey*. Respond to His mercy and grace, and in obedience, love Him and serve Him. Allow Him to continually grow and lift you, and to give you peace and fulfillment as you become all He created you to be. Then this promise becomes a reality in your life: "Where the spirit of the Lord is there is liberty" (2 Corinthians 3:17, NKJV).

# About the Author

Paul Taylor grew up in a blue-collar family in Cherryville, North Carolina, amongst hard-working, humble, loving people. He was blessed with loving parents in a warm, caring home where he was one of five children. He married his high school sweetheart, Lynette, and the two have now been married for over sixty-four years. They have been richly blessed with six children: Melinda, Paula (deceased), Bo, Sandra (deceased), Edwina, and Eugenia; ten grandchildren: Natalie, Brandon, Christopher, Tripp, Lane, Matthew, Julie, Jenny, Jackie, and Amanda; and the grandchildren are still adding to the number of great-grandchildren blessing the family.

Paul retired in 2001 as President of Southeastern Freight Lines, one of the most respected and trusted companies not just in trucking but in America. Prior to joining Southeastern in 1984, he had been with Carolina Freight Carriers Corp. since 1957, where he started as a day laborer and advanced to Senior Vice President of Operations. Paul fully acknowledges God's guidance and blessing upon his life. Paul became a Christian in 1969 and taught Bible study for over forty years. He was blessed to make twenty-one mission trips after retirement, some of which he shares in this book. He is a faithful member of First Baptist Church in Columbia, South Carolina.

In his spare time, Paul enjoys spending time with his family, reading, golfing, drawing/painting, flower gardening, surf fishing, and bird watching. Some of his family's happiest memories through the years have been at their beach condo.

*Bo and Paul Surf Fishing at beach condo*

In 2019, God impressed upon Paul the need to write this book with the purpose of sharing how his life was transformed by a most unexpected, supernatural, yet significant event. That event and the decision that resulted from it dramatically, positively, victoriously, and permanently impacted his life beyond his wildest imagination. This book is based on actual experiences and courageous attempts to follow God in whatever He wanted Paul to do.

Paul writes to encourage others not to fear or resist God's ways, His guidance, and His empowerment while revealing what God has done in his own life. Paul is certain the great impact Christ can have on anyone's life is a profound truth worth sharing and believes that this book will be beneficial to anyone seeking a more purposeful, peaceful, and fulfilling life. He desires others to be blessed with the same remarkable benefits as he has experienced.

Aware that Satan blinded and deceived him for many years, as he presently does so many others, into believing Christianity was the assurance of a weak, uneventful and anemic life, Paul encourages others to resist Satan's lie. Paul also reassures others by sharing the tremendous positive impacts from his experiences in knowing and yielding to Christ, the One willing to die, that we might truly live in victory. The enemy of God certainly does not want others to know and experience the life-changing power in Christ.

Paul discusses at length a powerful truth of an incredible Helper, a *Difference-Maker*, available to anyone who chooses Jesus and desires to live and achieve his or her fullest potential. On his *obedient journey*, Paul has come to understand the power that enables one to resist evil and live out their faith, concluding that it is our Creator who supplies the needed resources to live life victoriously!

Paul gives credit for his success not to his personal abilities but to God, to faith, and especially to his Helper, the *Difference-Maker,* who guided him into making right decisions on his life's journey. God's Spirit wonderfully helped him to know obedience would be the key to having God's continued peace in his life. Paul's guiding belief, because it both happened to him and he saw how it transformed many others, is that people can achieve beyond what they imagine possible if they give their lives to Christ and follow the best owner's manual ever written, the Bible. People can walk in obedience and can be empowered to stay on the path. Major themes included in the book include deliverance, Holy Spirit, discipleship, leadership, excelling, and others.

Also, Paul desires his younger family members to know who he is and what truly revolutionized and shaped his life. He hopes through this book they understand what gave his life real purpose and profound meaning. That purpose is "God has a better plan for every human being than we can ever create ourselves… and His plan includes glorious eternity! And God's Spirit wonderfully helped me know obedience would be the key to having God's continued peace in my life." Paul speaks from experience that our Creator's plan, when followed, will produce a life of indescribable peace and liberty "that passes all understanding" even in our most difficult times.

*Paul Grayson Taylor*

CPSIA information can be obtained
at www.ICGtesting.com
Printed in the USA
JSHW051421070822
28845JS00001B/4